DAM BUSTERS

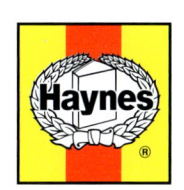

1943 onwards (all marks and models)

Acknowledgements

The author would like to thank all those who contributed to the text, images and discussion behind both, especially Ian Alder and Peter Elliott (RAF Museum), Mary Stopes-Roe, Rob Owen (617 Squadron official historian), Jim Shortland (617 Squadron historian), Dicky James (9 Squadron Association), Martyn Ford-Jones (15 Squadron official historian), Julian Temple (Brooklands Museum), 'Sandy' Sanderson and Harry Lewis (Custodian, EOD TIC), Les Munro (617 Squadron aircrew), Grant MacDonald (617 Squadron aircrew), Len Walley (Avro Heritage Centre, Woodford) and staff at the Science Museum Library, Wroughton.

© Iain R. Murray 2011

All rights reserved. No part of this publication may be reproduced or stored in a retrieval system or transmitted, in any form or by any means, electronic, mechanical, photocopying, recording or otherwise, without prior permission in writing from Haynes Publishing.

First published in August 2011

A catalogue record for this book is available from the British Library.

ISBN 978 0 85733 015 4

Library of Congress control no. 2011923594

Published by Haynes Publishing,
Sparkford, Yeovil, Somerset BA22 7JJ, UK.
Tel: 01963 442030 Fax: 01963 440001
Int. tel: +44 1963 442030 Int. fax: +44 1963 440001
E-mail: sales@haynes.co.uk
Website: www.haynes.co.uk

Haynes North America Inc.,
861 Lawrence Drive, Newbury Park,
California 91320, USA.

While every effort is taken to ensure the accuracy of the information given in this book, no liability can be accepted by the author or publishers for any loss, damage or injury caused by errors in, or omissions from, the information given.

Printed in the USA by Odcombe Press LP,
1299 Bridgestone Parkway, La Vergne, TN 37086.

DAM BUSTERS

1943 onwards (all marks and models)

Owners' Workshop Manual

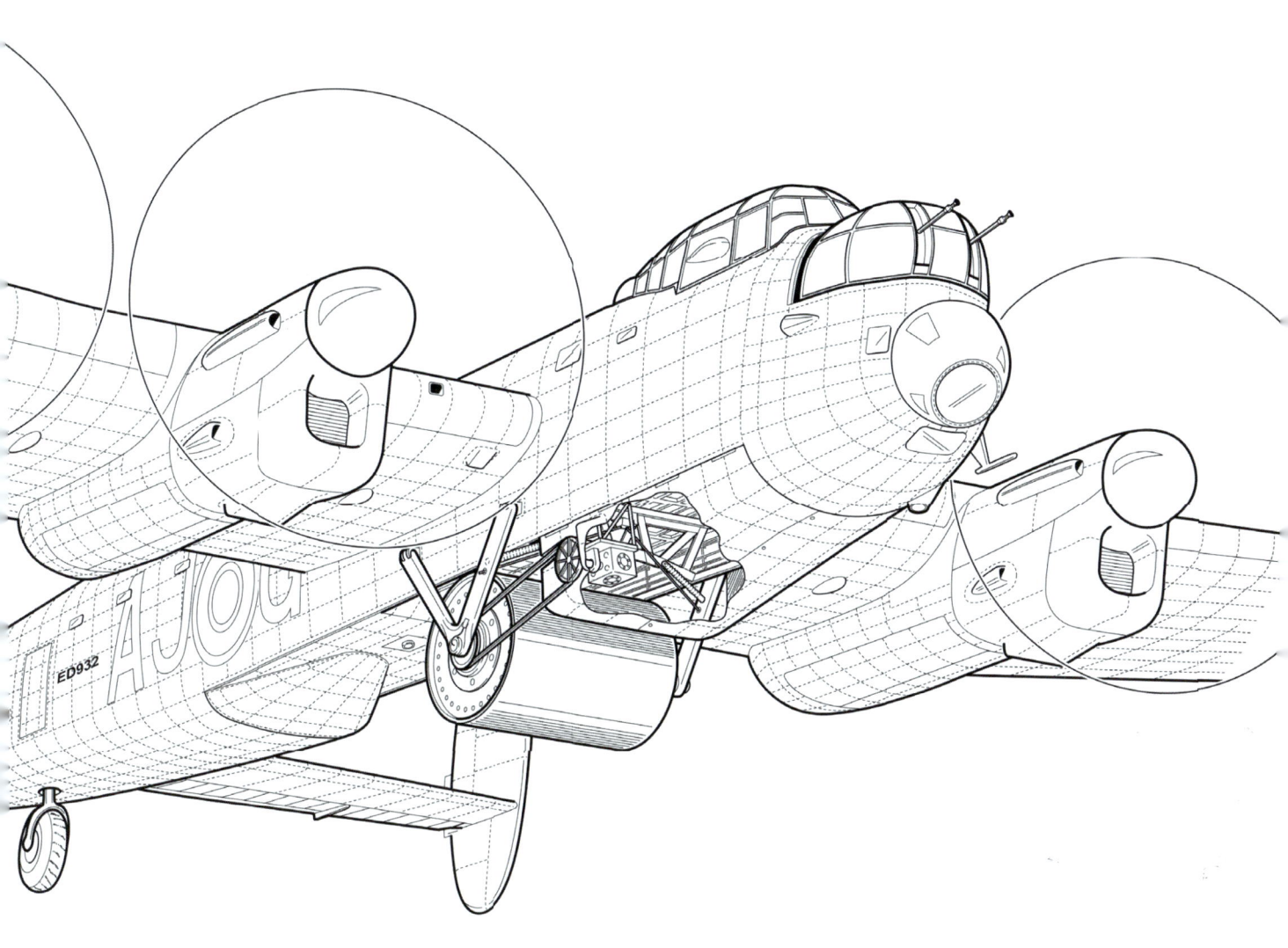

An insight into the weapons technology used against the dams and other special targets of Nazi-occupied Europe

Iain R. Murray

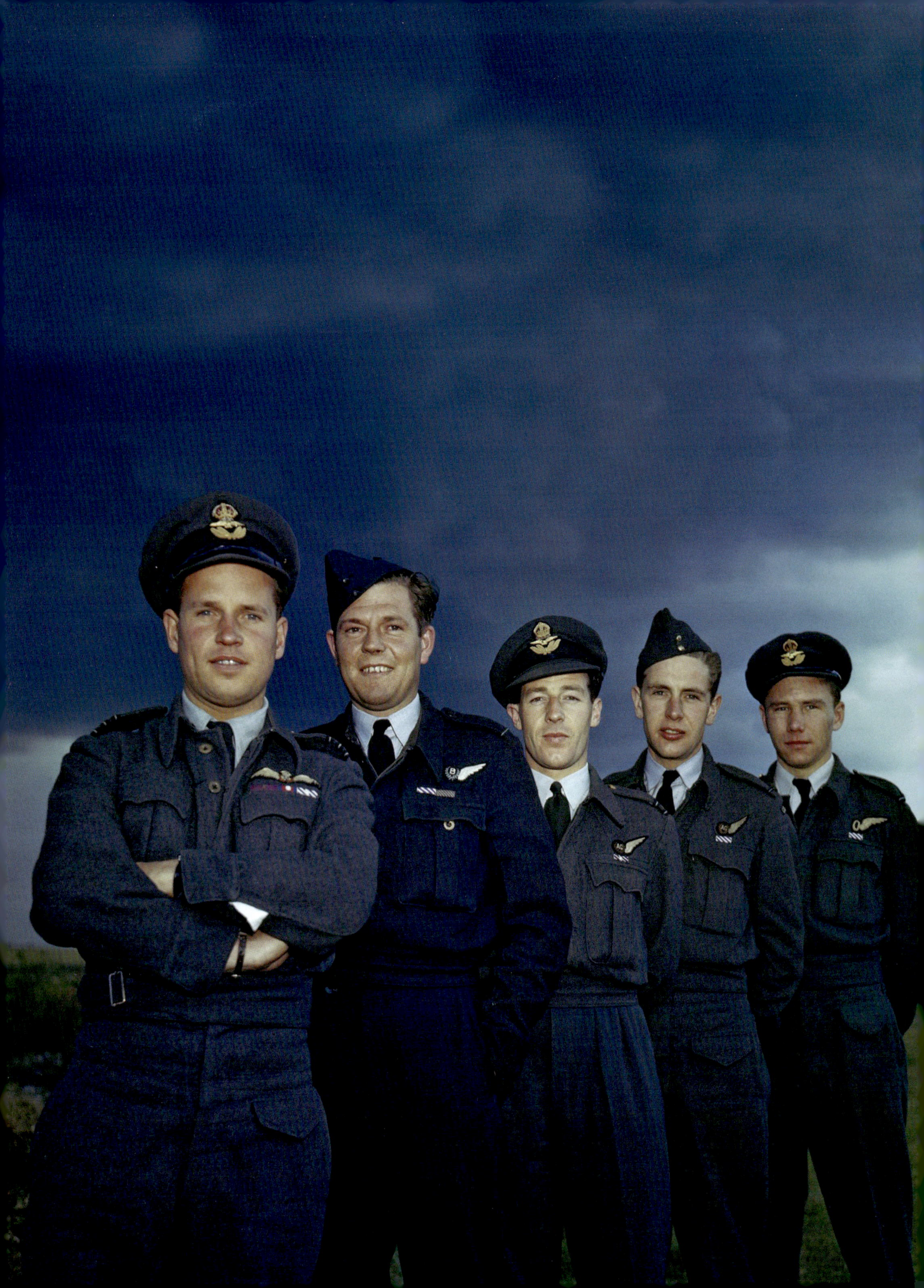

Contents

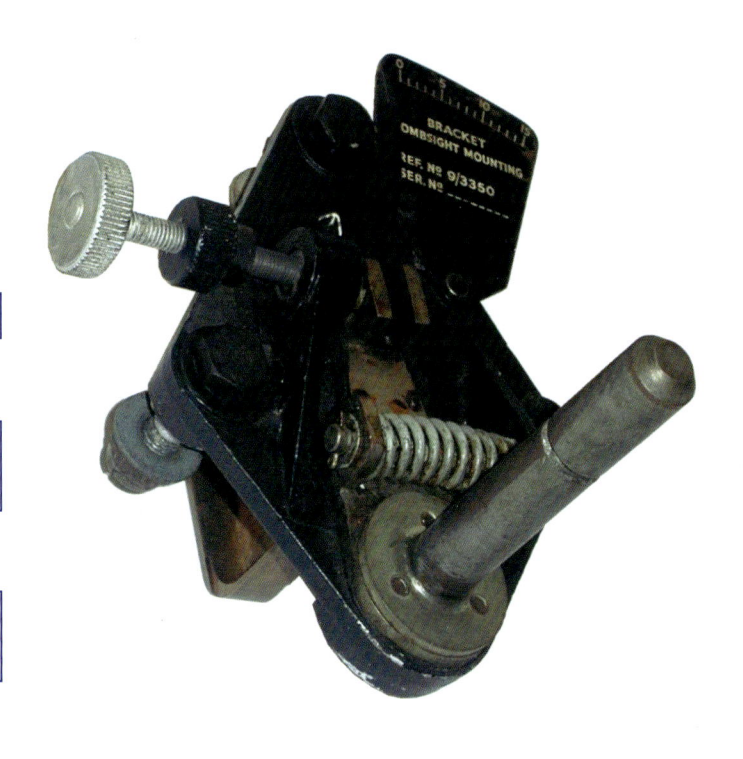

6	Introduction
The dams as targets	8

12	Development of the Bouncing Bomb
The Bouncing Bomb is born	14

38	Operation Chastise – The Dams Raid
A new squadron is formed	40
Further dam-busting operations	56

58	The 12,000lb HC Blockbuster Bomb
High-capacity bombs	60

68	Development of the Earthquake Bomb
What is an Earthquake bomb?	70
Development and testing of Tallboy	70
Grand Slam	91

94	The Earthquake Bomb Raids
Preparing for Tallboy	96
The V-weapon sites	100
The U-boat pens	110
Tirpitz	114
Dams again	118
Miscellaneous targets	121
Grand Slam arrives	125
Post-war developments	129

130	High-level Bomb Aiming
Bomb aiming	133

151	Appendices
Appendix 1 617 Squadron crews on Operation Chastise, 16–17 May 1943	152
Appendix 2 Type 464 Provisioning Lancasters	153
Appendix 3 Lancaster B.I Specials	154
Appendix 4 Bombs on display	155
Bibliography	157

158	Index

OPPOSITE 617 Squadron's first Officer Commanding, Wg Cdr Guy Gibson VC, DSO*, DFC*, with four members of his crew – Plt Off P.M. Spafford DFC, DFM (bomb aimer), Flt Lt R.E.G. Hutchinson DFC* (wireless operator), Plt Off G.A. Dearing DFC, and Fg Off H.T. Taerum DFC (gunners). *(Imperial War Museum TR1127)*

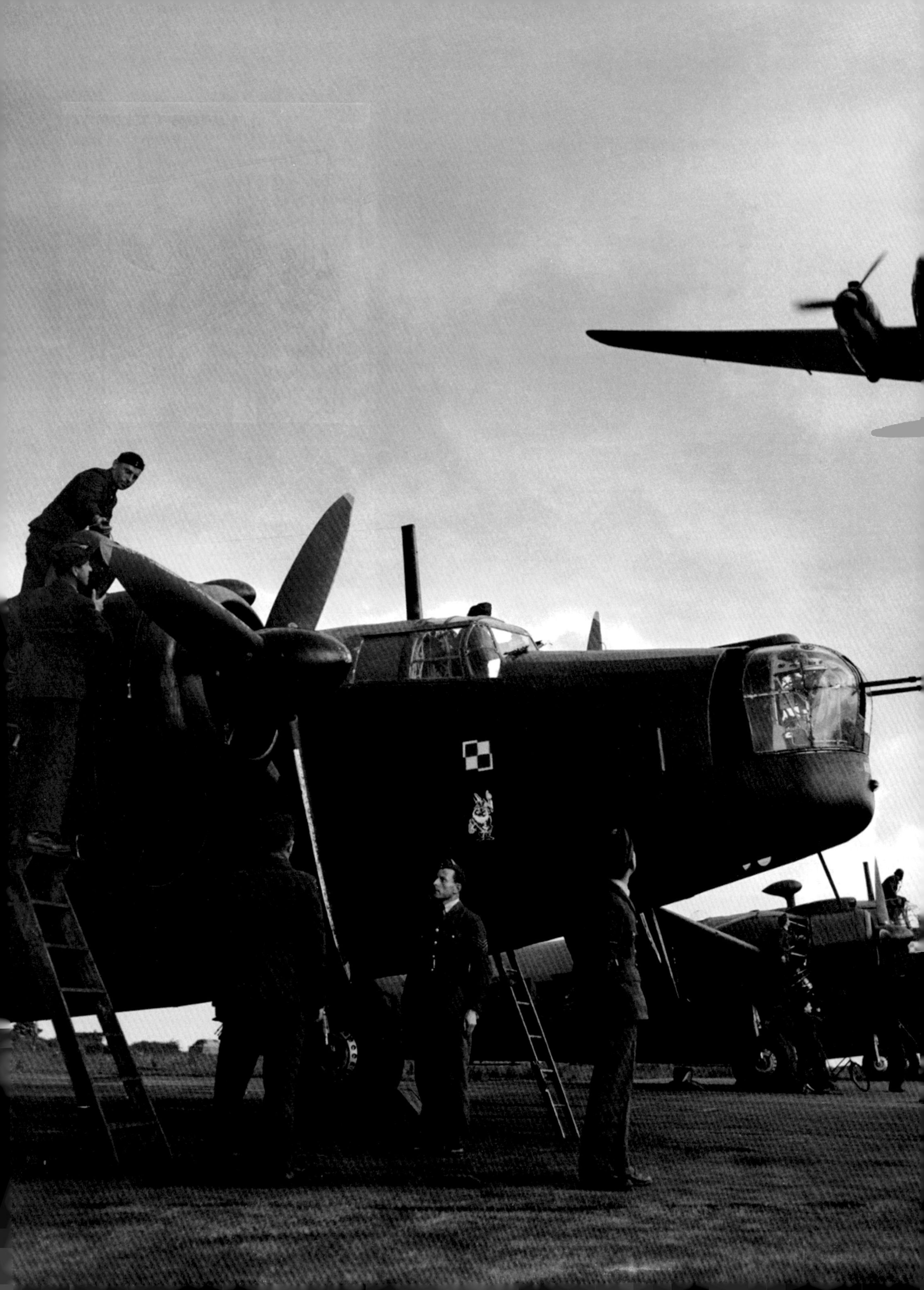

Chapter One

Introduction

At the start of the Second World War, aeronautical engineer Barnes Wallis asked himself what he could do to shorten the war. His answer was to develop a new range of weapons to attack special enemy targets that otherwise would have been invulnerable.

In the hands of specially-trained squadrons, these and other special weapons would punch above their weight in the fight against Nazi Germany.

OPPOSITE The Wellington was the mainstay of Bomber Command between 1939 and 1942; Barnes Wallis designed its geodetic airframe. *(Imperial War Museum CH10456)*

ABOVE **Barnes Wallis in his wartime office at Burhill Golf Club; the mantlepiece is adorned with Tallboy test specimens (see Chapter 5) and a photo of the Bielefeld Viaduct (see Chapter 6) is on the wall.**
(Mary Stopes-Roe)

The dams as targets

As the Second World War approached, Bomber Command of the Royal Air Force was portrayed to the British public as a powerful force, able to find and destroy pinpoint targets using self-defending formations of aircraft. However, in reality many of Bomber Command's aircraft were obsolescent, and heavy losses suffered on the first few daylight raids over Germany saw operations switched to predominantly night flying. Navigation was often problematic, especially in bad weather, and bomb aiming rudimentary. Even if a hit was made, the 250lb bombs that were in general use caused little damage.

To this problem came the mind of aeronautical engineer Barnes Wallis. Initially trained as a shipyard draughtsman, he had become involved in airship design, culminating in the successful *R.100* airship which flew to Canada in 1930. He then joined Vickers-Armstrongs Ltd at Weybridge, where he applied his skills in efficient structural design and light alloy to aircraft design, resulting in the 'geodetic' structure which was used in the Wellesley and Wellington bombers, the latter being the best aircraft in Bomber Command's arsenal in 1939 and which would continue in production until 1945.

Wallis quickly reached the conclusion that the best way to attack the enemy was to disrupt their war effort – rather than concentrate on the battlefield where targets were dispersed and able to shoot back, it was much more efficient to destroy the enemy's industry to cut off the supply of armaments at its source. In addition to the factories producing the arms, the infrastructure which supported the factories was also seen by Wallis as a tempting target – coal mines, oil storage, water, electricity – and the means to move raw materials – railways, canals, etc. From these possibilities, he selected dams as the best option, for several reasons: they were large and easy to find, they were impossible to disperse to new locations, and their destruction would not only remove a source of water and hydroelectric power, but also cause a deluge which would wash away factories, flood mines and destroy transport links. However, although unquestionably attractive targets, dams also posed the greatest challenge – as they were so massive, the small bombs then available would have had little effect on them.

Wallis was not unique in having realised the importance of the dams. Even before the war, the Air Staff had produced 'Western Air Plans' which offered operational guidance to the RAF in the event of war. These included WA4, describing attacks on rail, road and canal communications, and WA5, describing attacks on German industry. Although the plans were overtaken by events in the early months of the war, they had identified a number of key targets. Among these were the Ruhr dams including the Möhne Dam, a walled dam with a large reservoir, and the nearby Sorpe, an earth bank dam with a concrete core. Further to the east (and not part of the Ruhr system) was the Eder Dam, similar in construction to the Möhne with an even larger reservoir.

Early in the war, several schemes were proposed to attack the dams, from conventional

LEFT After the war, Wallis was based in the clubhouse at Brooklands; his office was on the first floor to the left. *(Author)*

bombing and torpedo attacks to more bizarre schemes such as using pilotless aircraft and winged torpedoes. A dam attack was even carried out in 1941 – at Tirso on Sardinia – using carrier-based Swordfish torpedo bombers, but the raid was unsuccessful, and it led to the installation of anti-torpedo nets at key dams including the Möhne.

The ten-ton bomb

Wallis spent most of 1940 working on the problem during the little free time he had from his day job as an aircraft designer at Vickers-Armstrongs. Although he had designed bombers, he knew little about the detailed workings of bombs, and resolved to find out what he could. He quickly discovered that the volume of material disrupted by an explosion is proportional to the cube of charge weight (for example, a 2,000lb bomb would have eight times the effect of a 1,000lb bomb), and that the pressure wave produced by an explosion was transmitted much more efficiently through the ground than through air. He thus

BELOW Wallis's original design for the ten-ton bomb appeared in his 'Note on a Method of Attacking the Axis Powers'. *(BAE SYSTEMS via The National Archives)*

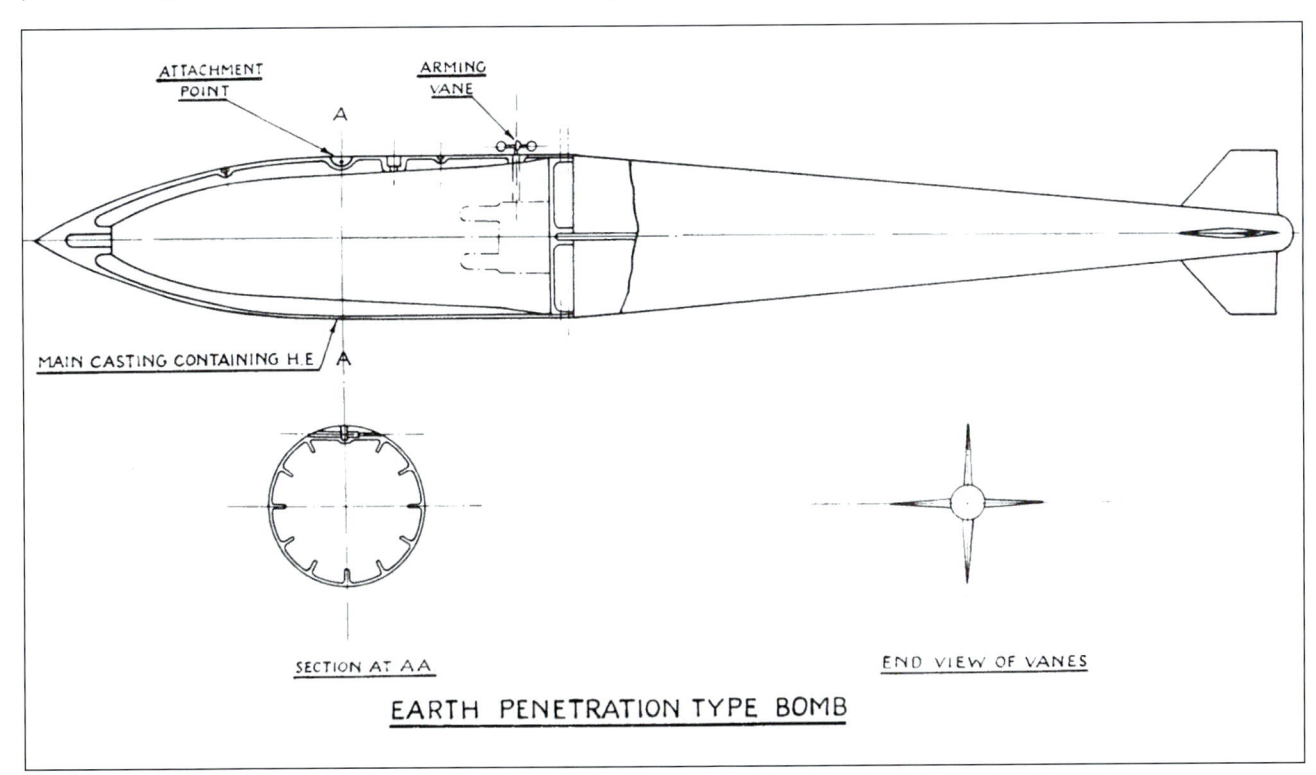

EARTH PENETRATION TYPE BOMB

realised that the ideal bomb would be a large one detonating deep in the ground where its effect would be felt over the greatest distance, and it might also create a 'camouflet' – an underground void left by the explosion – into which the target would then collapse. The size and power of this 'earthquake bomb' would be such that a direct hit would not be necessary, ideal considering that he was proposing to drop the bomb from 40,000ft for maximum penetration.

Wallis collected all his thoughts in a March 1941 paper entitled 'A Note on a Method of Attacking the Axis Powers'. The central tenet of this paper was a ten-ton bomb, a large cast-steel bomb able to penetrate the ground to a depth of over 100ft, and he included sketches of the bomb being dropped on the Möhne Dam and other targets such as underground oil storage tanks and coal mines. Recognising that this concept posed many practical problems, he included a treatment of all of them in his paper, such as the likelihood of being able to see a target clearly enough from 40,000ft and the need for an aircraft capable of carrying a ten-ton bomb (he included a design for one). Despite trying to close all the loopholes in his paper (and a subsequent appendix that he circulated a few months later to quash some of the criticisms levelled at it), his proposals were turned down. However, the Ministry of Aircraft Production set up an 'Air Attack on Dams' committee to investigate the possibilities.

Wallis asked the committee to support experiments to establish the smallest charge which would have a chance of breaking

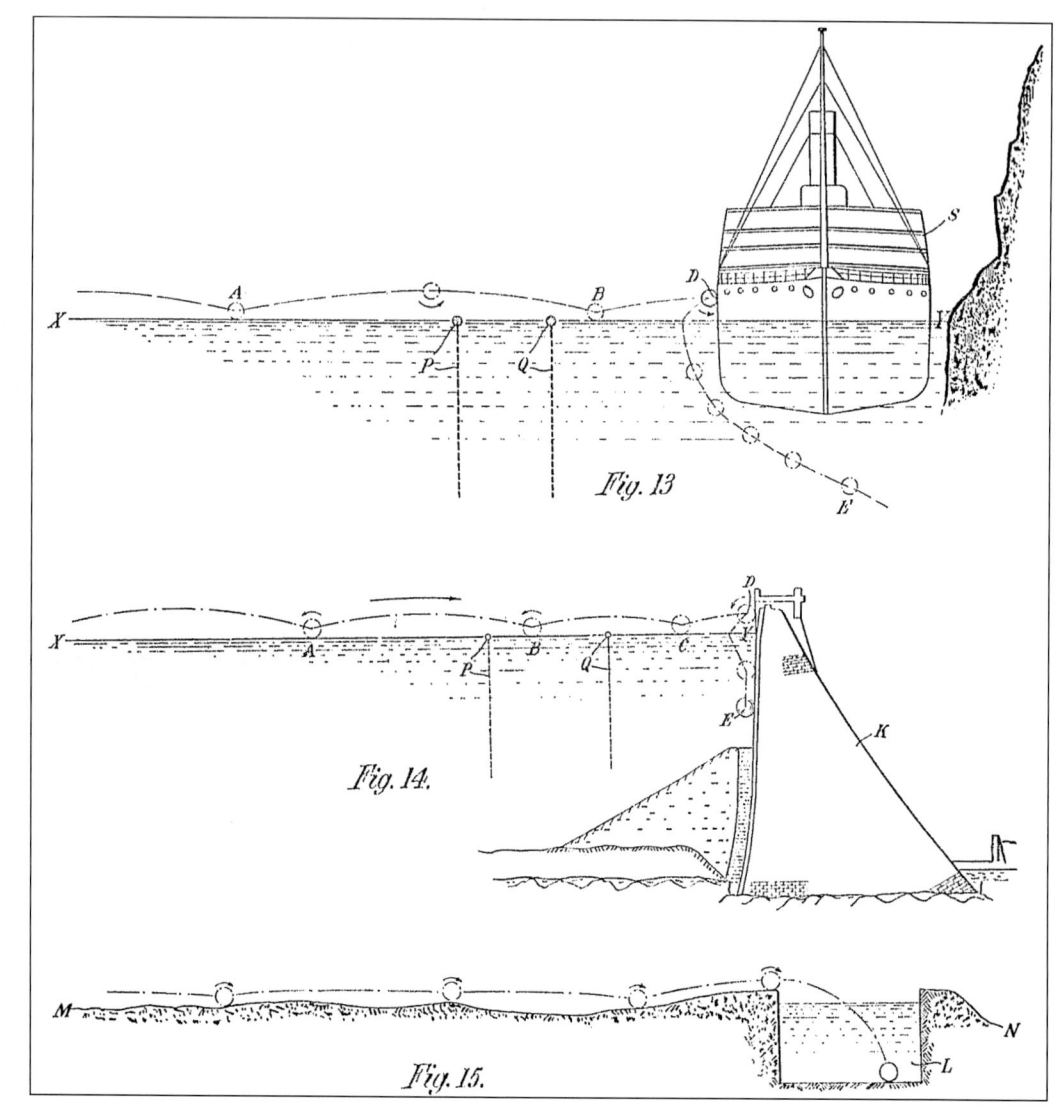

RIGHT **The three applications for the bouncing bomb in Patent GB937959 – backspun for use against ships and dams, and dropped over land into canals with forward spin.** *(BAE SYSTEMS)*

the Möhne Dam, and this work was given to the Road Research Laboratory (RRL) at Harmondsworth who built a number of one-fiftieth scale dam models there and on the site of the Building Research Station near Watford. Permission was also obtained to conduct experiments on a redundant dam at Nant-y-Gro near Rhayader in Wales, this being around one-fifth the size of the Möhne. Tests proceeded slowly, with disappointing results for scaled charges placed at a range of distances from the dam wall – these revealed that even a ten-ton bomb exploding just 50ft from the wall would be unlikely to cause a breach. However, a chance placement of a charge right against the wall produced dramatic results, leading to further experiments which revealed that a bomb of as little as two tons could break the Möhne wall – but only if it exploded in contact with the water face of the dam. This was confirmed by two tests at Nant-y-Gro – in the first, a scale charge equivalent to 30,000lb (well over ten tons) was placed a short distance from the wall and, as expected, failed to breach the wall. However, when a charge equivalent to only 8,000lb was placed right against the dam wall it caused, as predicted, a catastrophic collapse.

These experiments showed that a bomb of a practical size could be used to breach a dam as large as the Möhne – but there remained the problem of how to place it right against the face of the dam.

ABOVE One of the model dams remains at the Building Research Establishment near Watford – it is now a listed building. *(Author)*

BELOW The Nant-y-Gro Dam in Wales was where the theories developed on the model dams were successfully put to the test. *(BAE SYSTEMS via The National Archives)*

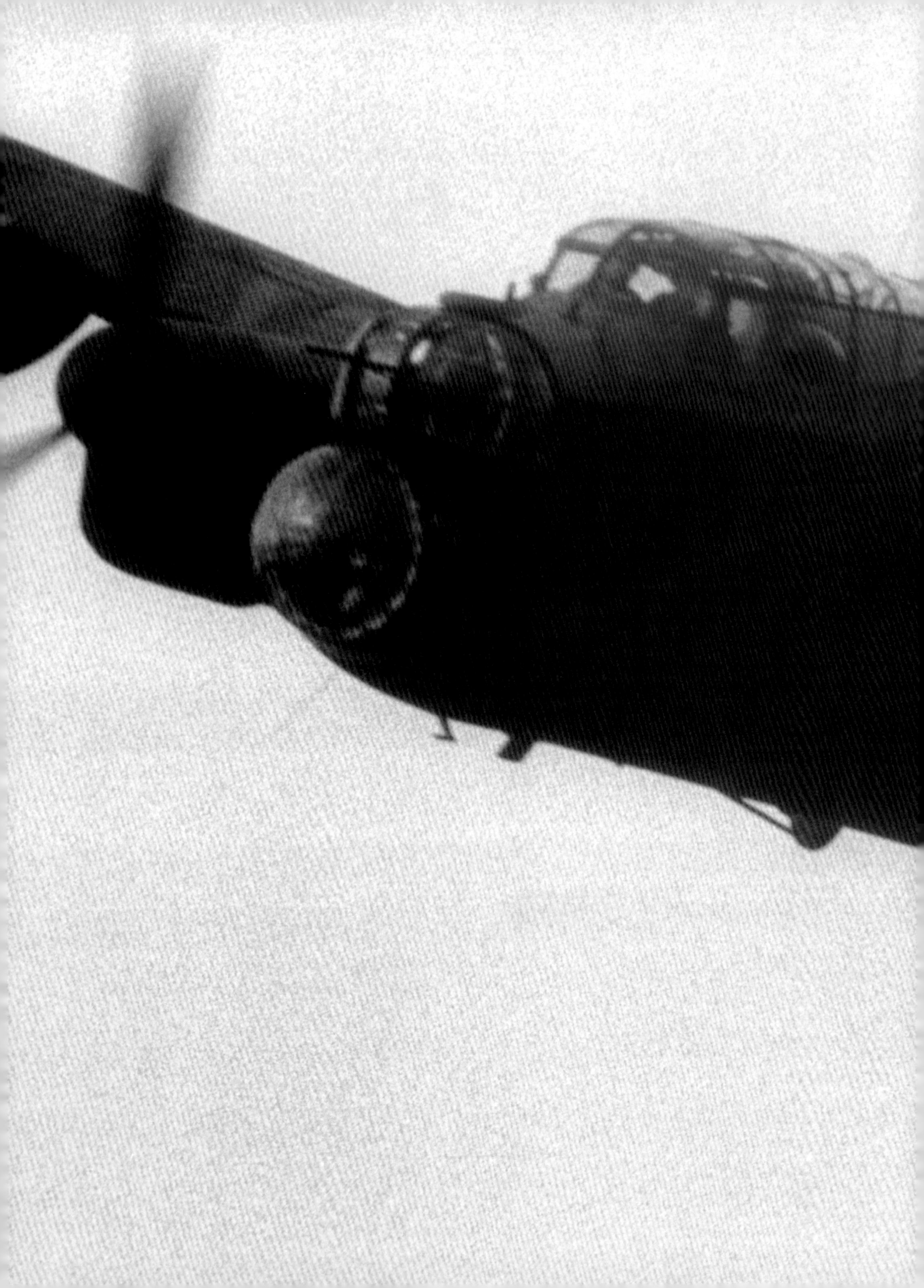

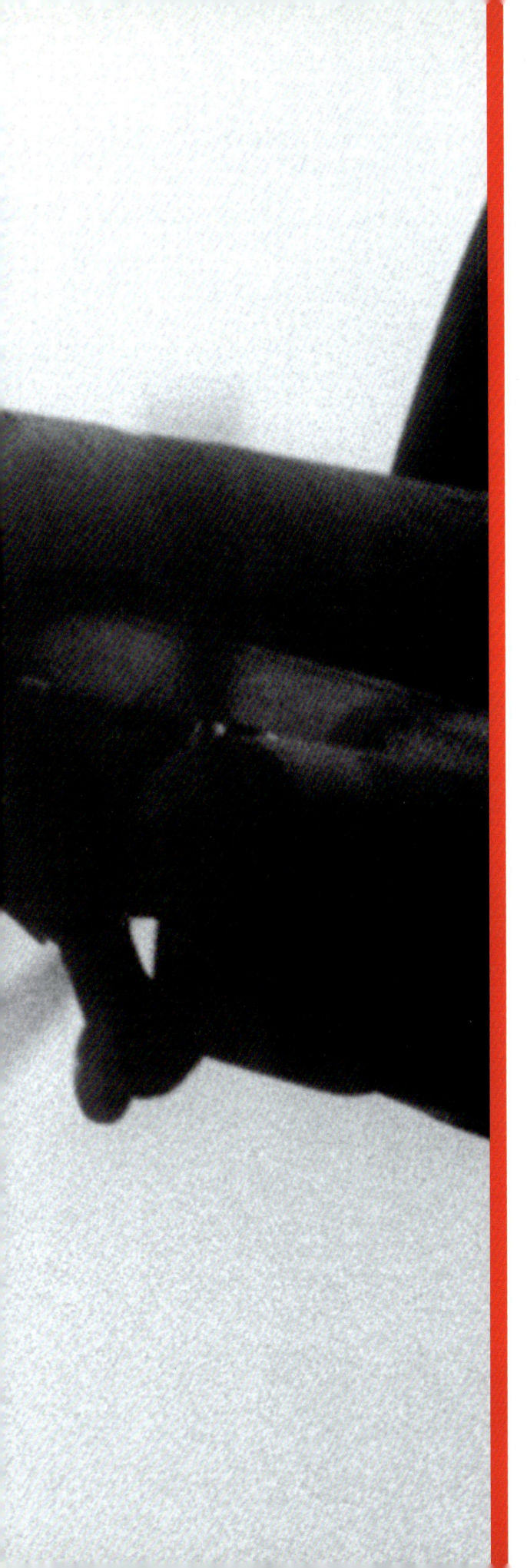

Chapter Two

Development of the Bouncing Bomb

The dams were formidable targets, and it was one of Wallis's characteristic flashes of genius which provided the means to attack them.

OPPOSITE Guy Gibson's Lancaster ED932 makes a low pass at Reculver; the tube behind the pitot head is the forward spot lamp and the calliper arms can be seen in their 'open' position. *(Imperial War Museum FLM00235)*

The Bouncing Bomb is born

With the model experiments having shown that a breach could be made with a warhead of only four tons, Wallis set about solving the problem of positioning the charge as required against the face of the dam. In early 1942, an idea began to form for a spherical mine which would be dropped at low level and skip over the lake in a series of bounces, losing energy and speed before coming to rest against the dam and sinking down beside it – this path would also allow it to skip right over anti-torpedo nets ahead of the dam. A preliminary experiment conducted along with his children using a tin bath full of water, a catapult and a collection of marbles proved that the skipping technique offered some promise, and further tests conducted shortly afterwards at Silvermere Lake near Weybridge using golfball-sized spheres of various materials and finishes, was also successful.

Wallis brought all of these ideas together in a report entitled 'Spherical Bomb, Surface Torpedo' written in April and May 1942. In this, he showed that a mine impacting the water at less than 7° would skip rather than sink, with subsequent water impacts being at less than 7° and hence the skipping would continue until all of its momentum was lost. The report also described the construction of the mine – an inner canister containing the charge, surrounded by a spherical structure for best aerodynamic performance, also giving control over the density of the weapon. The decelerating path of the mine would give the dropping aircraft (flying at over 300mph) time to get away to a safe distance before detonation.

Although he may not have originated the idea, Wallis realised about this time the benefits of adding backspin to the missile (that is, spin

BELOW The test rig for spinning and dropping prototypes; this one has fallen unevenly, a problem that would continue to plague Upkeep's smaller brother Highball. *(BAE SYSTEMS via Brooklands Museum)*

in the opposite sense to a wheel rolling beneath the aircraft). The main advantage was the generation of aerodynamic 'Magnus' lift caused by the interaction of the spin with the forward motion of the mine; this lift slowed the vertical speed of the mine, which gave several benefits. It prolonged the flight time (and hence distance) before the first water impact by around 20 per cent, as well as reducing the impact forces and reducing the effective angle of impact, which aided the mine's skipping performance. The other main benefit of spin was that, as the mine sank, the residual spin would push it forwards and so keep it in contact with the face of the dam, vital for the maximum explosive effect. Although the spin was assumed by some (including the Germans) to be for stabilisation, this was an incidental effect. The only problems posed by spin were those of actually carrying the mine in such a way that it could be spun up to the required 500rpm and released cleanly, and the need to carefully balance the mines before flight to prevent vibration.

Wallis was given access to the National Physical Laboratory's ship testing tanks at Teddington, and over a total of twenty-two days during the summer, he established to his satisfaction the rules governing the interplay of release speed, release height and the weight of the missile. This encouraged the Ministry of Aircraft Production to suggest a flight test, and permission was given to convert a Wellington for trials. The Oxley Engineering Company in Leeds was approached to produce some prototype mines, a diameter of 46in being selected as small enough to carry in the Wellington but large enough to adequately represent the full-sized weapon.

The first drops were made in early December on the Fleet, a long narrow lagoon between Chesil Beach and the Dorset coast, with Vickers Chief Test Pilot 'Mutt' Summers at the

BELOW **The first prototype Upkeeps were dropped from converted Wellington BJ895/G at Chesil Beach, with Wallis acting as bomb aimer; one smooth and one dimpled example are being carried here.** *(BAE SYSTEMS via Brooklands Museum)*

ABOVE To make Upkeep spherical, the charge cylinder was clad with wooden staves, but these broke away when the bomb hit the water.
(BAE SYSTEMS via The National Archives)

his idea in Whitehall, and on 26 March, the go-ahead for the raid was given. There were just eighty days until the ideal date to attack the dams, when the reservoirs were full after the spring rains and there was a full moon.

Constructing the bouncing bomb

Wallis's team set to work on drawings of the full-scale weapon, by now codenamed 'Upkeep', and these were completed in less than 36 hours. Although Wallis had conceived it as a spherical weapon 79in in diameter with flattened poles, it was too large to be easily fabricated as a sphere, so the charge was carried within a 60in long steel cylinder of 51in diameter, with wooden staves added to the cylinder to pad it out to a spherical shape. The pine staves were screwed to their neighbours and held onto the cylinder by several steel straps around the outside, giving the weapon the appearance of a fat beer barrel. On test drops, the straps often failed at the first water impact causing the wooden staves to fly off, but on several drops the bare cylinder bounced on itself. Adding extra straps and increasing their tension did nothing to prevent the failures, so in light of the performance already demonstrated by the cylinders, it was decided on 18 April to drop the cylinder 'bare', and all the wooden staves were removed.

The Upkeep mine's construction was relatively simple and similar to a conventional depth charge, consisting of two circular end plates and a cylinder formed from sheet steel. Two L-section rings 20in in diameter were bolted to the end plates to mate with the carrying discs which allowed the mine to be supported and spun, the rings being joined by six tie rods which passed through the cylinder from end to end to give rigidity. Within one end plate were four exploder pockets, one on the rotational axis and three positioned around it 120° apart. Surviving examples show variations in the exact construction (plate thickness, bolted/riveted/welded construction, number of bolts) over the development period; the operational weapons had ½in cylinders and ⅜in end plates, with 32 bolts. Some 6,600lb of Torpex explosive was used in each mine, making up just over 71 per cent of the overall

controls and Wallis himself acting as bomb aimer. The early tests were discouraging, with several bombs deforming or breaking on impact; release gear problems were also encountered, but by the end of January 1943, some successful drops had been made. Wallis brought together the theory of the weapon with the practical results in a paper entitled 'Air Attack on Dams', which was circulated to relevant Ministry and Forces personnel, some of whom also saw films of the drop tests. One of these was C-in-C Bomber Command, Arthur 'Bomber' Harris, who had previously been deeply sceptical of the whole idea. With his support secured, Wallis was able to weather a storm created by his zealous promotion of weight; Torpex was a comparatively new explosive intended for torpedoes, consisting of a mixture of 42 per cent RDX, 40 per cent TNT and 18 per cent aluminium powder. The mines were fitted with temporary protruding lugs, which would have allowed the mines to be stored on their ends and may also have been used when loading.

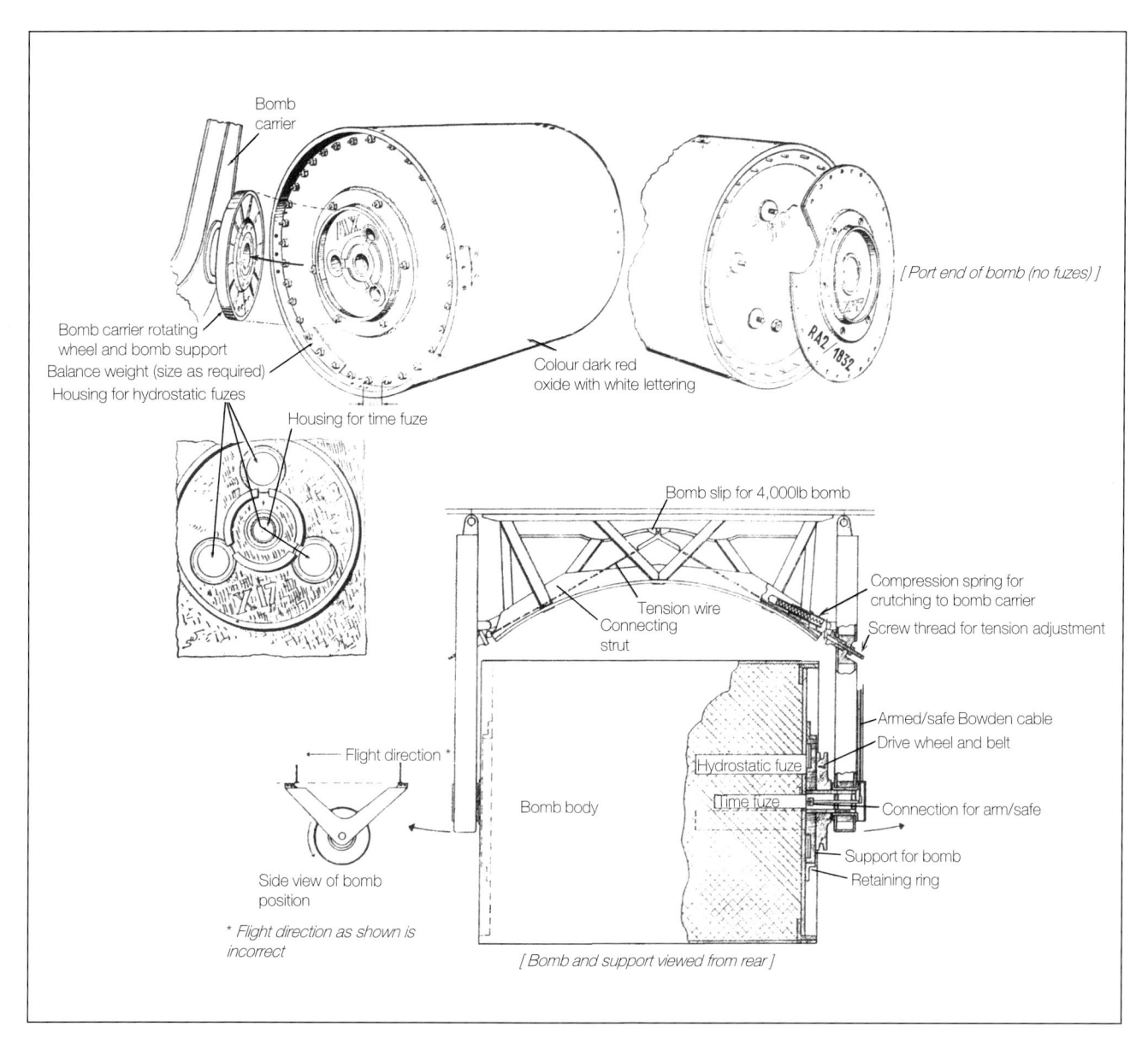

The Upkeep cylinders were manufactured at the Vickers works at Barrow-in-Furness and at Elswick and Walker on the Tyne. The HE-filled cylinders were prepared at the Royal Ordnance Factory at Chorley in Lancashire, and the inert ones at ROF Woolwich in south-east London; before the wooden shells were deleted, it had been planned to fit them at the RAF station.

Prior to loading, the mines would all have been carefully balanced on a rig at the RAF station, by adding small metal balance weights as appropriate onto the end plate bolts. In line with standard RAF practice, the inert mines were to have been painted grey and the HE-filled ones green. However, some crews painted theirs black, and at least one mine was delivered so late that it had only received its coat of red primer; the actual colours of all of the Upkeeps used on the operation is not recorded.

No original plans of Upkeep are known to have survived, and very few contemporary photographs were taken (even after the raid), although the many surviving test specimens have allowed detailed plans to be drawn post-war.

ABOVE The German bomb disposal drawings of Upkeep are the best surviving contemporary plans of the weapon (labels have been translated). *(Author's collection)*

Main particulars – Upkeep

Type	rotating depth charge
Length	60in
Diameter	51in
Weight	9,250lb (of which charge 6,600lb)
Charge/weight ratio	71.4 per cent
Casing thickness	0.5in (cylinder)/0.375in (end plates)
Filling	Torpex
Typical fuzing	three Mk.XIV hydrostatic pistols plus one No.42 fuze
Appearance	HE-filled – dark green overall, inert filled – grey (proposed)
Number expended on operations	17 (all by 617 Squadron)

RIGHT A close-up view of the outer face of the Mk.XIV pistol – the arming pin has been removed; water entered the pistol via the small holes. *(Philip French, Brenzett Aeronautical Museum)*

RIGHT One of the recovered prototype Upkeeps includes the three Mk.XIV hydrostatic pistols; the central hole was for the Mk.42 self-destruct fuze. *(Philip French, Brenzett Aeronautical Museum)*

Plans survive of the modifications made to the Lancaster to enable it to carry the weapon, though these are generally early drawings which may not reflect changes made later in the rapidly evolving development of the weapon. The Germans themselves produced detailed technical drawings within a few days of the raid, based on inspection of the crashed Lancasters and one of the Upkeeps which had been recovered intact. These details were published in *Beiehrungsblatt über Beseitigung Feindlicher Abwurfmunition*, a series of German bomb disposal information data sheets, and ironically these now form the most reliable description of the operational weapon; however, many technical and operational details of Upkeep cannot be verified with absolute certainty.

Fuzing

Detonation of the main explosive charge was required to occur at a depth of around 30ft against the face of the dam, and this was initiated by hydrostatic pistols (three were fitted to give some redundancy). Standard naval Mk.XIV pistols were selected (these were designed for use in depth charges which could be gun-launched from ships, and so were able to withstand the forces created by water impact) although the detonators contained extra

ABOVE Sectional view of Mk.XIV pistol showing mechanism. *(Author)*

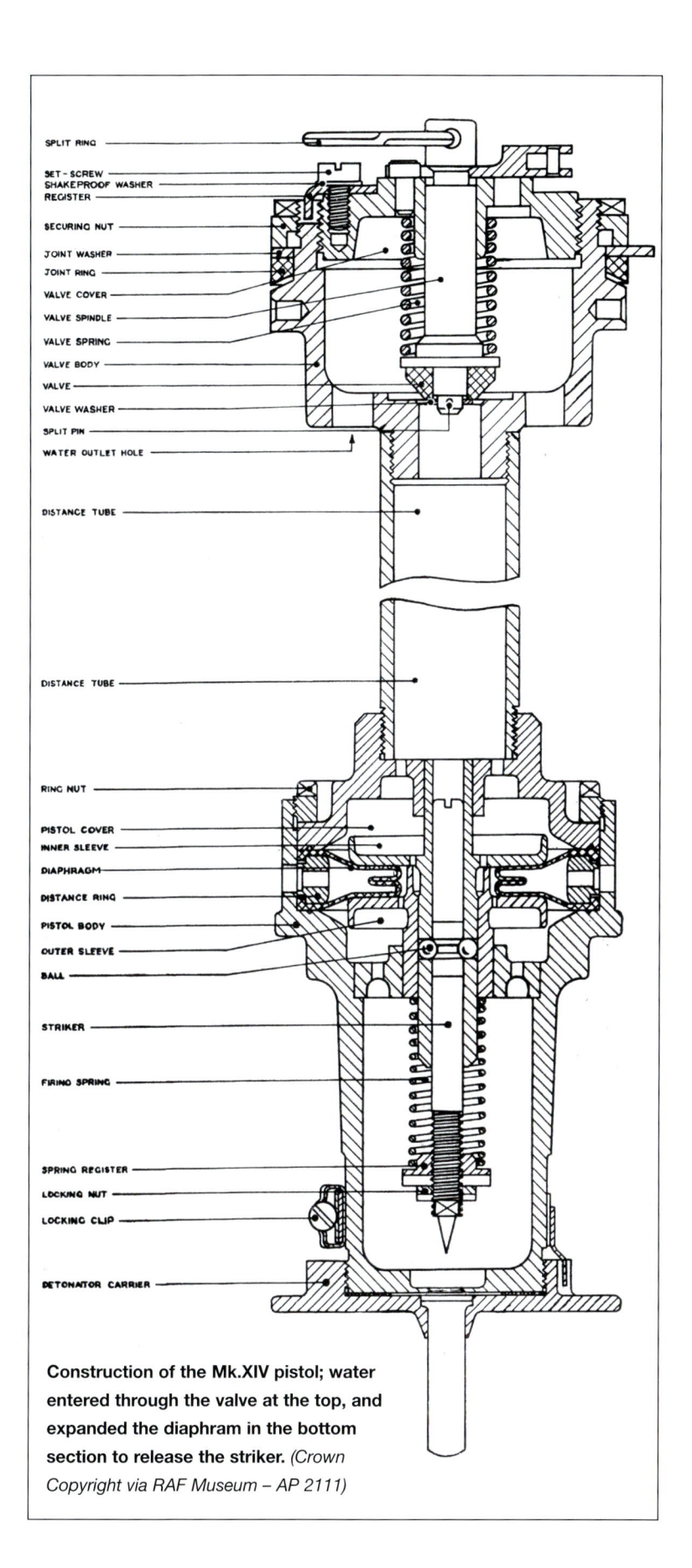

SPLIT RING	
SET-SCREW	
SHAKEPROOF WASHER	
REGISTER	
SECURING NUT	
JOINT WASHER	
JOINT RING	
VALVE COVER	
VALVE SPINDLE	
VALVE SPRING	
VALVE BODY	
VALVE	
VALVE WASHER	
SPLIT PIN	
WATER OUTLET HOLE	
DISTANCE TUBE	
DISTANCE TUBE	
RING NUT	
PISTOL COVER	
INNER SLEEVE	
DIAPHRAGM	
DISTANCE RING	
PISTOL BODY	
OUTER SLEEVE	
BALL	
STRIKER	
FIRING SPRING	
SPRING REGISTER	
LOCKING NUT	
LOCKING CLIP	
DETONATOR CARRIER	

Construction of the Mk.XIV pistol; water entered through the valve at the top, and expanded the diaphram in the bottom section to release the striker. *(Crown Copyright via RAF Museum – AP 2111)*

DEVELOPMENT OF THE BOUNCING BOMB

RIGHT Upkeep was triggered by a Mk.XIV depth charge pistol set to 30ft depth. *(Author)*

CE pellets (1.8kg each) to better initiate the large main charge used in Upkeep.

The Mk.XIV pistol (as described in Air Publication 2111A) comprised a valve unit and a pistol unit, separated by a distance tube, the whole unit being some 16in long and 3.5in diameter and weighing 9.5lb. The pistol could normally be dropped 'armed' (safety clip removed) or 'safe' (safety clip attached), but as it was impossible to arrange for removal of the three safety clips in flight (the mine was revolving and the pistols were covered by the supporting disc), these were removed before loading; this was considered safe as the mine would still have to be dropped into water for the pistols to fire and so would only have been a problem if the aircraft ditched with the Upkeep still attached. With the safety clip removed, a spring in the valve unit (on the outside of the mine) held closed a valve to prevent water entering the central tube. When the mine became submerged, water entered through holes in the valve unit into the space *outside* the central tube, and thence into a series of holes around the pistol unit. The water pressure forced a diaphragm to expand, pushing apart two sleeves, this action compressing the striker spring. On reaching the firing depth, the sleeves would have moved far enough to release ball bearings which locked the striker in place, the spring then forcing the striker down and firing the detonator beneath the pistol, which would trigger the main charge. Had the pistol been dropped 'safe', then the valve unit would have remained open, allowing water to reach *both* sides of the diaphragm, and with equalised pressures, it would not expand to release the striker.

Had an Upkeep been dropped on land, the hydrostatic pistols would not have been triggered so, given the highly secret nature of the weapon, a fuze was also fitted to the mine to act as a self-destruct device. The fuze selected was a No.42 time delay fuze, normally used in marker flares and designed to fire a detonator around 30 seconds after leaving the aircraft; it was modified for Upkeep to give a longer delay of around 90 seconds. The fuze consisted of a small canister containing a coiled length of Bickford tape (a slow-burning compound). When dropped 'armed', a Bowden cable (lanyard) would be pulled out to release a striker to fire a percussion cap which lit the tape. This would burn down slowly, eventually

Key principles – fuzing

For maximum safety, the main charge in a bomb is insensitive to rough handling, and a preset sequence of events is required to cause it to detonate. The usual explosive train (in the bombs discussed here) consisted of a pistol, percussion cap, detonator, exploder and finally the main charge. The detonation sequence began when a pointed striker impacted upon a percussion cap which contained a highly sensitive compound, typically ASA mixture (lead azide, lead styphnate and aluminium). The impact caused the ASA to burn rapidly, igniting Composition Exploding (CE) pellets (compressed TNT) in the detonator which produced a minor shock wave of sufficient strength to trigger an exploder containing a larger quantity of CE pellets, which in turn caused sympathetic detonation of the main charge. The striker and percussion cap were usually located within either a fuze (which contained some pyrotechnic element) or a pistol (which was purely mechanical), these devices being available in a variety of designs which were triggered under a range of different circumstances e.g. impact, barometric pressure, hydrostatic pressure or time delay. Detonators of the 'sensitive' type were typically used – these burned at different rates, the most common being the No.36, No.43 and No.49 which each gave a delay of 0.025 seconds (effectively instantaneous), and the No.35 which gave a delay of 11 seconds before triggering the exploder; all of these were 3.5in long and were interchangeable (colour codes were used to identify the different types).

The exploders and pistols were fitted shortly before the bomb was loaded into the aircraft. All pistols and fuzes were fitted with a safety pin which was only removed once the bomb was fully loaded and fitted with an arming wire, the latter being pulled out as the bomb fell away from the aircraft to arm the device. Certain types of fuzes and pistols could (if required) be dropped 'safe' by releasing the arming wire along with the bomb, hence preventing operation of the striker.

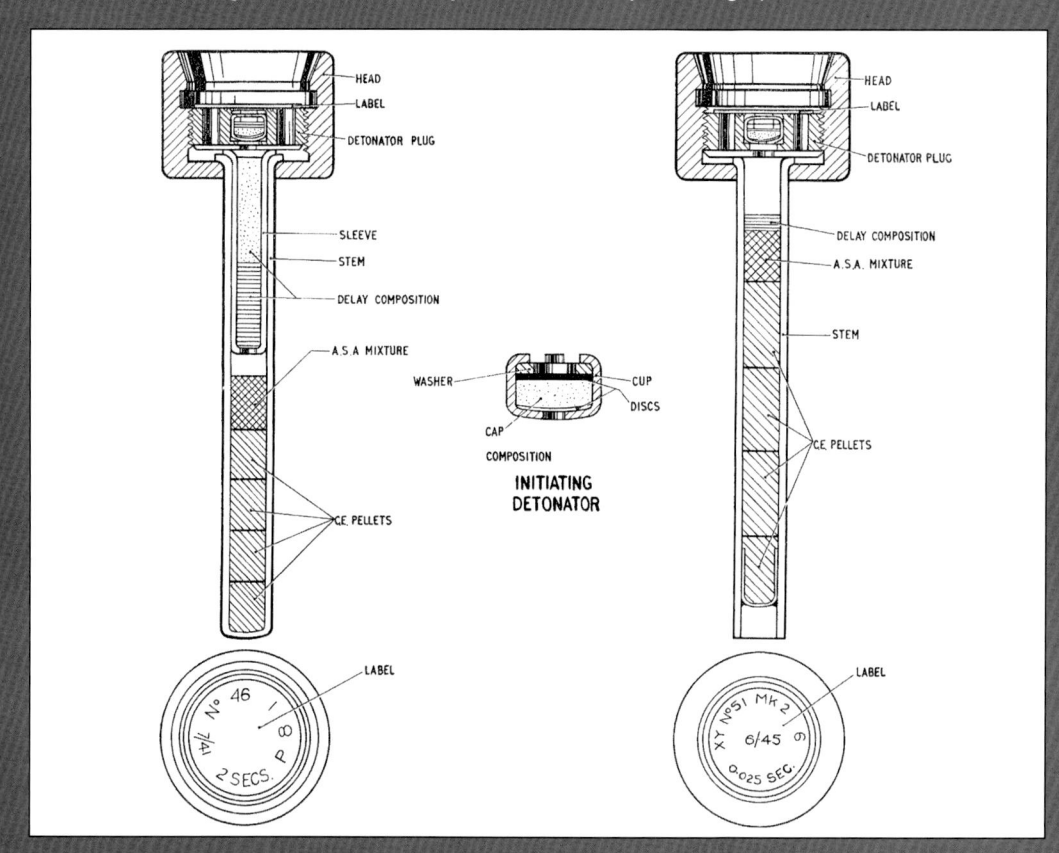

LEFT Construction of sensitive-type detonators similar to those used in Upkeep (and in the 'earthquake bombs'). *(Crown Copyright – AP 3196)*

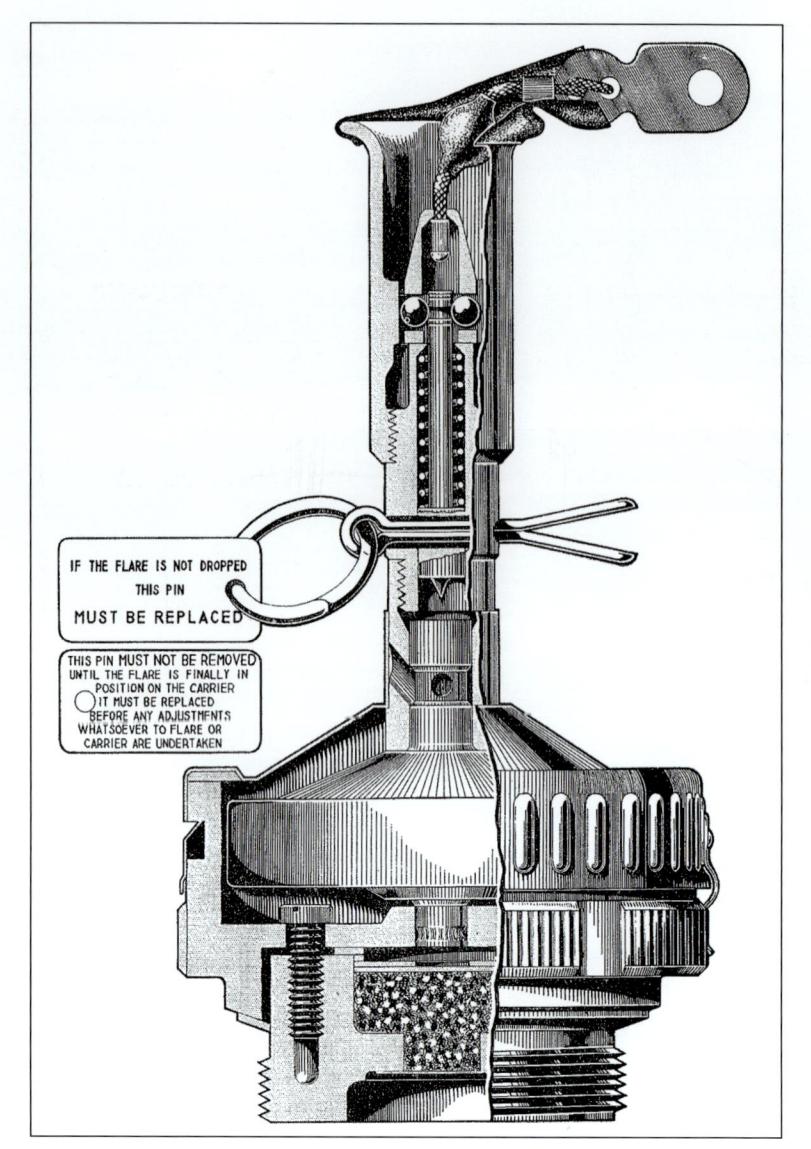

ABOVE Sectional view of No.42 fuze showing mechanism. *(Author)*

LEFT Construction of the No.42 fuze; pulling out the striker (top) lit the slow-burning compound within the drum, firing the detonator after 90 seconds. *(Crown Copyright – AP 3196)*

RIGHT A No.42 fuze was used in Upkeep to act as a self-destruct mechanism; the standard 30-second delay was extended to 90 seconds. *(Author)*

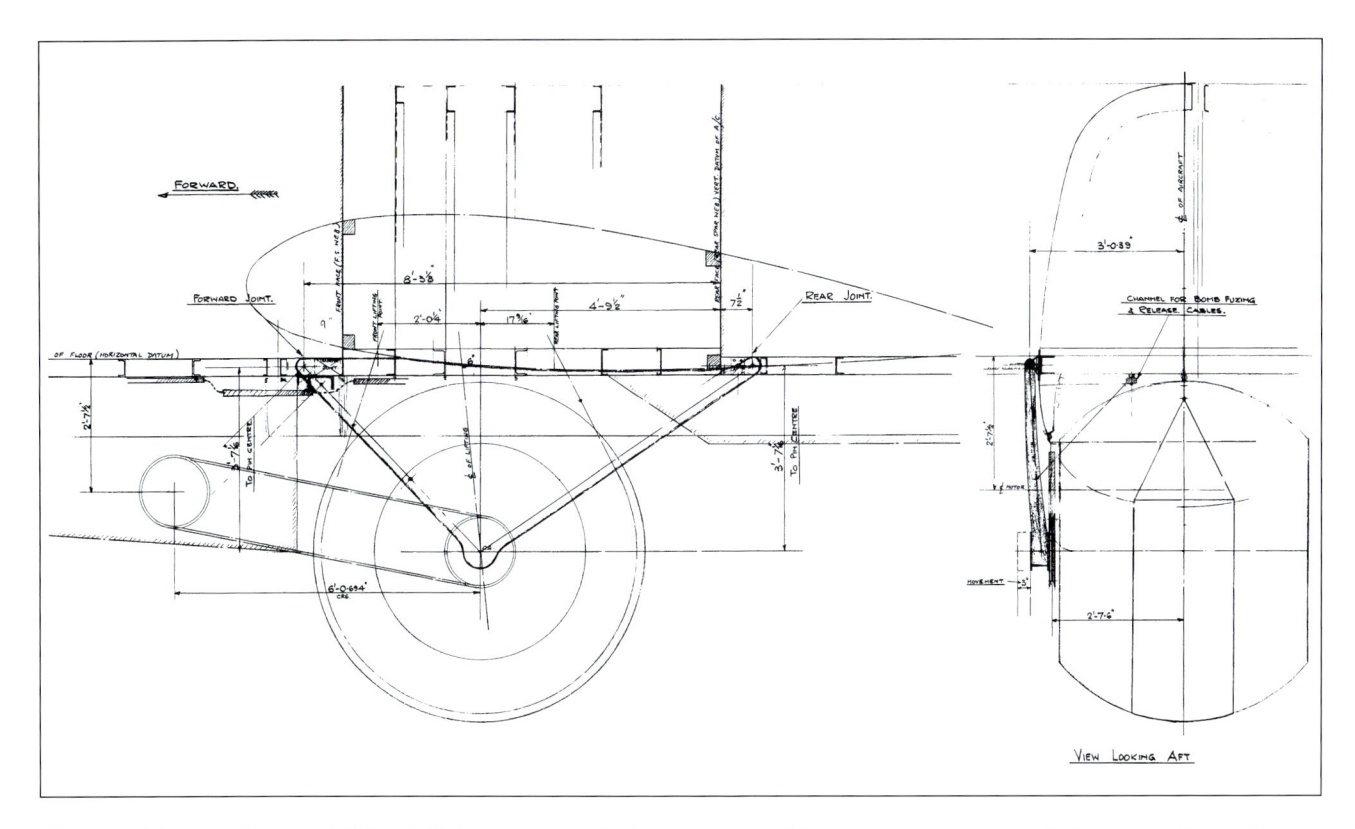

ABOVE This early draft Type 464 Lancaster installation shows the relative positions of the spherical Upkeep (including lifting harness), hinges and calliper arms, although the latter would be a simpler shape in practice. *(BAE SYSTEMS via Avro Heritage Centre)*

firing the detonator (1.3kg of CE) to initiate the main charge to destroy the mine. If dropped 'safe', the Bowden cable was dropped with the mine so the tape was not lit. The No.42 fuze was fitted in Upkeep's central exploder pocket (on the axis of rotation) to allow the mine to be spun up without the fuze being lit; the Bowden cable was connected (through the centre of the support disc) to a fuzing unit mounted on the outside of the forward arm, and so would be pulled out at the moment of release as the calliper arms opened. Five aircraft were brought down en route to the Ruhr, four of these over land, and in three of these the bomb was destroyed either in the crash or by operation of the self-destruct mechanism. However, it seems that Barlow's Upkeep stayed attached to the calliper arm so the fuze was not activated, allowing the Germans to recover his mine and learn all of its secrets (it is possible that the fuze had not been armed, but this should have been done when crossing the enemy coast).

The Type 464 Provisioning Lancaster

Originally, authorisation was given for the conversion of 30 Avro Lancaster heavy bombers for the Dams Raid, but only 23 were actually converted, under the supervision of Roy Chadwick, designer of the Lancaster. As this was a Vickers project, the special Lancasters were assigned the Vickers Type 464 (all Vickers projects were allocated a type number in roughly chronological order) and also given the nondescript codename 'Provisioning Lancaster'.

The aircraft were Lancaster B.IIIs (with four Packard Merlin 28 engines, each delivering 1300hp) with modifications carried out by Avros on the production line, and the additional parts being manufactured or supplied by Vickers (although the three prototype aircraft were modified by Vickers engineers at the Royal Aircraft Establishment at Farnborough); late alterations were made at RAF Manston (trials station) and RAF Scampton (operational station).

The modifications were mostly additions and detail changes, and involved little alteration to the main structure of the aircraft, aiding the planned

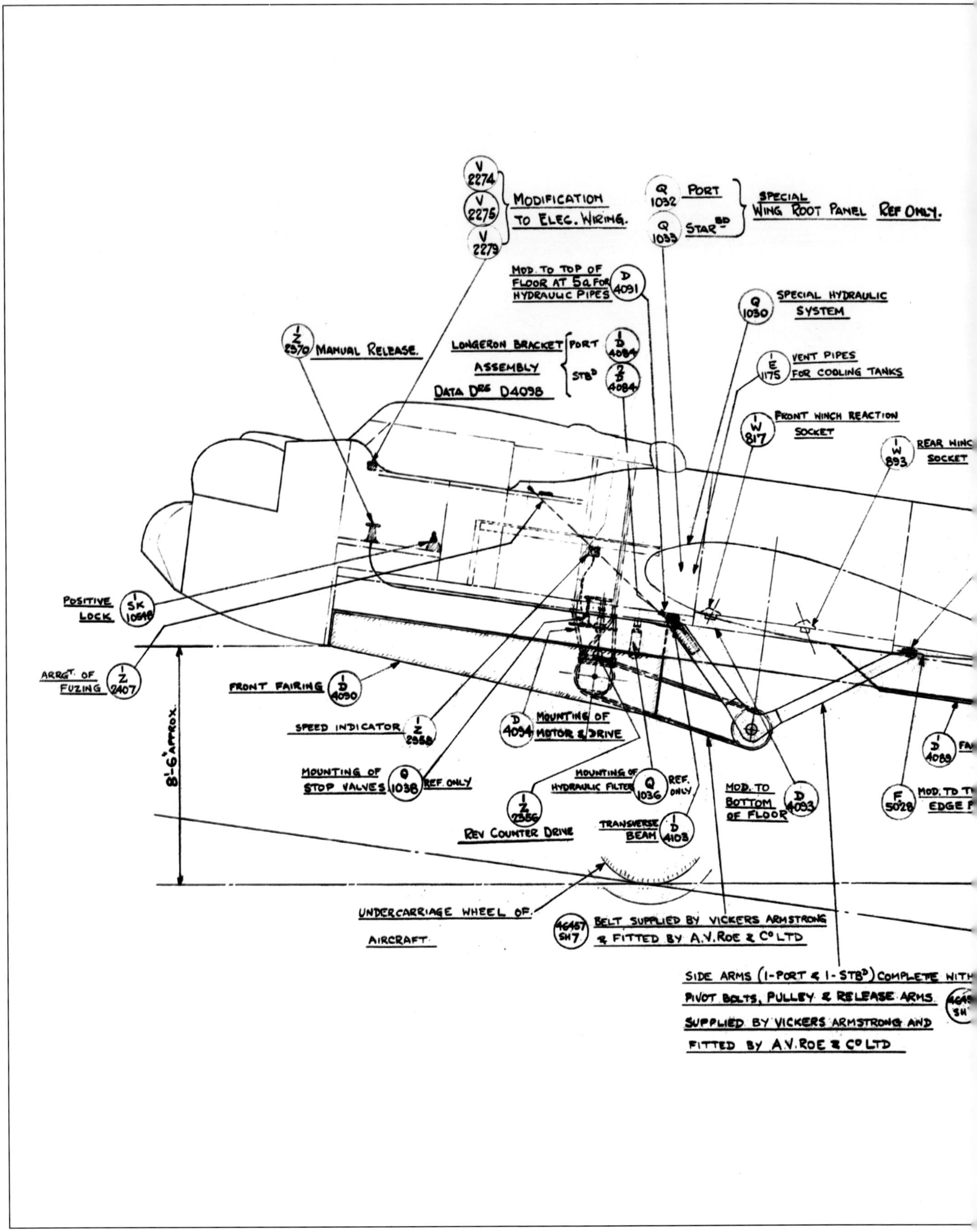
V 2274
V 2275
V 2279
MODIFICATION TO ELEC. WIRING.
Q 1032 PORT
Q 1033 STARBD
SPECIAL WING ROOT PANEL REF ONLY.
MOD. TO TOP OF FLOOR AT 5Q FOR HYDRAULIC PIPES
D 4091
Q 1030
SPECIAL HYDRAULIC SYSTEM
Z 2370 MANUAL RELEASE.
LONGERON BRACKET ASSEMBLY
DATA DRGS D4098
PORT 1 D 4084
STBD 2 D 4084
E 1175
VENT PIPES FOR COOLING TANKS
W 817
FRONT WINCH REACTION SOCKET
W 893
SOCKET
POSITIVE LOCK
SK 10548
ARRGT. OF FUZING
Z 2407
FRONT FAIRING
D 4090
SPEED INDICATOR
Z 2358
D 4094
MOUNTING OF MOTOR & DRIVE
MOUNTING OF STOP VALVES
Q 1038 REF. ONLY
MOUNTING OF HYDRAULIC FILTER
Q 1036 REF. ONLY
Z 2356
REV COUNTER DRIVE
TRANSVERSE BEAM
D 4103
MOD. TO BOTTOM OF FLOOR
D 4093
D 4089
F 5028
8'-6" APPROX.
UNDERCARRIAGE WHEEL OF AIRCRAFT.
46457 SH7
BELT SUPPLIED BY VICKERS ARMSTRONG & FITTED BY A.V. ROE & CO LTD
SIDE ARMS (1-PORT & 1-STBD)
PIVOT BOLTS, PULLEY & RELEASE ARMS.
SUPPLIED BY VICKERS ARMSTRONG AND
FITTED BY A.V. ROE & CO LTD

Avro drawing Z2352 gives the clearest overall view of the modifications to the Lancaster (the numbers in the circles are references to other drawings); although from the same batch of aircraft, the serial number shown was not used on a Type 464, and the ventral gun was not carried.
(BAE SYSTEMS via Avro Heritage Centre)

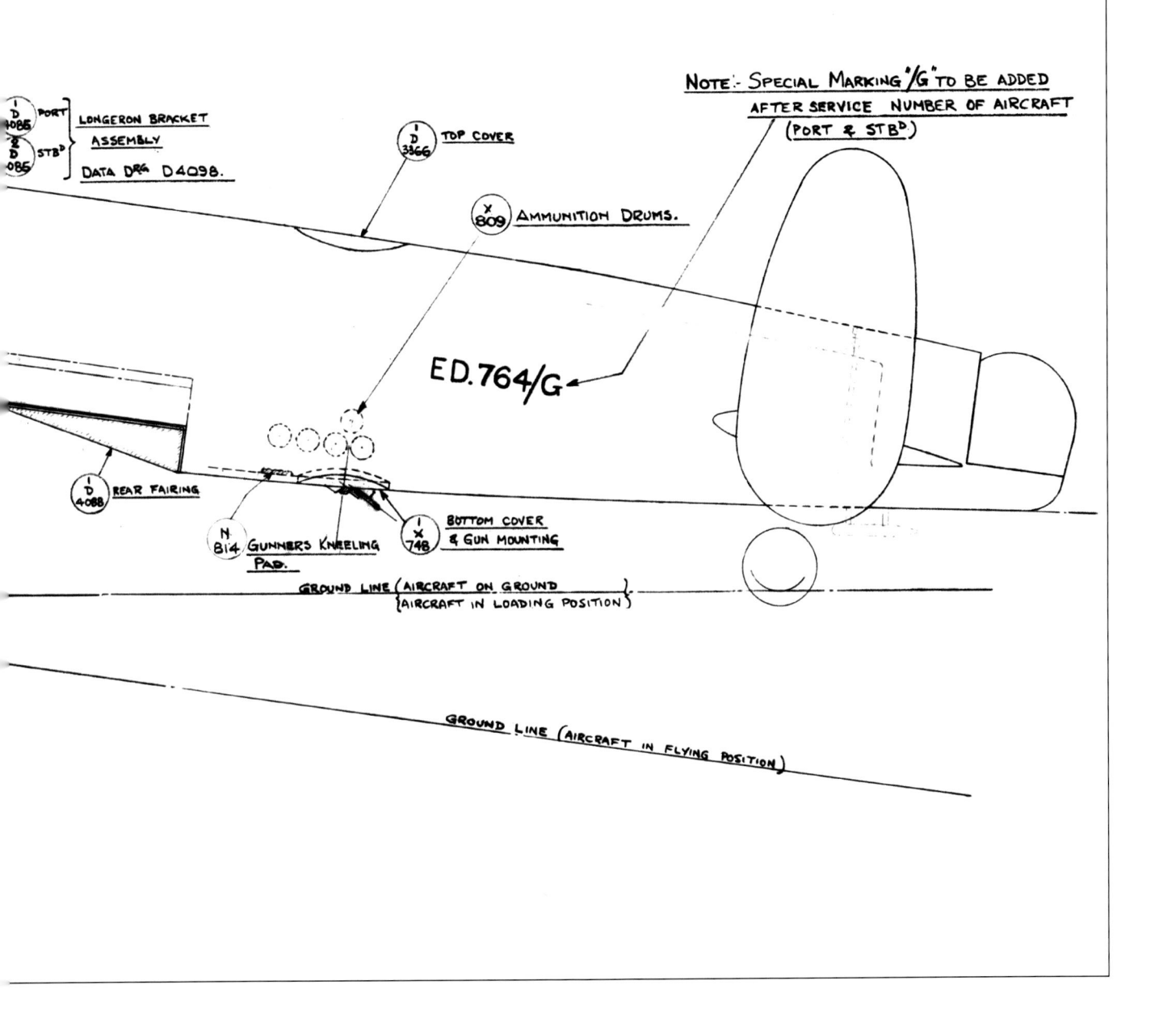

DEVELOPMENT OF THE BOUNCING BOMB

ABOVE Type 464 Lancaster ED825 was tested at A&AEE Boscombe Down – the calliper arms and belt drive are clearly visible. Allocated as the spare aircraft, it flew on Operation Chastise and attacked the Sorpe Dam. *(Imperial War Museum ATP11384B)*

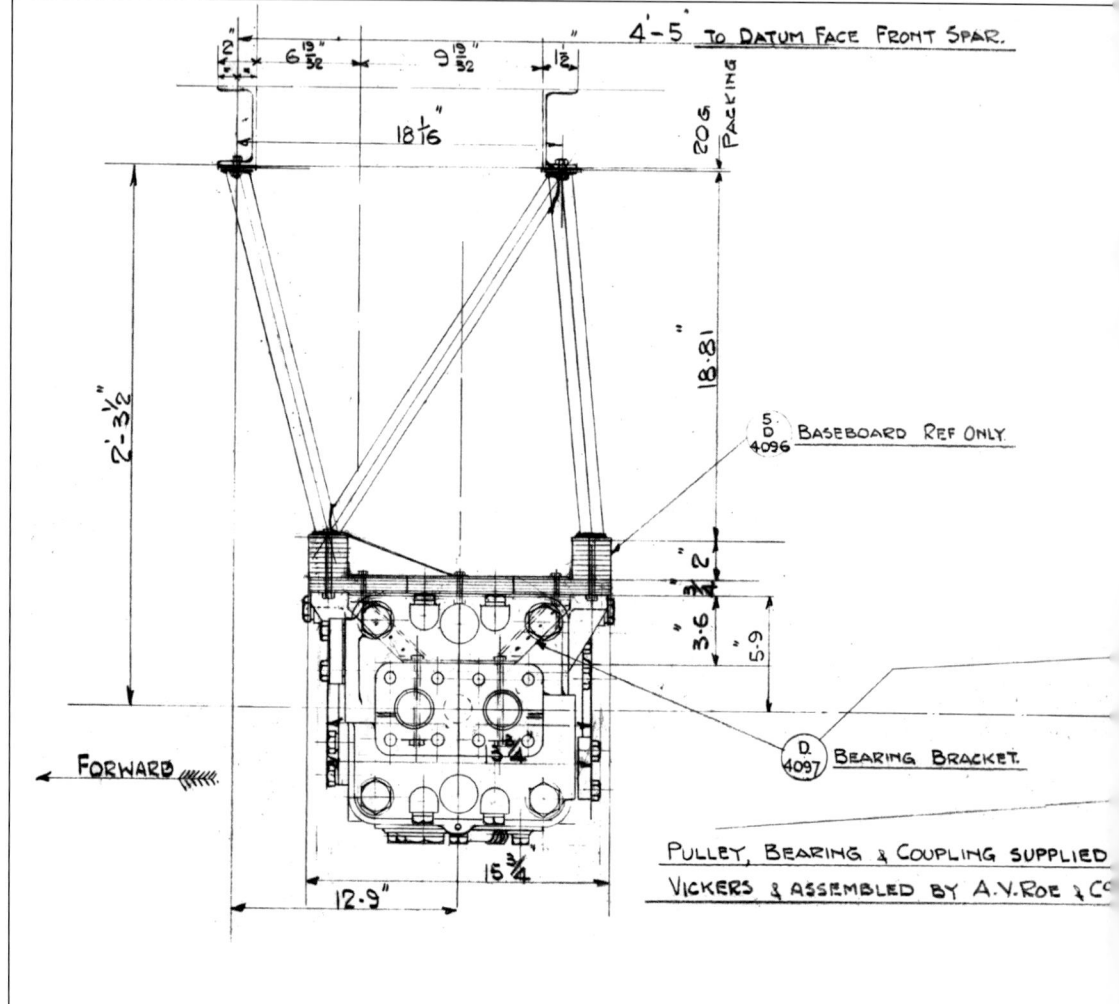

RIGHT Detail from Avro drawing D4094 shows the Variable Speed Gear hydraulic pump from a submarine, which was used in reverse as a motor to spin the bomb up to 500rpm. *(BAE SYSTEMS via Avro Heritage Centre)*

conversion back to standard bomber aircraft after the raid. The changes from the standard Lancaster specification were as follows:

Removal of bomb doors and mid-upper turret

The most obvious modifications to the aircraft were the removal of the bomb doors (to accommodate the Upkeep, which protruded below the aircraft) and, at Chadwick's suggestion, the mid-upper turret (to save weight and drag). The earliest converted Lancasters were towards the end of a production run which included fittings for a ventral gun; at least four of the Type 464 aircraft included these fittings, and the ventral gun itself can be seen in some of the pre-raid photos. However, the gun was not carried on the raid itself due to the low-level nature of the operation.

Calliper arms

The principal addition to the aircraft was the fitting of two V-shaped calliper arms to carry the Upkeep. These were made from rectangular-section metal tube, and hung from brackets attached to the bomb bay roof structure through the fuselage sides. At the bottom of the V, each arm was fitted with a free-pivoting disc which mated with the support ring on the ends of the Upkeep; the starboard disc was also fitted with a pulley for the V-belt from the rotation motor, and a fuzing unit was fitted on the outside of the forward starboard arm.

Hydraulic motor and belt

In order to spin the Upkeep at the required 500rpm, a hydraulic motor was fitted in the forward bomb bay. The motor was attached to a wooden board held approximately 18in clear

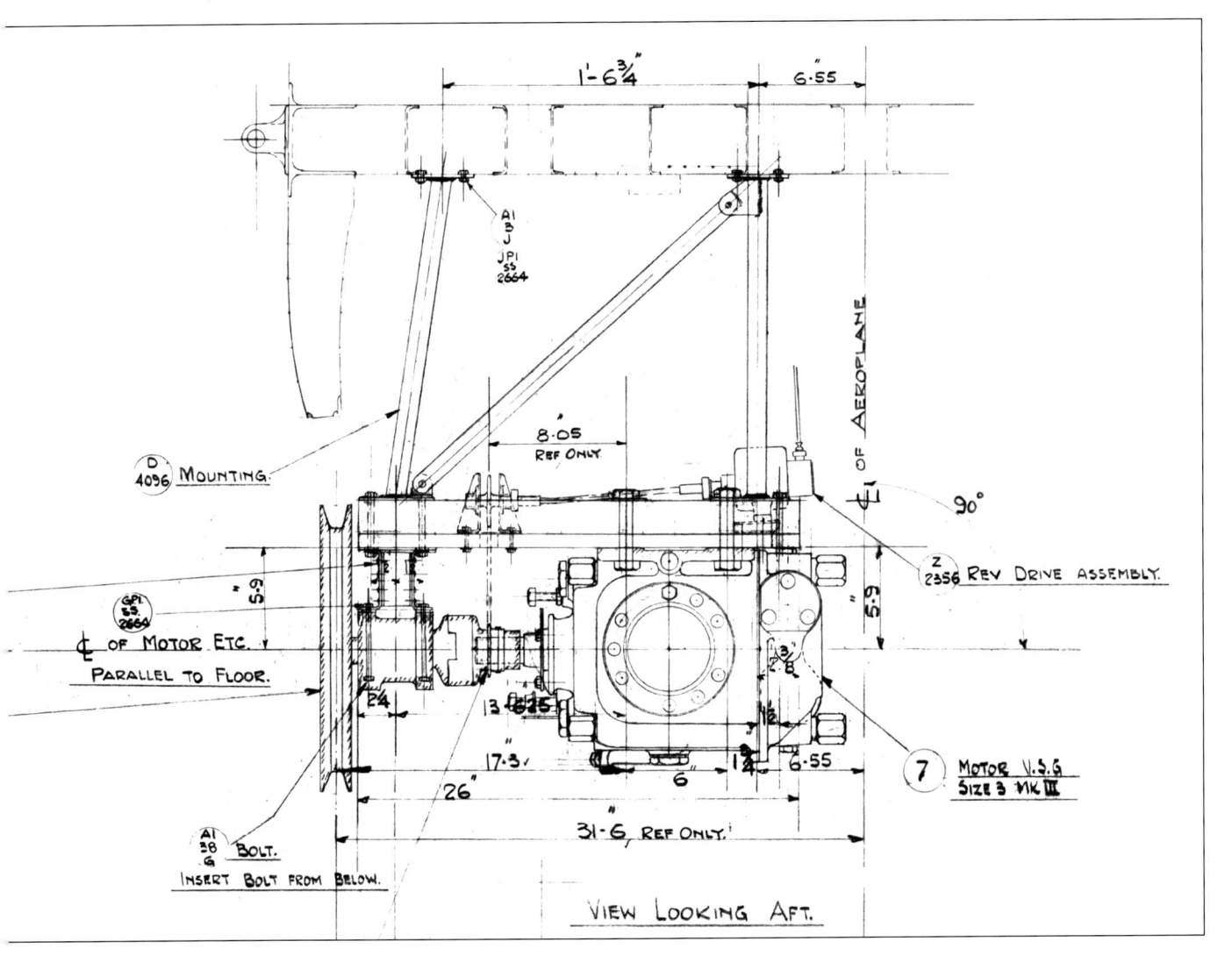

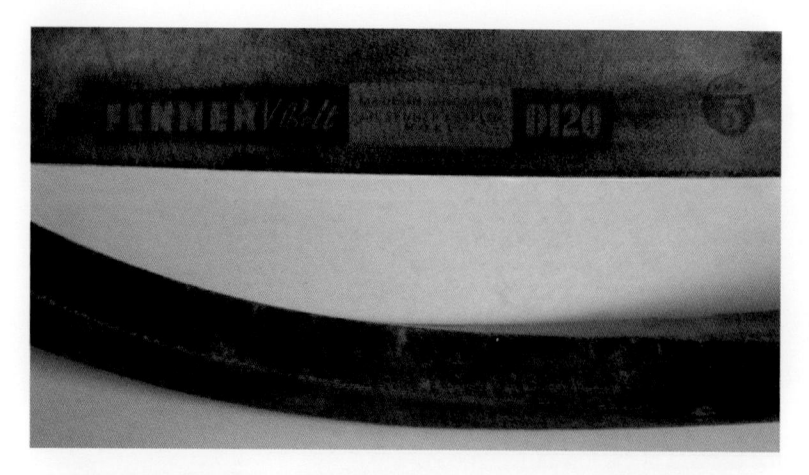

ABOVE This Fenner drive belt held by the RAF Museum is very similar to the ones used to spin Upkeep, although this example is actually too short at only 120in. *(Author)*

ABOVE RIGHT Detail from an Avro drawing gives the main dimensions of the pulleys and belt, which was 194in long. *(BAE SYSTEMS via Avro Heritage Centre)*

of the bomb bay roof by six supporting legs. Wallis designed a suitable motor himself, but when the drawings were sent for fabrication, it was found that a very similar motor was already in production at the Vickers-Armstrongs yard on the Tyne. The Vickers-Jassey Variable Speed Gear was used in submarines, although it operated in the opposite sense – the VSG was mechanically driven to pump hydraulic fluid to pistons which operated the control surfaces. The S-class submarines (built 1930–45 for the Royal Navy) used three VSGs for the rudder and hydroplanes fore and aft, and the succeeding A-class (built 1944–47) used one for the rudder only. In the Lancaster, the motor was powered from the hydraulic connection for the bomb bay doors (or possibly the connection for the mid-upper turret) and drove a 17in-diameter pulley on the starboard side of the aircraft; a 194in V-belt (made by Fenners of Marfleet, Hull) connected this to the pulley on the support disc of the Upkeep. The motor speed was controlled by the wireless operator (although at least one flight engineer reports being in charge of the spinning) using a valve and a rev counter (taken from a motorcycle) which was driven from an attachment on the output shaft of the motor and mounted on a bracket fixed to the navigator's table. There is no record of Upkeep having been spun electrically, although this was tested for spinning Highball. The Upkeeps dropped at the Sorpe were not to be spun.

RIGHT The Variable Speed Gear motor came from the steering gear in submarines like HMS *Alderney*, which was launched by Barnes Wallis's wife Molly in June 1945. *(Author's collection)*

Forward and rear fairings in bomb bay

With the bomb bay doors removed, aerodynamic fairings were added ahead of and behind the Upkeep. The front fairing followed approximately the profile of the bomb bay doors, stopping just short of the Upkeep. The fairing was in two parts, hinged along the upper edge in the same manner as the original doors; it was held together along the aircraft centreline by four fasteners, and it could be opened to give the groundcrew easier access to the weapon. The motor pulley protruded through the starboard side of the fairing, and the belt ran in two grooves in the side; a shallow fairing just ahead of the pulley was added on to divert the airflow around it. The rear fairing was in two parts – a flat section at the level of the door hinges with an inclined section connecting it to the bomb bay roof, and a curved fairing to connect the flat section to the curved profile of the lower fuselage aft of the bomb bay.

Transverse beam and bomb slip

To carry the bomb slip which would release the Upkeep, a new L-profile beam was inserted through a hole cut in the starboard side of the fuselage and bolted to the bomb bay roof. A standard Type F bomb slip was bolted to this beam, angled down to an angle of approximately 45° in line with the forward arms. Cables attached to the forward arms were used to pull the arms inwards to secure the Upkeep; the exact nature of attachment of the cables into the jaws of the bomb slip remains unknown – the German drawings show the two cables meeting at an attachment, though a simple ring around the cable may have been used. When the slip was released, the arms were able to move apart slightly (a movement of just a few inches or 5° rotation of the arms was enough to release the Upkeep), but the cables remained connected to the arms and prevented them from swinging significantly. Some post-war diagrams show four cables connecting the arms to the bomb slip, and it has also been suggested that the arms were pushed

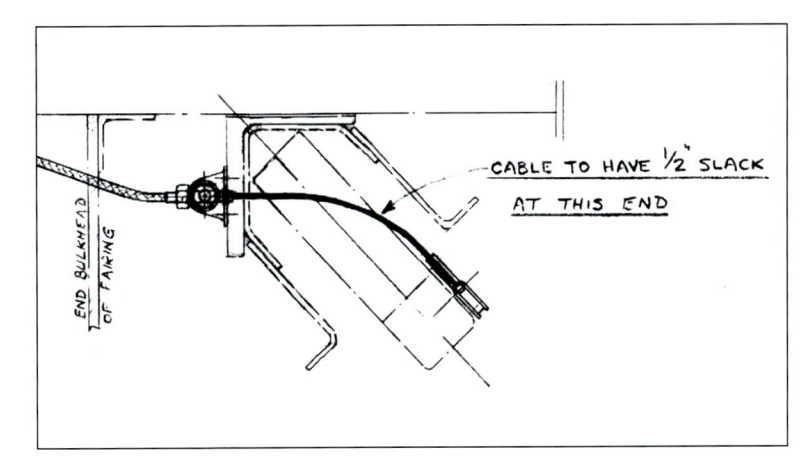

ABOVE A detail from Avro drawing Z2370 shows the new transverse beam carrying the bomb slip, with its manual release cable; the beam shown in the German drawings must have been attached to the bracket on the right. *(BAE SYSTEMS via Avro Heritage Centre)*

LEFT A standard Type F bomb slip was used to release Upkeep; it normally carried a 4,000lb HC 'Cookie'. *(Author)*

out by hydraulic jacks (having been spring-loaded inwards), but there is no firm contemporary evidence for either of these arrangements.

Manual bomb release
In case an emergency jettison was required, a cable was run from the release lever on the bomb slip to a handle on the pilot's floor, the handle coming from a glider tug (where it would have been used to release the tow).

Height lamps
One late change to the aircraft which was not shown on the original plans was the addition of two Aldis lamps for setting the correct height. One of these was fitted in the place normally reserved for the bomb aimer's camera, but the exact location of the other lamp remains open to conjecture; the most likely location seems to be within the panelling forming the rear bomb bay fairing. A surviving document with instructions for adjusting the lamps shows the rear lamp positioned exactly 20ft aft of the forward lamp, but this would place it in the sloping part of the fairing and also very close to the Upkeep, so it seems likely that it was further aft than this. Underside views of the Lancasters from the test drop films show a perceptible square marking on the horizontal rear fairing panel, and this may indicate the location of the lamp. It is possible that in early experiments with the height lamps, the rear lamp was fitted even further aft, perhaps in the ventral turret position.

The 'German beam'
The most intriguing modification is the substantial beam within the bomb bay shown in the German drawings – because this does not appear in any of the British drawings, nor is any attachment to the aircraft apparent. However, such a beam was required to carry the springs to push out the calliper arms at the moment of release. The beam's shape suggests an early genesis, as it has a clearance gap for the outer shell of the early Upkeep. The drawing appears (from its general arrangement and the hinges in

BELOW This drawing shows the configuration of the Upkeep mechanism within the Lancaster's bomb bay. Note also the two Aldis lamps fore and aft. (Haynes)

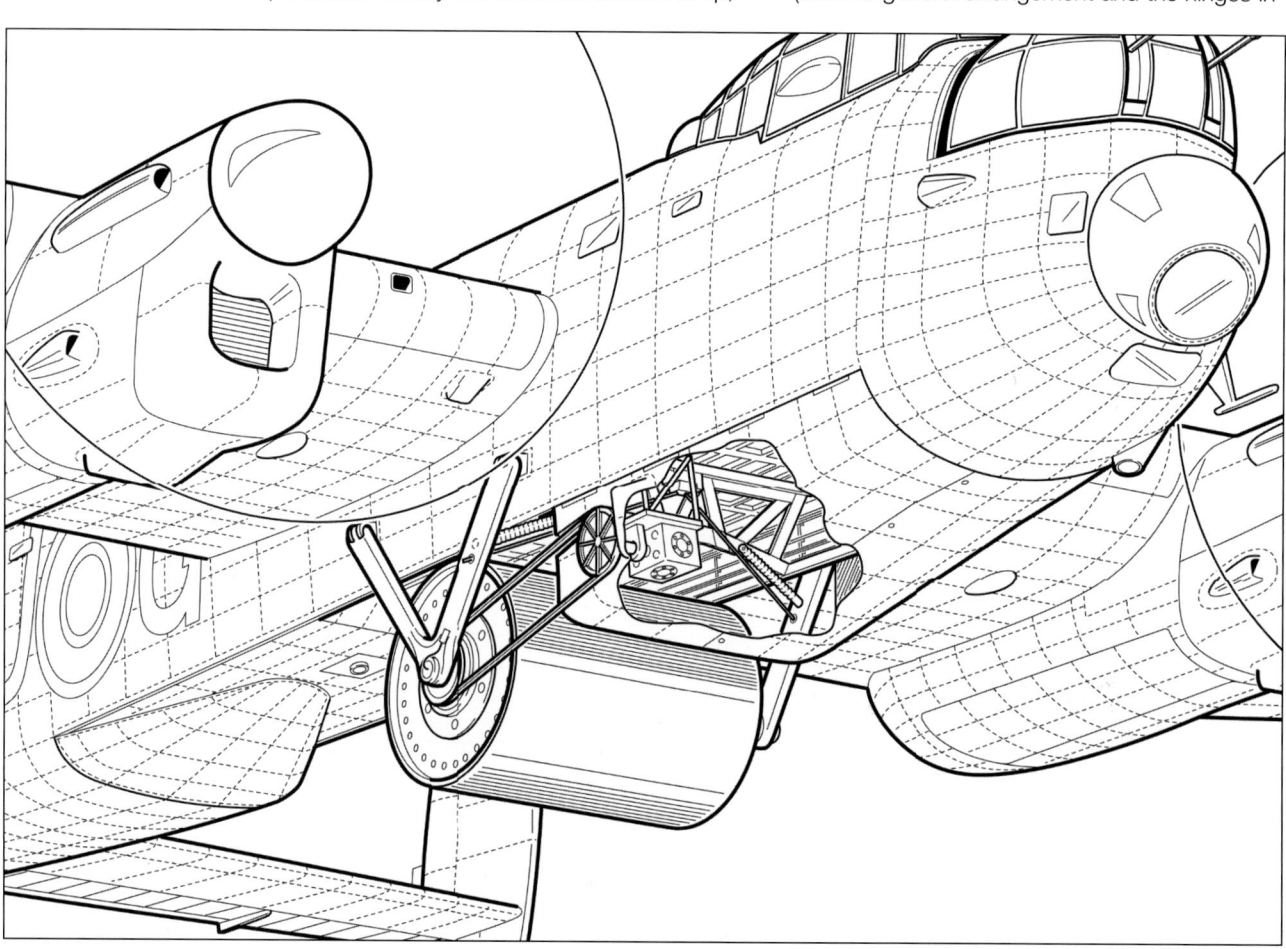

particular) to be a view from the rear, but there is not enough clearance between the mine and the bomb bay roof for the beam to fit as shown. Investigation points to the beam being inclined in line with the forward calliper arm, and attached to the L-shaped transverse beam just aft of the bomb slip (hence no other attachment point is required). The springs were attached to the calliper arms at a level just below the sides of the bomb bay, and just above the attachments for the cables which held the arms in. The springs themselves were encased in telescopic tubes, probably to keep them straight when under compression.

Miscellaneous small modifications

Minor changes were made to the electrical system, the hydraulic system and the bomb bay roof; '/G' was added to the aircraft serial number (indicating that it was to be guarded when on the ground), although this was removed prior to the raid. TR1143 VHF radios were fitted to allow voice communication between aircraft when over the target area (normally bombers only used wireless telegraphy with their base, and any communication between aircraft was by signal lamp; the latter was unsuitable for this operation although the former procedure was used). The front gun was usually manned by the bomb aimer, but as both roles were required at the target on this operation, stirrups were fitted to the turret to prevent the gunner's legs from hanging down in front of the bomb aimer. The aircraft were fitted with the 'deep' (i.e. hemispherical) bomb aimer's blister, which was already becoming standard fit in preference to the flatter type fitted to early Lancasters.

Loading Upkeep

Avro drawings specified a Type E bomb trolley for carrying the Upkeep, although this was a new type at the time, so older types available on the stations may actually have been used; two battens were fixed across the trolley to hold the Upkeep. When carried on a trolley, the

BELOW **A detail from Avro drawing Z2353 shows the two bomb winches used to lift the Upkeep into the bomb bay – note also the detail of the wooden rear fairing, within which the rear Aldis lamp would have been mounted (not shown).** *(BAE SYSTEMS via RAF Museum)*

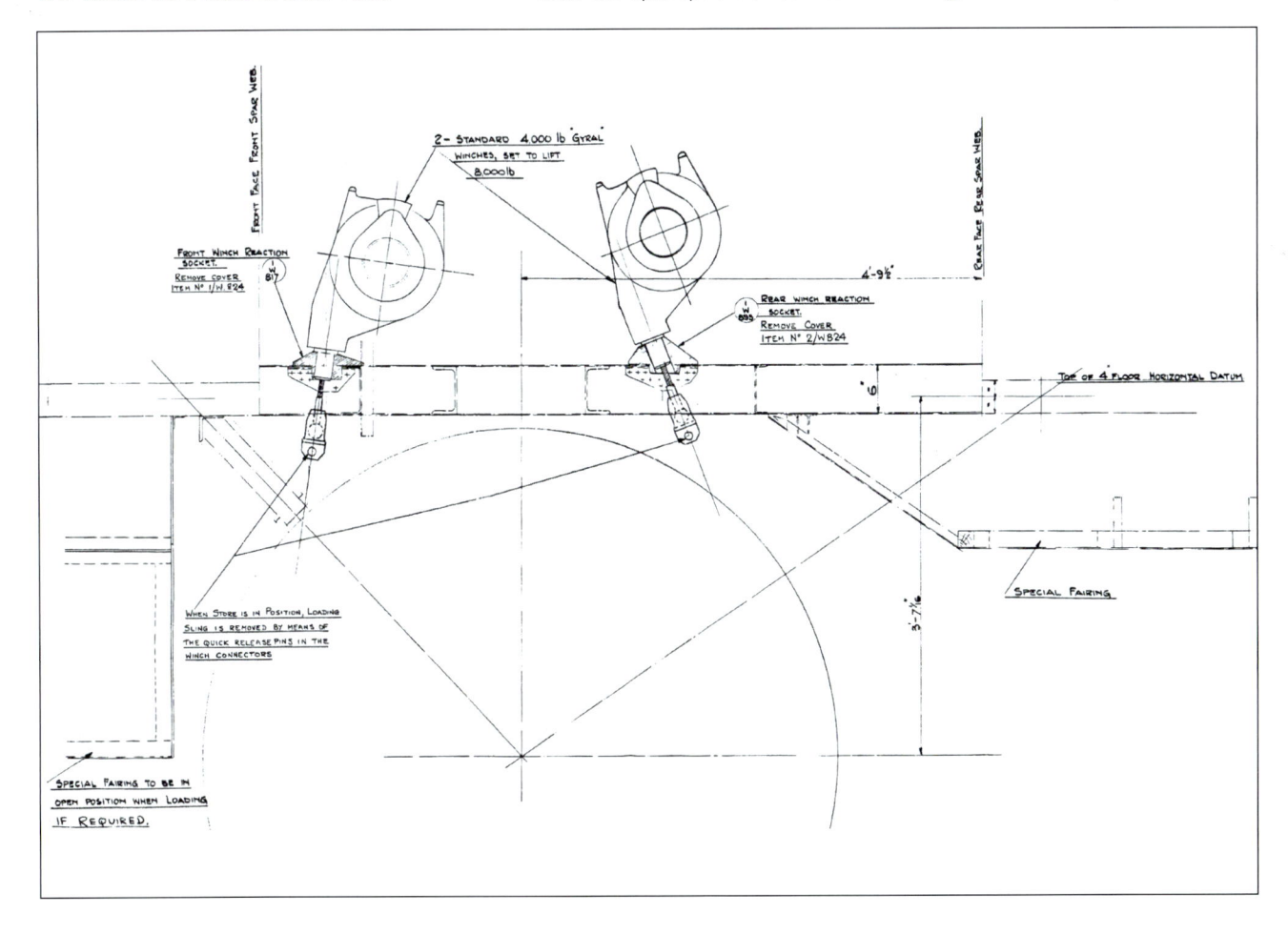

ABOVE In its original form, Upkeep was too large to fit beneath the Lancaster's nose, so the tail had to be lifted to allow the bomb to be loaded at the rear. This simulation of the loading is based on an Avro drawing in the RAF Museum. *(Author)*

prototype Upkeep would not fit beneath the Lancaster for loading like a conventional bomb load. Consequently, a scheme was devised whereby the tail of the Lancaster would be lifted by a crane (using an eyebolt which could be attached to the aircraft just forward of the rear turret), allowing the bomb trolley to be pushed in from the rear with just a few inches clearance; once Upkeep was in position beneath the bomb bay, the tail wheel was lowered back down onto the tarmac. A wire harness was then put around the Upkeep, and this connected via cables to two standard 4,000lb Gyral bomb winches fitted (as was standard for normal bomb loads) in sockets above the bomb bay roof; the winches were each adjusted to lift 8,000lb. The harness cables terminated in wire-spliced loops, which were connected to the winch cables (for speed of manufacture, the first sling had solid stainless steel ends fitted, but these did not offer sufficient flexibility, and one of Wallis's staff had to use a sledgehammer to reshape them to fit).

Once winched up, the fitting on the release cables was attached to the bomb slip, thus pulling the calliper arms together, compressing the release springs and clamping the Upkeep in place; the nuts connecting the screwed ends of the cables to the arms were then used to adjust the tension in the cables. With the Upkeep secure, the harness could be removed, and the winches could be removed from the aircraft. The weight of the Upkeep was thus supported by the flanges engaging the discs on the calliper well on the smooth cylinder, it is probable that the lifting cables were attached to the lugs bolted to the ends of the cylinder, or that some intermediate cabling and lifting beam was used. The lugs were unbolted and removed prior to flight, leaving triple sets of holes on the rims, which can be seen on the German drawings.

In order for the Upkeep to follow the desired trajectory and arrive accurately at the dam travelling at low speed, it was necessary to release it at a closely specified height, speed and distance from the dam. After early trials showed that the planned release height of 150ft was impractical, Wallis recalculated these as 60ft, 232mph and 475yd respectively. Although the airspeed was easy to achieve (this was almost full speed for the laden Lancaster at low altitude), Wallis had given little thought as to how the height and distance could be achieved accurately, and ultimately these problems were solved by others using similar principles.

Setting the release height

Although judgement of height by eye was satisfactory for test drops in daylight, this was not practical at night. Cockpit altimeters and radio altimeters were not accurate enough for the job, and attempts to hang weights down beneath the aircraft were unsuccessful. The problem was solved by Benjamin Lockspeiser, Director of Scientific Research at the Ministry of Supply, employing a technique tried by Coastal Command for low-flying U-boat searches – the beams from two lamps could be set to converge at the required height. In the Lancaster, the forward lamp was in the bomb aimer's camera position slightly to port of the aircraft centreline, and this shone directly to starboard at 30° from the vertical. The second lamp in the rear bomb bay shone to starboard at 40° from the vertical and slightly forward so that its spot touched the spot from the forward lamp when the aircraft was at the required height of 60ft. The spots were just ahead of the wing line and were observed by the navigator through the starboard cockpit blister; as the spots travelled in different directions as the aircraft varied its height (the forward spot went sideways, the rear spot moved diagonally), the navigator could tell whether the aircraft was too

arms, and there was very little force placed on the bomb slip.

Finally, the drive belt (which would have been placed round the aft pulley before the Upkeep was loaded) could then be put in place around the forward pulley, and the aircraft was ready to fly.

With the removal of the outer shell following the decision to use the bare cylinder, the tail lift loading method was no longer necessary, as the cylindrical mine on its trolley could fit beneath the nose of the aircraft (if the forward fairing was opened) with sufficient clearance beneath the hydraulic motor. It is thus likely that this method was used for loading the aircraft for the later test drops and for the operation itself. As the wire harness would not have gripped

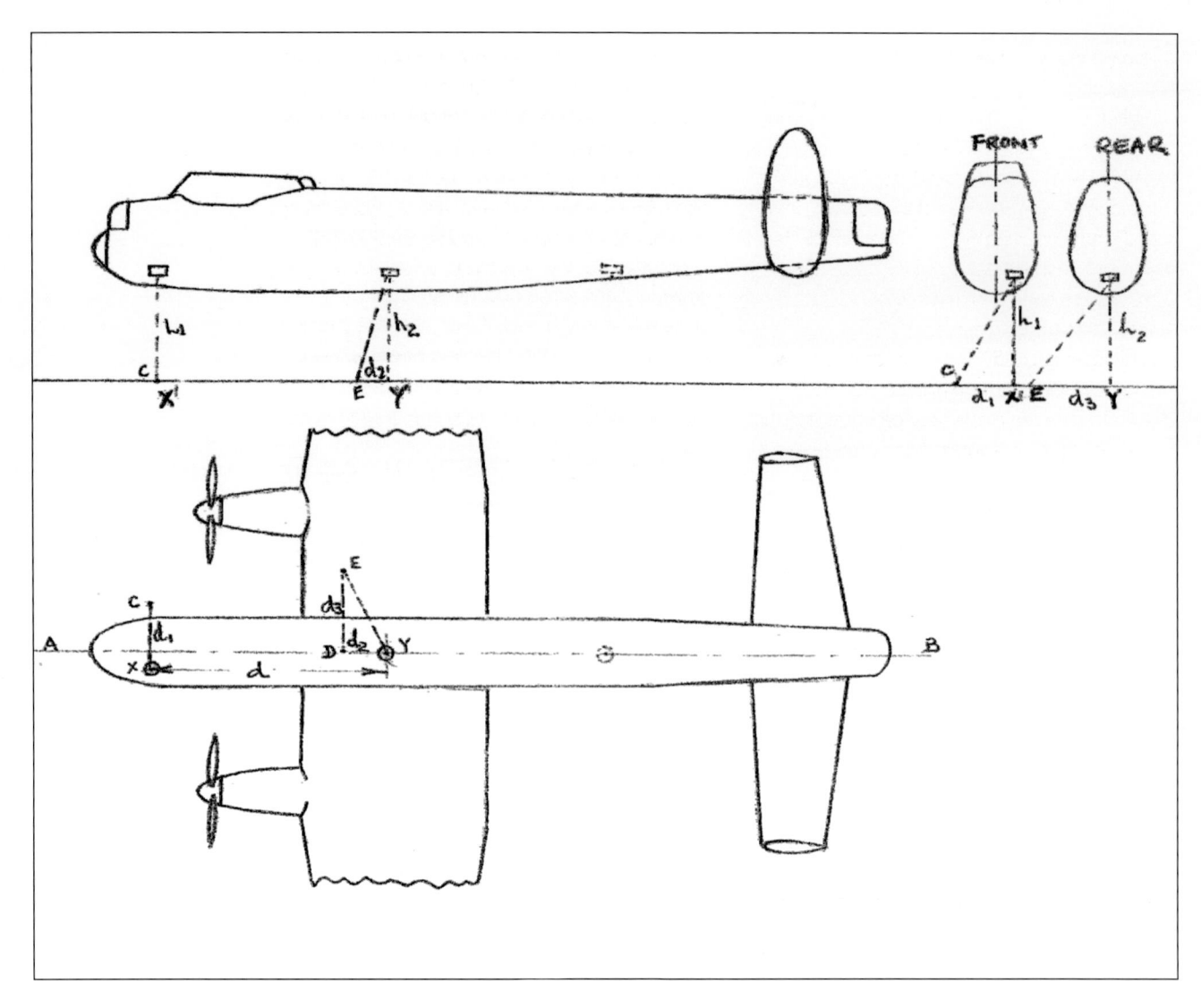

ABOVE This drawing shows the original configuration of the Aldis lamps used for judging height over the water. *(RAF Museum DC72/28)*

high or too low from the pattern they made, and direct the pilot accordingly.

A handwritten document describing how the height lamps were to be correctly adjusted (in the Lancaster on the ground) has survived in the RAF Museum's collection (it dates from immediately after the use of the lamps was adopted, as it assumes a lamp spacing of 20ft and the original drop height of 150ft):

1. Jack up aircraft until riggers' fore and aft datum line is horizontal within ±¼°.
2. Check that aircraft is level transversely i.e. it is not standing with one wing low; tolerance is ±1°.
3. Adjust lamps as follows, using a 'combination set': front lamp – pointing 30° from the vertical out to starboard, level fore and aft; rear lamp – pointing 40° from the vertical out to starboard and $\tan^{-1} d/150$ forwards.
4. From suitable points on the underside of the fuselage, one near the nose and the other near the tail, drop a plumb line and mark off the fore and aft line on the floor (AB) or draw a string tightly between them.
5. From the centre of the glass of the front lamp, drop a plumb line and mark the floor point X. Measure this distance (h_1). From the tables, read off the appropriate value of d_1. Using the jig provided, draw the line X'C perpendicular to line AB such that X'C=d_1. Mark clearly point C.
6. From the centre of the glass of the rear lamp, drop a plumb line and mark the floor point Y. Measure this distance h_2. From the tables, read off values of d_2 and d_3. Using the jig provided, draw the line DY=d_2 parallel to AB and DE=d_3 perpendicular to AB. Mark clearly point E. Check that the fore

and aft distance between X and Y is approx. 20 feet.
7. Switch on the lamps and adjust front lamp so that the centre of light spot on the ground coincides with point C and rear lamp so that the centre of light spot coincides with point E. Tighten up wing nuts on lamp brackets and drill each bracket. Fit locking bolts so that lamps cannot change their settings (two locking bolts per bracket).
8. After locking bolts have been inserted, switch on again and check. It is essential that the adjustments are made very carefully and that the light spots are within ¼in of the desired points.

Note: h_1 and h_2 are measured from the lamp fronts. A correction has been applied to the tables to allow for the fact that the measurements should be made from the centre of the filaments.

The tables referred to in these instructions gave some pre-calculated values of d_1, d_2 and d_3, derived from the formulae:

$d_1 = [(h_1+1in) \times \tan 30° - 0.7in]$ feet
$d_2 = [(h_1+1in) \times \tan 40° - 0.7in]$ feet
$d_3 = (h_2+1in) \times d/150$ feet

When the drop height was changed to 60ft, the values would have been recalculated and the lamps adjusted accordingly. The height setting was checked by flying the aircraft across the airfield using the lamp altimeter and measuring its actual height using a theodolite.

Setting the release distance

Triangulation was also the solution to the distance problem, which was solved by Wg Cdr Dann, the Supervisor of Aeronautics at the Aircraft & Armament Experimental Establishment (A&AEE). Noting that the two main target dams had two sluice towers, he devised a triangular sight that allowed the bomb aimer to view two pins which would align with the towers when the correct distance was reached. In practice, it was found extremely difficult for the bomb aimer to keep the sight steady while holding himself up and grasping the release button in his other hand. Consequently, many of the bomb aimers used a variation on this technique, attaching a length of string between two screws on opposite sides of the clear view panel in the nose blister. Pulling the string taut to their eye with a nail, they could line up the towers with marks drawn onto the clear view panel using a chinagraph pencil.

The bombing run thus called for great co-ordination by the crew – the flight engineer controlling the aircraft speed, the navigator calling out changes in height, the bomb aimer calling out changes in line, and the pilot orchestrating all of these while keeping the aircraft flying straight and level. The bomb aimer had to be completely satisfied that all of the release parameters were correct at the instant the release point was reached before pressing his button (on the raid,

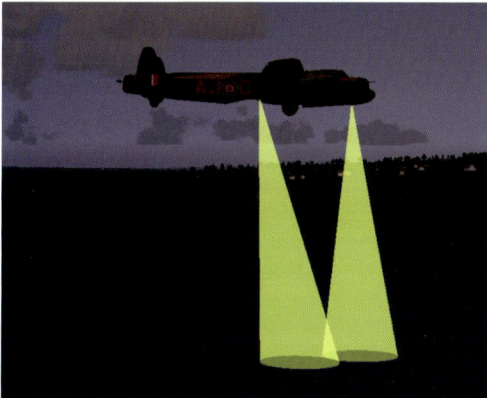

LEFT Simulation of the light spots on the water with the Lancaster at 60ft including front-on (top) and side-on (middle); many drawings mistakenly show the spots directly under the fuselage. *(Author)*

RIGHT The principle of similar triangles – the triangle is the same in all cases. *(Author)*

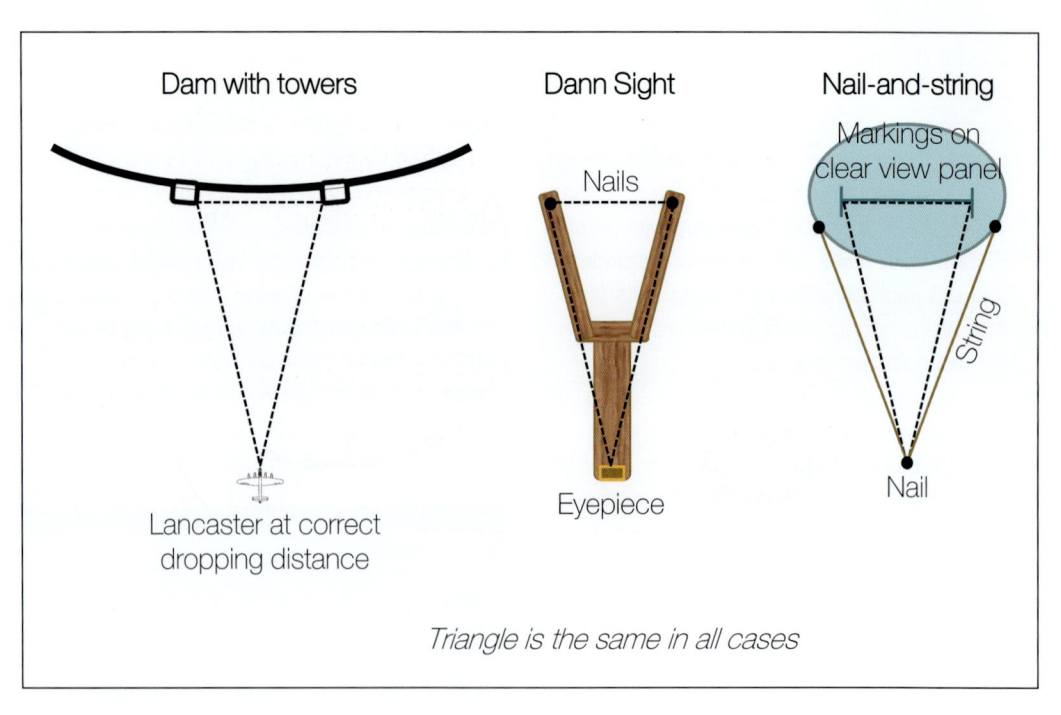

Dam with towers
Lancaster at correct dropping distance

Dann Sight
Nails
Eyepiece

Nail-and-string
Markings on clear view panel
String
Nail

Triangle is the same in all cases

BELOW The Dann sight used by Maltby's bomb aimer is the only one to have survived. *(David Worrow)*

many 'dummy runs' would be called because the bomb aimer was unhappy with some aspect of the approach). This caused the solenoid in the bomb slip to operate and separate the slip jaws. This released the cables between the calliper arms, which were then rapidly forced apart by the compressed springs, allowing the Upkeep to fall clear. The pilot would then pull up, the navigator would note the spin speed at release before turning off the spin motor, and the rear gunner was tasked with observing the path of the Upkeep.

Final preparations

With the prototype mines and Lancasters ready, test drops began on 13 April at Reculver on

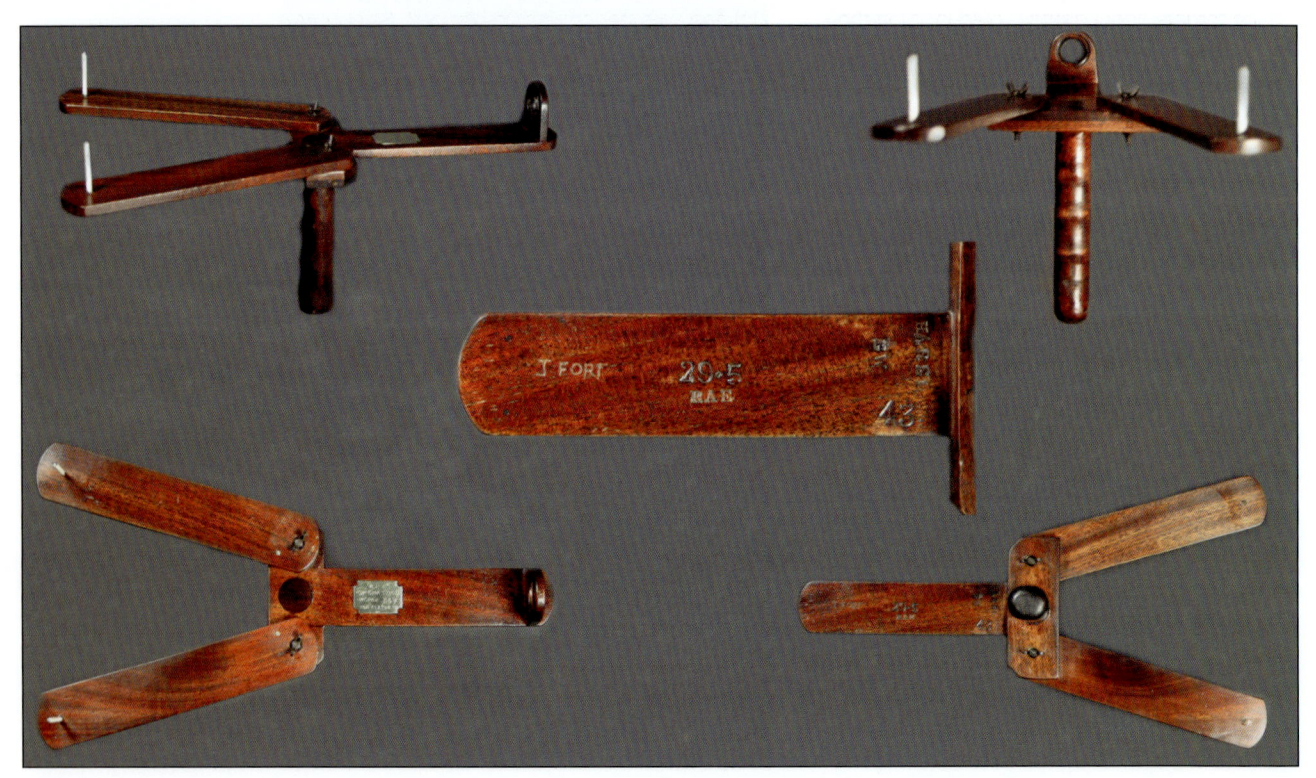

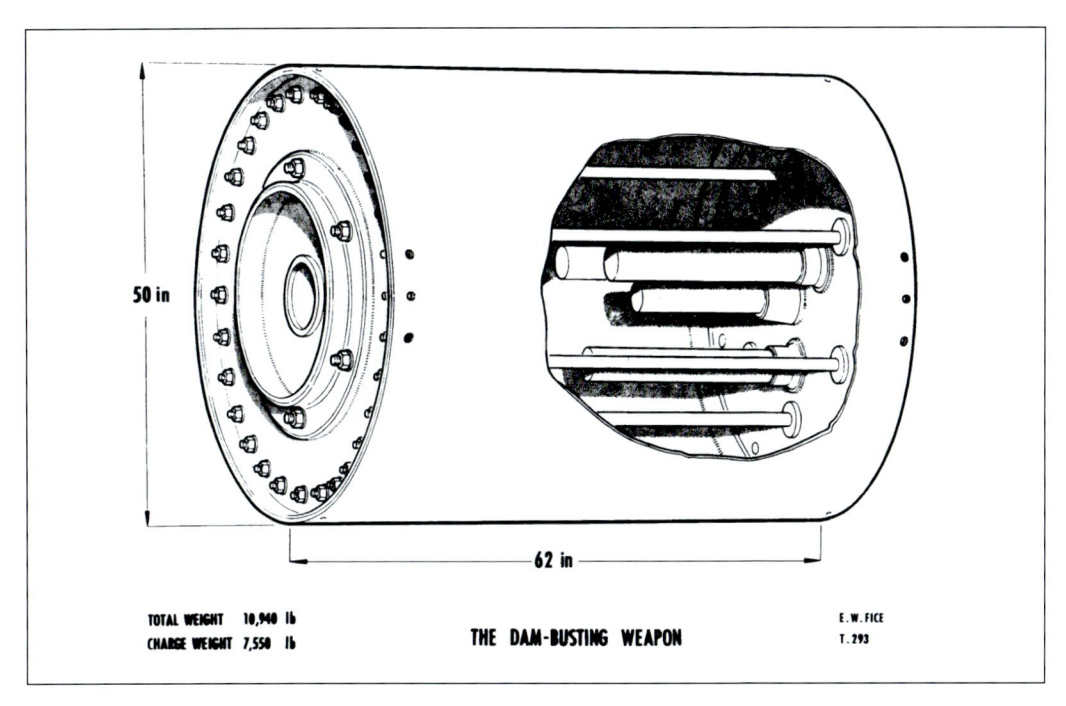

LEFT The Upkeep patents were published in 1963, and one of the first jobs given to new draughtsman Ted Fice was to draw the weapon for release to the press; the four exploder pockets and six tie-bars can be seen inside. *(BAE SYSTEMS via Ted Fice)*

the north Kent coast, flying from nearby RAF Manston. Reculver was a reasonably isolated location, and the gently shelving beach would allow drops to be made at high tide and the mines to be inspected or recovered at low tide. Early drops were made parallel to the beach, later drops being made towards the beach, with screens erected in place of the sluice towers on the targets. Ideal drops would land on the surf line, though some fell short and some cleared the back of the beach, spinning into the lagoon behind. At the end of April, one aircraft (ED825/G) also underwent a series of flight tests at the A&AEE at Boscombe Down in Wiltshire, in order to establish its handling characteristics and fuel consumption, both loaded and unloaded; the maximum permissible take-off weight was 63,000lb.

By the second week in May, Upkeep was behaving well enough to allow the 617 Squadron pilots to practise for themselves – it was planned to allow each crew two test drops. These were also largely successful, although on at least two occasions the water splash from the mine caused damage to the dropping Lancaster, one so badly that it could not be repaired before the raid.

Two additional test drops were made further out from the coast. The first, on 13 May, was a drop of a live Upkeep, the mine making seven bounces over 800yd before sinking and detonating successfully, producing a spectacular water plume over 1,000ft high. The second, two days later, was an impact test, the Upkeep being dropped from 500ft, unspun and with no pistols fitted. As expected, when it hit the water it did not break up or explode.

Testing and training were complete, and Upkeep was performing as planned. Final approval from the Chiefs of Staff (who were visiting Washington with Churchill) was given on 15 May, and the raid – codenamed Operation Chastise – was to go ahead at the 'first suitable opportunity'.

LEFT An arming pin from the live Upkeep dropped off Broadstairs on 13 May 1945, which pilot Sqn Ldr 'Shorty' Longbottom kept as a souvenir. *(Courtesy of Dominic Winter Book Auctions)*

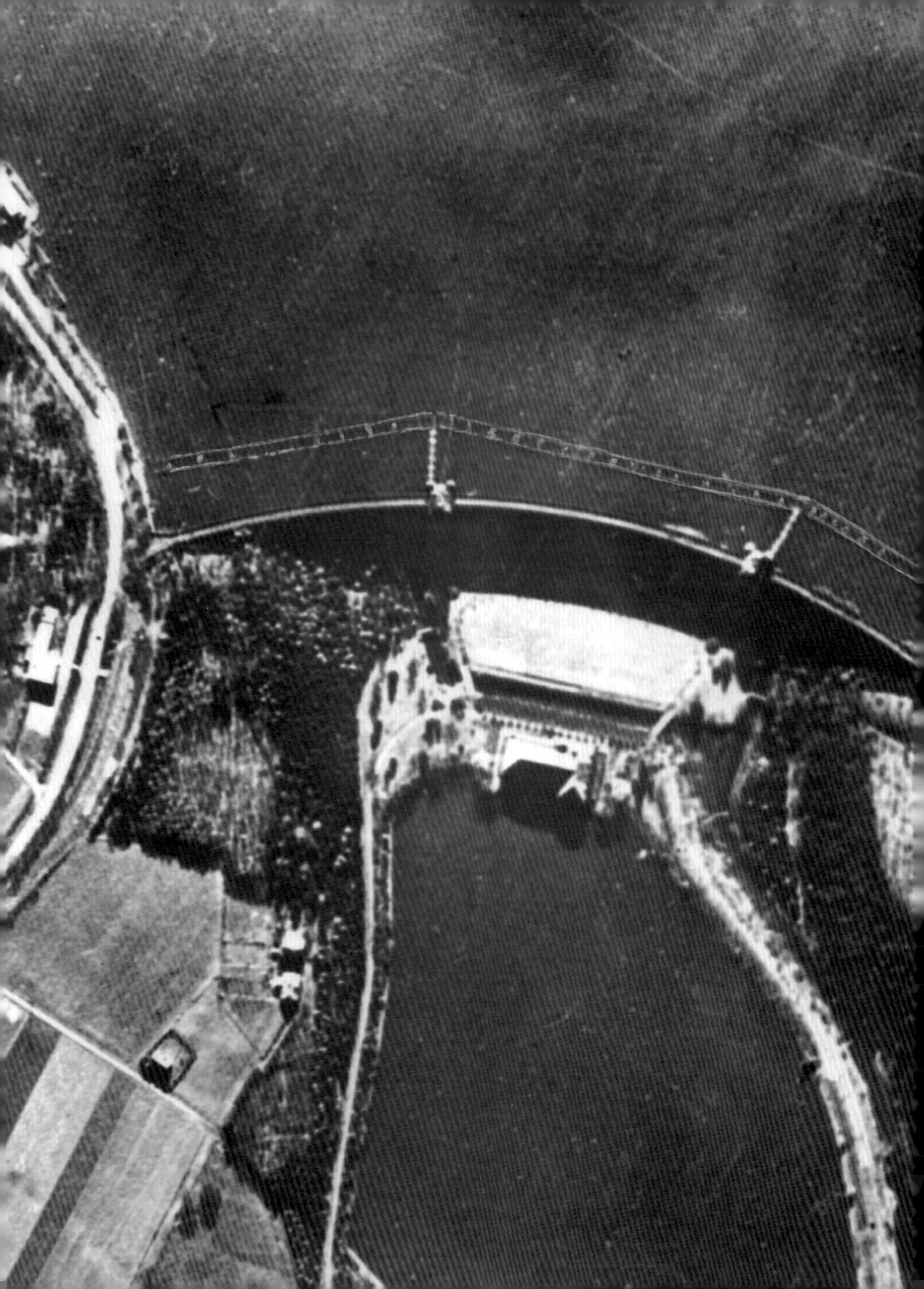

Chapter Three

Operation Chastise – the Dams Raid

With the reservoirs full after the spring rains and a full moon, Operation Chastise was set for the night of 16–17 May 1943. The raid would become the stuff of legend.

OPPOSITE Primary target X – the Möhne Dam; Gibson thought it looked 'squat and heavy and unconquerable' when he first saw it. *(Imperial War Museum C3717)*

A new squadron is formed

From the moment he gave his approval for what would become Operation Chastise, 'Bomber' Harris had planned to create a new squadron specifically for the mission. To avoid depleting existing squadrons, he ordered the AOC of 5 Group, AVM the Honourable Sir Ralph Cochrane, to form the squadron from tour-expired aircrew, and to command the squadron he had selected Wg Cdr Guy P. Gibson who had just completed his second tour on bombers – having had a third on night fighters in between. Highly experienced, Gibson was respected by those who knew him, but was often found to be arrogant and domineering by new acquaintances, especially the lower ranks. He was rarely to be seen without his faithful black Labrador, Nigger. Gibson was allowed to choose many of the aircrew for the new squadron, but contrary to myth, all came from 5 Group and not all were highly experienced, some having only flown a few missions; some were volunteers, others were not.

The squadron was formed at RAF Scampton in Lincolnshire on 17 March, formally becoming 617 Squadron nine days later; this station was due to be closed while its grass runways were replaced with paved ones, and one of its two squadrons had already moved out.

Secrecy surrounded the new squadron, to the extent that even its CO was not initially told the target they would be attacking, even after he met Wallis for a briefing on Upkeep. However, the squadron was told to practise low flying over water at night, which they set to using standard Lancasters pending the arrival of the modified aircraft that they would use on the operation. Night after night, cross-country navigation exercises were conducted at low level, including passing over many lakes and reservoirs around the country. Navigators were not used to working at such low levels, and relied on the bomb aimers calling out landmarks as they passed over, some crews devising clever ways of folding or rolling maps to keep up with the rapidly changing landscape. To allow training to continue during the day, synthetic night flying equipment was introduced

BELOW Training flights were flown over several British dams, including the Derwent Dam in Derbyshire, now often the site of raid commemorations. *(Author)*

– this consisted of blue celluloid fitted to the windows and yellow celluloid fitted to the pilot's goggles; he could thus read his instruments clearly, but the outside view was that of a moonlit night.

When the problems of target distance and height estimation were solved, the crews also began training with the wooden bomb sights and Aldis lamp altimeters, testing these out at the Wainfleet range on the Wash (using screens on the shore in place of towers), the Howden and Derwent Dams in the Peak District, Eyebrook Reservoir in Leicestershire and Abberton Reservoir near Colchester; the latter two had no towers, so RAF personnel manned small boats fitted with tall masts to aim at. The low-level training resulted in some heart-stopping moments, but with a full mission profile flown successfully on the evening of 6 May, Gibson declared the squadron ready for action. Navigation training continued, with the addition of test drops of the weapon at Reculver from 11 May, culminating in a full 'dress rehearsal' training flight, involving long-distance navigation and a simulated attack, on the evening of 14 May, which went without a hitch.

Final preparations and briefing

The operational Provisioning Lancasters had been arriving at Scampton since 8 April, with twelve on the station by the end of the month, but the last of the twenty did not arrive until 12 May. By the day of the raid, repairs to Maudslay's ED933 had not been completed; thus only nineteen aircraft were available, so ED825 (one of the prototype aircraft) was ferried up from Boscombe Down to act as a reserve (although there was no time to fit it with height lamps or VHF radio). Although twenty-one crews had trained for the raid, Wilson and Divall's crews were ruled out through illness, so nineteen crews were available also. The planned fifty-six HE-filled Upkeeps were available on the station.

The tight security surrounding the squadron meant that the aircrew were not told the nature of their targets until the day of the raid, although the two flight commanders and the squadron's bombing and gunnery leaders had been briefed the evening before. Following this meeting, Gibson was informed that, earlier in the day, Nigger had been killed by a car just outside the Scampton gates; ignoring this potential bad omen, Gibson requested that he be buried at the same time as the raid would be reaching its climax over Germany.

The final version of the operation order was prepared on the morning of 16 May, and in the afternoon, the pilots and navigators were briefed on the targets while the wireless operators were separately briefed on the radio signals procedures that had been devised, and these (together with a series of operation codewords) had to be memorised before take-off.

The final briefing for all aircrew began at 18:00, when they were told the targets and nature of their mission by Gibson, and Wallis gave a presentation on the functioning of

BELOW Once the outer casing was removed, the cylindrical Upkeep could be loaded from the front without lifting the Lancaster, if the front fairing was opened. *(Author)*

Signal code words

Pranger	Attack Möhne (target X)
Nigger	Möhne breached, attack Eder (target Y)
Dinghy	Eder Breached, attack Sorpe (target Z)
Danger	Attack Lister (target D)
Edward	Attack Ennepe (target E)
Fraser	Attack Diemel (target F)
Gilbert	Attack last resort targets
Mason	all aircraft to return to base
Goner 1	Upkeep released, but failed to explode
Goner 2	Upkeep released, overshot
Goner 3	Upkeep released, exploded over 100yd from dam
Goner 4	Upkeep released, exploded 100yd from dam
Goner 5	Upkeep released, exploded 50yd from dam
Goner 6	Upkeep released, exploded 5yd from dam
Goner 7	Upkeep released, exploded in contact with dam
Goner 8	No apparent breach in dam
Goner 9	Small breach in dam
Goner 10	Large breach in dam

'Goner' codes were to be combined with the target letters e.g. 'Goner 79F' would have signalled a strike on the Diemel resulting in a small breach.

Upkeep. Cochrane was also present to wish the crews well, along with Gp Capt Whitworth, the Scampton station commander. There was some relief among the crews that the target wasn't the *Tirpitz*, but they were under no illusion that it was going to be an easy mission. After the briefing ended at 19:30, the aircrew enjoyed the traditional pre-operation meal of bacon and eggs.

Photo interpreters at RAF Medmenham had been keeping an eye on the dam defences and water levels in the reservoirs, and produced detailed terrain models of the principal targets; the Möhne and Sorpe models were available for the briefings, but the Eder model was not completed until after the raid. There had been a scare when the interpreters had spotted mysterious objects along the top of the Möhne; these were actually artificial trees intended (completely unsuccessfully) to camouflage the dam.

BELOW Gibson (on ladder) and his crew board Lancaster ED932 for their flight into history; the '/G' has been removed from the serial number. *(Imperial War Museum CH18005)*

ABOVE This image of ED932 is probably the clearest which survives showing the Upkeep mechanism; note the fuzing unit on the forward arm. *(Imperial War Museum HU69915)*

LEFT This front view of ED932 shows the cylindrical Upkeep and the ends of the two tie rods which protrude from the calliper arms; the rectangles on the front of the wing are barrage balloon cable cutters. *(Jonathan Falconer collection)*

OPERATION CHASTISE – THE DAMS RAID

RIGHT Although this map was drawn to show the location of the Arnsberg Viaduct (centre – see Chapter 6), it also shows the location of the Chastise primary targets, and has been augmented to show the locations of the Lister (D), Ennepe (E), Diemel (F), Henne (H) and Bever (B) dams.
(RAF Museum B3253)

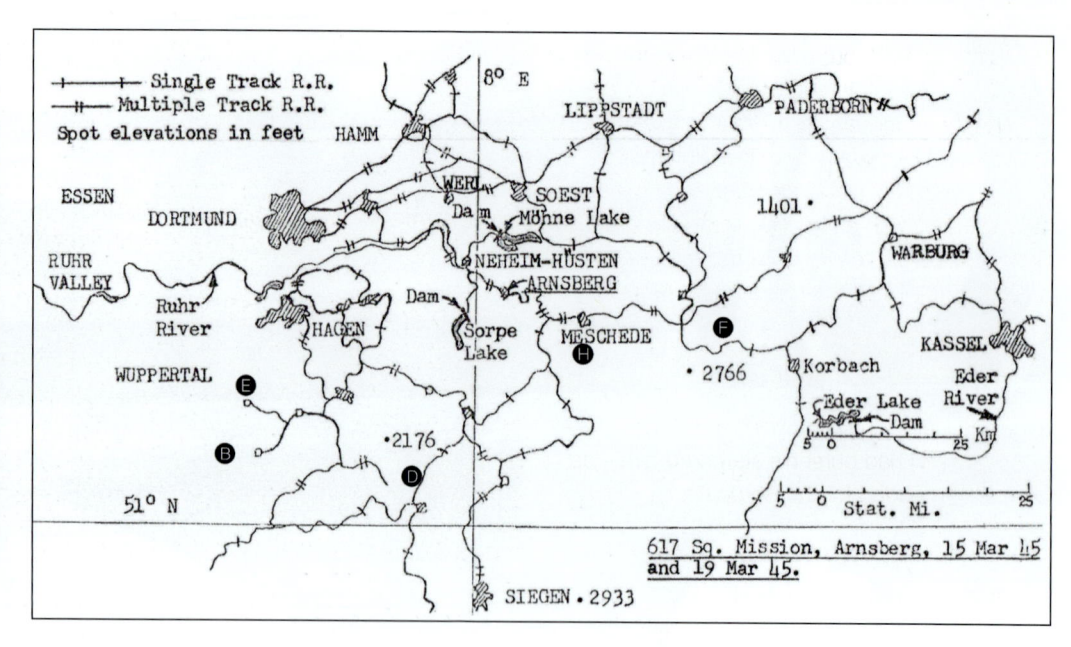

Out at the aircraft dispersals, final preparations for the operation were under way, including fuelling the aircraft, swinging the compasses both with and without Upkeep in place and fitting ammunition for the two turrets. This had a tracer round in every fourth slot, to enable to the gunner to see where his shot was going at night and to offer some 'scare' effect.

The squadron was split into three waves, the first and third following a southerly route heading east from the Scheldt estuary, the second taking a northerly route between the Dutch islands and south across the IJsselmeer; the first two waves should have crossed the enemy coast at the same time, in an effort to confuse the enemy defences. The second wave were to depart first as their route, the most northerly, was also the longest. The first two waves were to meet at the Möhne then proceed to the Eder, all under the guidance of Gibson (in the role that would become known as Master Bomber), while the third wave were to independently attack the secondary targets and also act as a reserve force (all aircraft could be redirected as required by radio). The mines were to be fuzed just before crossing the enemy coast. The crews were briefed to fly as low as possible at all times in order to avoid night fighters and the heavier flak guns, and several aircraft would fly beneath high tension cables on their way to the Ruhr. Wallis and Cochrane saw the first two waves off, then proceeded to the 5 Group HQ at Grantham, where they were joined by Harris.

A full list of Operation Chastise aircrew can be found in Appendix 1.

Take-off

At 21:10, a red Verey light signalled the crews to start their engines, and at 21:28 the signal came for the first aircraft to go. However, McCarthy found that he had a coolant problem with this aircraft, and had to hurriedly change to the reserve aircraft, meaning that Barlow was first away, followed at one-minute intervals by Munro, Byers and Rice; despite a problem with ED825's compass deviation card and his own parachute, McCarthy finally got away about thirty minutes late, though he managed to make up some time en route. The wave did not fare well – Byers was hit by flak passing the Dutch islands, and crashed into the sea. In the same area, flak also hit Munro's aircraft, which disabled the aircraft intercom – with no means for the crew to communicate in the final stages of an attack, there was no point in proceeding, so he reluctantly took his Upkeep back to Scampton (some sources say that the crews were briefed not to return with their Upkeep on board, but surviving aircrew say that this was not the case). Passing the islands safely, Rice flew too low, and his mine was torn off by the sea – he only just managed to keep his aircraft in the air, but was also forced to return home and make a careful landing with damaged hydraulics and without a tail wheel, which had been torn away by the Upkeep; lost in water too shallow to trigger the hydrostatic pistols and apparently having damaged the self-destruct fuze, the mine did not explode, though it may have gone off with a high tide some days later. Barlow managed to reach Germany, but after crossing the Rhine, hit an electricity pylon and crashed just north-east of Rees. The aircraft exploded, killing the crew, but the Upkeep rolled clear. Of this wave, only McCarthy remained, acquiring just a single hit which (he would discover later) had burst his starboard tyre – as briefed, he headed for the Sorpe Dam.

Gibson led the first wave off at 21:39, this consisting of three flights of three aircraft departing at ten-minute intervals. With Hopgood and Martin, Gibson was supposed to reach the enemy coast at the mouth of the River Scheldt, but strong winds had pushed him further south over the island of Walcheren and he had to quickly correct his course. Following a series of turning points, clearly seen in the moonlight, they arrived successfully at the Möhne. The second flight of Young, Maltby and Shannon made landfall more accurately and, despite some course deviations when over Germany, also reached the Möhne without serious incident. The third flight of Maudslay, Astell and Knight departed Scampton shortly before 22:00. Between the Rhine and Dülmen, Astell fell behind and his aircraft was seen caught in the fire from two guns, crashing to the ground where the Upkeep exploded.

The third wave departed at one-minute intervals, Ottley leading off at 00:09 following (like all in this wave) the southerly outward route, but near the rail yards at Hamm, his aircraft was hit by flak and exploded in mid-air; only his rear gunner survived the crash and the explosion of the Upkeep. Burpee met a similar fate – straying off course, he passed over a heavily defended airfield, and was shot down, the detonation of his Upkeep destroying numerous buildings on the airfield. Brown was next away, and although he encountered flak along the way, he arrived safely at the already-breached Möhne and made his way to the Sorpe. It was a similar story for Townsend, who received instructions along the way to attack the Ennepe Dam. The last aircraft to depart, at 00:15, was flown by Anderson.

ABOVE RAF briefing photo of the Möhne Dam. *(RAF Museum)*

Attacking the Möhne

Meanwhile, Gibson's flight had arrived at the Möhne and quickly identified guns in the two towers on the dam, one on the east end of the dam, and others in the fields beyond it, and the front and rear gunners fired on all of these as the opportunity presented. As Gibson made a dummy run over the dam to test the defences, the second flight arrived, the waiting aircraft entering a left-handed circuit to the east of the dam. On instruction from Gibson, the aircraft were briefed to start their runs at the Körbecke Bridge on the northern arm of the reservoir, flying west to overfly a spit on the Heversberg peninsula between the two arms, then turn north-west to find the dam straight ahead. At 00:28, with his Upkeep already spinning, Gibson

BELOW Cross-section of the Möhne Dam. *(Crown Copyright via The National Archives)*

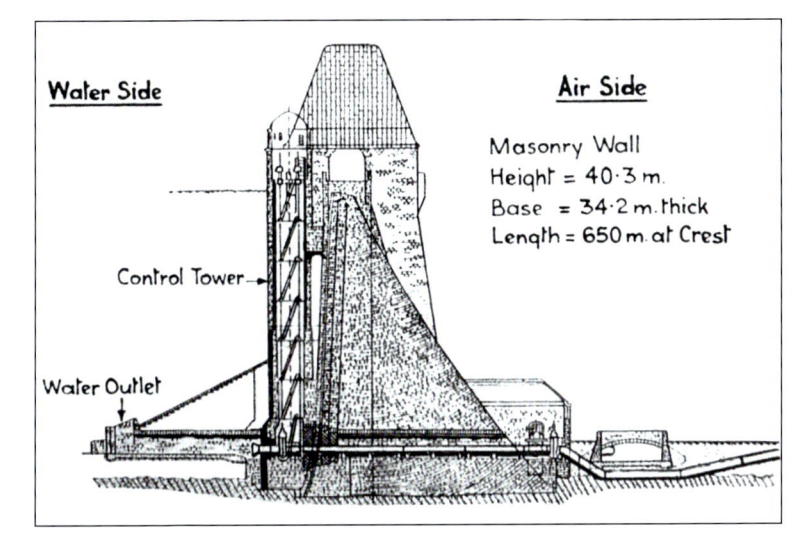

TARGET PROFILE

Möhne Dam (primary target X)

Type:	walled gravity dam
Location:	51° 29' 23" N 8° 3' 33" E (near Günne, North Rhine–Westphalia, Germany)
Built:	1909–13
Length:	777m
Width:	8m (top)/31m (base)
Height:	37m
Reservoir capacity:	135 million m³
Attacked:	17 May 1943 (5 Upkeep mines), wall breached

The Möhne Dam is the most important source of water for the Ruhr industrial area, and stands at the confluence of the Möhne and Heve rivers; outflow from the dam joins the Ruhr at Neheim some five miles south-west of the dam. Built of limestone, sandstone and diorite, it contains 267,000m³ of masonry and has two prominent sluice towers 170m apart – these fed a hydroelectric power station in front of the dam, plus a smaller one at the side of the compensating basin. Behind the dam was a bank of silt, so Upkeep was set to detonate before it reached the silt. The dam was protected by twin anti-torpedo nets running the length of the dam, and flak guns in both sluice towers and in the fields north of the dam; it was the only dam with any such protection. There were no barrage balloons or searchlights near any of the target dams.

The breach at the Möhne was 77m wide and 28m deep, the result of 12,500m³ of masonry having been washed away, and an additional 6,800m³ was so severely cracked that it had to be replaced, effectively widening the breach to 105m. Following the attack, the loose masonry around the breach was removed; repairs commenced on 9 July and were completed by the end of September 1943 – a remarkable feat involving the reinstatement of 250m³ of masonry per day. The main power station was not replaced, and the shape of the compensation basin remained largely as the flood waters had left it. Various defences against further attack were added – as well as balloons, flak guns and smoke generators, floating boards were installed on the water side to catch any above-surface bombs, and on the air side, netting was hung on booms to catch any bombs falling on that side. Cables were also hung across the lake to snag any low-flying aircraft, and as the role of the towers for sighting was known, the tower roofs were dismantled.

The dam remains in use; despite the speed of repair, the same materials were used as in the original construction, so the area of the breach can now hardly be seen.

went in first, the Aldis lamps being turned on as the aircraft crossed the spit. The correct line, height and speed were quickly found, and the Upkeep was released, the wireless operator firing a red Very cartridge as the aircraft passed over the dam to signal the release. The rear gunner observed three bounces but the mine fell short and sank near the anti-torpedo nets. There was a huge explosion, and when the spray settled, the dam was unaffected. Gibson's radio operator signalled 'Goner 68A' meaning that an Upkeep had exploded 5yd from the Möhne but there was no breach.

During the pause to let the waves subside, Maudslay and Knight arrived and joined the circling aircraft, and Hopgood was called in to attack. The gunners now knew what to expect, and his aircraft was hit in both wings during the approach; the Upkeep was dropped late, bouncing over the dam parapet and onto the power station below. Hopgood struggled to gain height but the aircraft was engulfed in flames and Hopgood ordered his crew to bail out; despite the lack of height, three did so before the aircraft exploded, although only the bomb aimer and rear gunner survived the landing, the latter with serious injuries. The self-destruct fuze destroyed the Upkeep and the power station with it; the smoke from the burning remains would cause some problems for the later attackers.

Martin was called in next, with Gibson flying on his starboard side and slightly ahead to draw off some of the flak. He also dropped his Upkeep at the first attempt, but his wings may not have been level, as the Upkeep veered off to the left and blew up about 20yd from the dam.

The fourth attack was made by Young, with Martin flying shotgun alongside while Gibson circled on the air side of the dam to draw the flak further away. After three bounces, the mine reached the dam and another huge plume of water went up. The crews of the circling aircraft watched with eager optimism, but as the water cleared, the dam appeared unaffected and 'Goner 78A', indicating a hit but no breach, was radioed back to Grantham.

Maltby made the fifth run, and yet again a release was made at the first attempt. However, as they overflew the dam, Maltby realised that it was already starting to collapse – Young's mine had worked after all. However, Gibson had

LEFT This famous reconnaissance photo was taken on 17 May, by which time most of the water had gone. *(Crown Copyright)*

LEFT The same from ground level, water still pouring through the huge breach made by Young and Maltby's Upkeeps. *(Author's collection)*

OPERATION CHASTISE – THE DAMS RAID

ABOVE The rebuilt dam was left without towers and had nets and other passive defences added on both sides. (Author's collection)

not seen this, and following the explosion of Maltby's mine, called in Shannon. He had barely done so when it became apparent that the dam had been breached, a surge of water cascading into the valley and erasing the remains of the power station. It was 00:56 when Gibson told his wireless operator to send the signal 'Nigger' to Grantham, the codeword (in honour of his dog) for a breach in the Möhne. The mood in the operations room had become increasingly sombre with each failure signal, but it changed dramatically when this signal was received, Wallis punching the air and accepting the congratulations of the staff officers.

Aircrew duties during attack with Upkeep

The attack phase required a large amount of teamwork – the duties of each member of the aircrew during the attack were as follows:

Pilot	controlling aircraft, with verbal line guidance from bomb aimer and height guidance from navigator; aim – to have aircraft at correct height and heading straight towards dam with wings level at moment of release.
Flight engineer	using throttles to maintain steady aircraft speed during approach; aim – to achieve speed of 232mph at moment of release.
Navigator	switching on Aldis lamps, then looking out of starboard cockpit blister to observe light spots on surface of the reservoir; aim – to call out height directions to pilot to maintain steady correct height during approach.
Wireless operator	at the navigator's table to control the speed of Upkeep rotation; aim – to achieve speed of 500rpm at moment of release, then to fire a red Verey cartridge when crossing dam to indicate to other aircraft that a weapon had been released.
Bomb aimer	observing dam towers via Dann sight or nail-and-string sight; aim – to determine moment of release at correct range from dam, and to release Upkeep if other release parameters judged to be correct.
Front and rear gunners	giving suppressing fire to enemy defences; rear gunner also to observe path of Upkeep following release.

RIGHT RAF briefing photo of the Eder Dam.
(RAF Museum)

Attacking the Eder

Martin and Maltby then turned for home, while Shannon, Maudslay and Knight (accompanied by Gibson and Young) headed for the Eder some 50 miles to the south-east. It proved harder to find, being nestled between higher hills; Gibson and Young found the dam first, firing red Verey lights to gather the other aircraft. The dam was undefended, except by the forbidding nature of the surrounding terrain. The plan of attack was to pass Waldeck Castle, situated on a hilltop north of the dam, diving towards a promontory on the western shore, then turn left by 90° to head for the dam on a south-easterly heading. Shannon went first but, after the dive and turn, was unable to find the correct height and speed in time; he tried three more times, but each time the bomb aimer was not satisfied and the mine was not released. Maudslay then tried, but twice had the same problem. Shannon tried again, and after two more unsuccessful runs, at 01:39 released his Upkeep, which bounced twice then appeared to strike the dam before exploding. Maudslay then made his third run and dropped his Upkeep – but it was dropped late, struck the parapet of the dam and exploded immediately. His aircraft was beyond the dam and so shielded from the worst of the explosion, but it must have sustained some damage as only a faint response was heard to a call from Gibson; no more was heard from this aircraft, which later crashed in Holland – probably shot down, or it may have succumbed to damage acquired in the explosion. Gibson then called Astell to attack, apparently not appreciating that he had not made it to the dams – thus he realised that only one Upkeep remained. Knight's first attempt was also unsuccessful, but on his second, the Upkeep was released. His rear gunner observed three bounces and when the mine exploded, saw a hole punched through the dam. As the torrent began, the rush of water washed away the masonry above the hole and began to widen the breach – it was 01:52, less than 90 minutes since the first attack at the Möhne.

TARGET PROFILE

Eder Dam (primary target Y)

Type:	walled gravity dam
Location:	51° 11' 0" N 9° 3' 30" E (near Waldeck, Hesse, Germany)
Built:	1908–14
Length:	400m
Width:	6m (top)/36m (base)
Height:	48m
Reservoir capacity:	300 million m³
Attacked:	17 May 1943 (3 Upkeep mines), wall breached

The Eder Dam is similar in size and construction to the Möhne, although its reservoir holds far more than the Möhne. The dam was built for generation of hydroelectric power by two power stations sited at the foot of the dam, and to control the water levels in the River Weser and the Mittelland Canal. As such, the Eder is not part of the Ruhr catchment area, and it was thus of less strategic importance than either the Möhne or Sorpe dams.

Having been created by only one mine, the breach in the Eder was slightly smaller (70m wide and 22m deep) than at the Möhne, but there was extensive cracking and damage to the internal drainage system in the wall, which had to be made good, so the reservoir was not filled to capacity until 1948. The overflow sluices in the area of the breach were not restored, so the location of the breach is more apparent than at the Möhne. The dam remains in use, although the power stations are no longer operational, one containing a museum.

RIGHT Reconnaissance photo of the Eder, with the morning sun nicely showing the breach in the dam. *(Crown Copyright)*

OPPOSITE The Eder valley the day after the raid, showing the effects of the flooding, including broken bridges. *(Crown Copyright via 617 Squadron)*

BELOW The Eder Dam from the lake after the raid; the emergency sluices were not restored in the repaired section. *(Author's collection)*

The signal 'Dinghy' heralding the breach was sent back to Grantham, prompting more jubilation in the ops room. Harris telephoned Washington to give the news to ACM Portal (Chief of the Air Staff) and thence to Churchill.

Attacking the Sorpe and other dams

Of the second wave, only McCarthy remained and, after his delayed departure, he reached the Sorpe without incident, although mist made the target hard to locate. Due to its different method of construction, alternative tactics were to be used at the Sorpe. The crews were briefed to

RIGHT RAF briefing photo of the Sorpe Dam. *(RAF Museum)*

51

OPERATION CHASTISE – THE DAMS RAID

RIGHT Cross-section of the Sorpe Dam, showing a different method of construction from the other primary targets. *(Crown Copyright via The National Archives)*

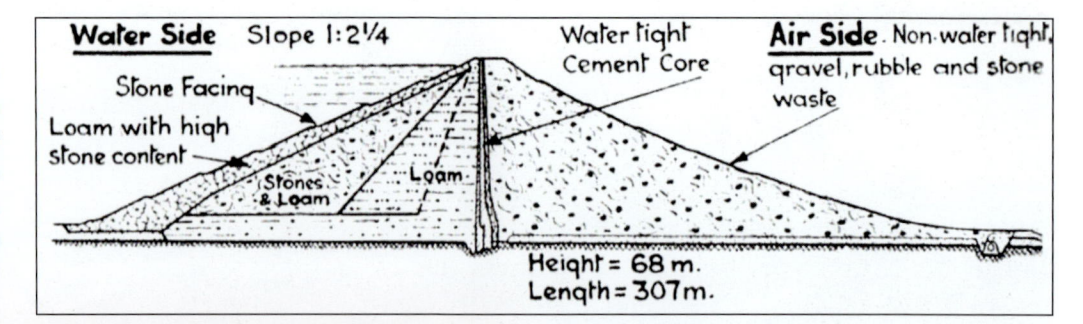

TARGET PROFILE

Sorpe Dam (primary target Z)

Type:	earth bank dam with concrete core
Location:	51° 21' 3" N 7° 58' 6" E (near Langscheid, North Rhine–Westphalia, Germany)
Built:	1926–35
Length:	700m
Width:	6m (crest)/380m (base)
Height:	69m
Reservoir capacity:	70 million m³
Attacked:	17 May 1943 (2 Upkeep mines), crest damaged /15 October 1944 (16 Tallboys), crest and other parts damaged

The Sorpe was of different construction to all the other dams on the target list, having a concrete wall at its core supported on either side by banks of earth, the water side being faced with masonry. It was thus realised that an attack using Upkeep was much less likely to succeed against this target; however, Wallis was of the opinion that four or five Upkeeps might crack the core, allowing water to leak through the dam, creating an outflow which would build up until it eventually breached the dam. This was perhaps wishful thinking, but the importance of the Sorpe, which was second only to the nearby Möhne, meant that it was retained as a priority target. This view was confirmed by the Germans themselves – Albert Speer, Minister of Armaments and War Production said later that, had the Sorpe been breached also, the effect on the Ruhr would have been far greater than breaching the Möhne alone.

Uniquely, the Sorpe was also attacked with Tallboys, 9 Squadron dropping 16 on the dam in October 1944 (the dam, previously undefended, now having barrage balloons and flak guns). The main purpose of this raid was to destroy the busy railway line along the Ruhr valley below the dam which, like the dam itself, had been repaired after Operation Chastise. However, despite two hits on the crest (exposing the core) and other hits on the air side, no outflow of water was achieved (the water level of the reservoir was deliberately being kept low) and so the dam was not breached. It remains in use.

attack along the line of the dam, with the port outer engine above the parapet. Upkeep was to be dropped with no spin in the middle of the dam, from where it would roll down into the water and explode; drop height was less critical, which was fortunate as the reserve aircraft was not fitted with height lamps. Hills at both ends of the dam made this approach as tricky as at the Eder, and a church spire on the north side added an unexpected complication. However, McCarthy quickly realised that he could use the spire as a marker to line up his approach to the dam. Despite this, it was not until the tenth run over the dam that the bomb aimer was satisfied and released the Upkeep, at 00:46. The explosion sent up a plume of water and damaged the face of the dam, but despite circling for several minutes, no breach was observed and the crew turned for home.

Arriving at the Sorpe some two and a half hours later, Brown found even more mist. He also made several runs over the dam, releasing the mine on what was reckoned to be his sixth attempt; it caused damage similar to that done by McCarthy.

Townsend had difficulty finding the Ennepe Dam due to the mist which was by now filling the valleys. As the mine was spun up, a significant vibration was felt in the aircraft, suggesting that it had not been balanced correctly. The bomb aimer was not satisfied with the approach the first three times, but released on the fourth attempt. Flying back over the target, a circular pattern of waves was observed, suggesting that the mine had fallen short of the dam. Subsequent analysis of the evidence from Townsend's attack indicates that it was not the Ennepe that he attacked, but the Bever, some seven miles south of the Ennepe.

Anderson had been the last to depart, and on arrival in the target area, experienced the worst of

LEFT Reconnaissance photo of the Sorpe after Operation Chastise, showing damage to the crest and discolouration in the compensating basin from water washed down the air side. *(Crown Copyright)*

LEFT Reconnaissance photo of the Sorpe after 9 Squadron's visit in October 1944. Despite the accuracy of the Tallboy attack, there was no outflow of water, so the dam held. *(Crown Copyright)*

TARGET PROFILES

German dams (secondary targets)

Name	Type	Location	Length	Height	Reservoir Capacity
Lister Dam (secondary target D)	walled gravity dam, built 1908–12	51° 5' 40" N 7° 50' 15" E (near Albringhausen, North Rhine–Westphalia)	265m	40m	22 million m³
Ennepe Dam (secondary target E)	walled gravity dam, built 1902–4	51° 14' 29" N 7° 24' 33" E (near Filde, North Rhine–Westphalia)	275m	51m	12 million m³
Diemel Dam (secondary target F)	walled gravity dam, built 1912–23	51° 22' 40" N 8° 43' 40" E (near Helminghausen, Hesse)	194m	42m	20 million m³
Henne Dam (originally secondary target F, but dropped from the target list shortly before Operation Chastise)	walled gravity dam, built 1901–5	51° 20' 7" N 8° 16' 27" E (near Meschede, North Rhine–Westphalia)	376m	56m	38 million m³
Bever Dam (not on the target list, but attacked in error by one crew)	rockfill dam, built 1935–38	51° 8' 31" N 7° 22' 13" E (near Hartkopsbever, North Rhine–Westphalia)	520m	49m	24 million m³

All dams are currently in use; the original Henne Dam was replaced by a rock-fill dam 1952–55

RIGHT After the Lister, the Diemel Dam was the most important of the secondary targets. *(Public Domain)*

BELOW The Lister Dam post-war, showing its single sluice tower; the water at the foot of the dam is part of a larger reservoir downstream that was created in 1965. *(Ray Morley)*

the mist. He was to attack the Diemel Dam, but at 02:28 received orders to divert to the Sorpe.

Return

Now there remained the flight home. Maltby and Martin had departed first from the Möhne, and returned via the northern route over the IJsselmeer without incident, landing at Scampton at 03:11 and 03:19 respectively. Shannon had followed a similar route back from the Eder, landing at 04:06. Gibson followed about ten minutes later, having flown back via the Möhne to view the squadron's handiwork there, then via a route to the south of the others; he too had an uneventful trip back, other than seeing another aircraft shot down in the distance. Knight followed a similar route to Gibson, landing at 04:20, as did Young, but he was not so lucky. Passing close to IJmuiden, his aircraft was hit by flak and crashed into the sea just off the coast – there were no survivors.

From the Sorpe, McCarthy headed the few miles north to the Möhne, where he observed the flood in progress. Flying so low, they experienced some navigational difficulties en route, straying into some defended areas, but managed to reach Scampton safely at 03:23. Following the same path hours after McCarthy, Brown's crew were astonished by the level of destruction now apparent beneath the Möhne, but with the sky lightening rapidly, they had no time to linger. Brown also had some close encounters with flak, taking some hits as they crossed the coast, the multiple holes around the cockpit which were found when they reached Scampton at 05:33 suggesting that they had been lucky not to sustain any injuries.

Thirty minutes behind Brown, Townsend also used the Möhne as the first waypoint for his return flight. The sky was now quite light, causing him to push the Lancaster as low and as fast as he dared in his dash for the coast, and his height may have saved them from the shells of a flak gun on the Dutch islands. An apparent oil leak caused him to shut down an engine over the North Sea, and he made a bumpy landing at Scampton in front of the other crews and staff officers who had gathered to welcome the last of the aircraft to return.

Anderson was unable to locate the Sorpe, or any of the other target dams, so turned

Debriefing

SUMMARY OF DEBRIEFING QUESTIONNAIRES FROM CREWS WHICH ATTACKED

Dam	Pilot	Bounces	Spun?	Runs	Results
Möhne	Gibson	3	500rpm	1	Two holes in dam*
Möhne	Martin	Not seen	480rpm	1	None visible
Möhne	Maltby	3	Yes	1	Breached before attacking
Eder	Shannon	2	Yes	3 **	Gap 9ft wide east side**
Eder	Knight	3	Yes	2	Large breach 30ft below top of dam
Sorpe	McCarthy	N/A	N/A	10	Crown crumbled 15–20ft
Sorpe	Brown	N/A	N/A	10	Crown crumbled 300ft
(Bever)	Townsend	1	Yes	3	No damage

* evidently refers to raid, rather than result of his own mine
**contradicts other accounts

for home still carrying his Upkeep, arriving at 05:30, the last aircraft to return. Gibson was not pleased with his failure to press home an attack and saw to it that he was posted out of 617.

From nineteen departing aircraft, there had been two early returns, eight aircraft which had attacked a dam and one which hadn't. Of the fifty-six men in the eight aircraft which failed to return, only three survived, all spending the rest of the war as PoWs.

The usual debriefing procedures were applied to the returning crews, though the crews had to complete an additional questionnaire regarding the aircraft parameters at the time they dropped their weapon, and observations on its behaviour.

The effects of the raid

Some 116,000,000m^3 of water were released from the Möhne reservoir, and 154,000,000m^3 from the Eder reservoir, and this caused immense devastation in the valleys below the two dams. At the Möhne, the main power station was destroyed, another two were flooded and others affected; eleven factories and an iron foundry were destroyed and one hundred and fourteen factories damaged; twenty-five bridges were destroyed and twenty-one damaged; many pumping stations and waterworks were damaged. The Eder's two power stations were damaged and in the mainly agricultural area below the dam, fifty hectares of arable land was washed away; Fritzlar airfield was partially flooded; 30,000m³ of silt had to be dredged from the River Fulda, plus 5,000m³ from the River Weser and 5.5km of the Fulda's banks had to be rebuilt. At the Sorpe, there were only two craters around 8m deep just below the waterline; however, much of the water in the reservoir had to be released in order to effect repairs, so this water was also lost.

Secondary effects, such as loss of livestock and damage to housing, were widespread. Water supplies to industry and to agriculture and the population were slashed, but the effects of this were relatively short-lived, and the manufacturing industries were not affected nearly as severely as had been hoped. Electricity-generation capacity was also reduced, although the transmission grid meant that this was not serious.

Loss of life was substantial, officially recorded as 1,341 (the vast majority at the Möhne, including hundreds of Ukrainian women forced labourers who were housed in a camp in the valley). This had a large effect on the morale of the local population who lived in fear of a repeat for the rest of the war.

Work on reconstructing the dams was begun almost immediately, and despite the scale of the damage, was largely completed by the autumn in time to catch the winter rains, meaning that the hoped-for effects of long-term water loss were not realised. The manpower required for such a gargantuan task was substantial – up to 7,000 men – most coming from the Atlantic Wall, which in consequence was incomplete in places on D-Day the following year.

Another incidental benefit to the Allies was the substantial effort to design, install and maintain enhanced defences on the target dams (and more than twenty others) – barrage balloons were in place within twenty-four hours and, once the operation of Upkeep was understood, netting and floating barricades were put in place to thwart further attacks with the weapon. Searchlights, smoke apparatus and flak guns were stationed around the dams, and special methods were employed to deter low-level attacks, including towers carrying trailing cables and even mines in the reservoirs, which could be detonated remotely if aircraft flew over. These countermeasures were one reason why the reconstruction works were not attacked, and why Upkeep was not used in anger again.

In Britain, the raid gave a major propaganda victory, with reconnaissance photos of the smashed dams appearing in all the newspapers, accompanied by tales of the attackers, daring and the devastation meted out to the enemy. Many of the aircrew received decorations, including a Victoria Cross for Gibson; Wallis and Chadwick were awarded the CBE. On a visit to Scampton, the King gave his assent to the squadron badge showing a broken dam surmounted by lightning bolts, and its motto 'Après moi le déluge'.

However, Barlow's Upkeep had been recovered intact and safely defused by German bomb disposal officers. Within two weeks of the raid, they had a full technical specification of the weapon and the Type 464 Lancaster (although they did not fully understand the reasons for the spin). From this, they reverse engineered the mine to produce their own smaller version, codenamed Kurt, although this was primarily intended as an anti-ship weapon. British Intelligence learned of the recovery and, worried about the possibility of reprisal attacks, defence plans were hastily drawn up for key British dams, including the Derwent.

Further dam-busting operations

Following the raid, the Provisioning Lancasters were initially retained while many possibilities were considered for using Upkeep again. These included further German dams as well as dams in Italy and one in Finland which served an important nickel smelter. Canal banks and the Rothensee Ship Lift, at the junction of the Mittelland Canal with the River Elbe, were also considered, but the target which received initial interest was viaduct piers – it was hoped that a forward-spun Upkeep could come to rest against a pier and so bring it down, and trials conducted during June were promising. Dummy piers were set up on the bombing range at Ashley Walk in the New Forest, and 617 conducted some test drops there in August. These showed that Upkeep's path over land could be somewhat erratic, and the tests were halted when one of the low-flying Lancasters crashed into the ground, badly injuring two of the crew. The target which attracted greatest consideration was the Bissorte Dam in the French Alps, with a view to destroying the road and railway in the valley below, which were being used for transporting military reinforcements to Italy. This remained a possible target well into 1944, but was eventually discounted due to the likely large number of civilian casualties; attacks on the Italian dams were ruled out for the same reason. Towards the end of 1944, in support of troop advances into Germany, Upkeep was considered for an attack on the Urft Dam. This dam had a greater curvature than those attacked previously, and further model work was carried out, but the plans were ultimately scuppered by a realisation that the surrounding terrain offered no practical approach to the target, which was also likely to be protected by low-level cable defences. Despite all the possibilities, Upkeep was not used in action again, and several of the Provisioning Lancasters were converted back to conventional configuration, although some were retained until the end of the war, their final mission being Operation Guzzle, the disposal of the remaining HE-filled Upkeeps at sea. For details of the history of the Provisioning Lancasters, see Appendix 2.

Highball

Wallis had always viewed dams as the primary target for the bouncing bomb, but he hedged his bets and also offered it to the Navy as a potential anti-ship weapon – and, initially, it was the Navy which showed the greatest interest in it. The naval version, codenamed Highball, was smaller than Upkeep – 35in in diameter and weighing 1,200lb, of which half would be the warhead. It was planned to carry two in de Havilland Mosquitoes and four in Vickers Warwicks (although the latter never materialised). When clearance was given to proceed with Upkeep, clearance for Highball was also given, with a view to carrying out a raid on the dams and a Highball raid (possibly two) at the same time. The primary target for Highball was the German battleship *Tirpitz* (see Chapter 6), secondary targets including the Italian fleet in the Mediterranean, U-boat pens and (again) the Rothensee Ship Lift.

Although developed in tandem with Upkeep, Highball encountered more teething troubles. Casing problems were also experienced in early tests, although these were solved by adding a wide metal plate over the wooden staves. More serious initially was a wobble caused by uneven release from the calliper arms, which meant the Highball did not run in a straight line. This had not been resolved satisfactorily by the time the deadline for the dams raid approached, and very few Mosquito conversions had been completed, so it was decided to press ahead with the Upkeep operation alone. Highball development continued through the summer of 1943, with test drops being made at Reculver and also at Loch Striven in Scotland by test pilots and pilots of 618 Squadron, which had been formed to deliver Highball. In the autumn, an attack by X-craft submarines disabled the *Tirpitz*, and 618 was then largely transferred to other duties, but in 1944 it was decided to use Highball against Japanese warships in the Pacific, so the squadron was built back up to full strength and crews underwent further training over the summer, including performing carrier landings. Embarked on two escort carriers, 618 was ferried to Australia, arriving just after Christmas, but although further training was done 'down-under', no suitable targets could be found for the weapon, and the squadron was disbanded even before the end of the war, the Highball stockpile being blown up. The Americans also experimented with Highball carried by an A-26 Invader under the codename Speedee, but on one test drop in Florida, the mine was dropped from too low a height, and it bounced into the tail of the aircraft, causing it to crash into the sea; no further experiments were conducted.

A further version of the bouncing bomb intended for use on motor torpedo boats and codenamed Baseball was also developed at the same time by the Navy's Department of Miscellaneous Weapons Development at Weston-super-Mare, but it too never saw action.

Thus, despite the successful outcome of Operation Chastise and serious consideration given to many other possible uses of the bouncing bomb, neither Upkeep nor the other versions were ever to be used operationally after 17 May 1943. The technical details remained secret until 1963, when the two patents covering the concept (GB937959 and GB937960) were published.

12,000

4000

2000

1000

Chapter Four

The 12,000lb HC Blockbuster Bomb

Retained as a special operations unit, 617 Squadron were selected to drop another new type of bomb – the largest in the RAF's armoury.

OPPOSITE The 'Blockbuster' was the largest of the RAF's HC blast bombs, dwarfing the 4,000lb 'Cookie' and 2,000lb HC bombs, and the 1,000lb and 500lb GP bombs. The 8,000lb 'Super Cookie' is missing from this line-up.
(Imperial War Museum CH12450)

High-capacity bombs

Although Wallis's original 'big bomb' theory had been rejected, the need for bombs larger than the standard 500lb and 1,000lb bombs had been realised, with the expectation that the blast from a larger bomb would have more widespread effects. The bombs developed were known as high-capacity (HC) or light-case bombs (LCBs), as they had a relatively thin case made of sheet steel (compared to the cast bodies of other bombs), which gave them a greater charge-to-weight ratio (up to 70 per cent) as well as making them easier to fabricate. The bombs comprised a simple steel cylindrical section containing the charge, plus a tail which, in the smaller bombs, was simply a plain cylinder continuing the line of the bomb body. Early bombs had a conical nose with a single pistol at the apex (plus side fuzes in some versions), but later this was superseded by a blunt nose with three pistols in line across it, all acting upon the same exploder. To prevent damage on impact, early types were fitted with drogue parachutes to reduce impact forces. Impact or delay pistols could be used; the latter allowed the bombs to be dropped from low level while allowing the dropping aircraft time to escape the blast.

The first of the HC bombs was the 4,000lb 'Cookie', which was 30in in diameter. Generally used by the four-engined 'heavies' as part of a mixed bomb load (with General Purpose bombs or incendiaries), it could also be carried by modified Wellingtons and (when they became available) Mosquitoes. The first use of the Cookie was at the end of March 1941 when two were dropped on Emden by 9 Squadron, and around 68,000 were dropped before the end of the war.

The 8,000lb HC 'Super Cookie' was conceived at about this time. It consisted of two 4,000lb sections bolted together (these were 38in in diameter, so were not the same as the Cookie cylinders), the nose cylinder being slightly domed at the forward end and fitted with three nose pistols. The cylinders were fabricated from ½in steel plate, and had an exploder core running up the centre of the bomb to ensure that both sections of the bomb would explode simultaneously. These bombs could only be carried by the Lancaster and Halifax, the first being released on Essen from a 76 Squadron Halifax in April 1942. The first to be dropped on Italy was in November 1942 by 106 Squadron aircraft (one of which was piloted by Guy Gibson), just over 1,000 being used during the war.

The Blockbuster

By adding a third similar section, the 12,000lb HC 'Blockbuster' was created (this name was sometimes used to refer to any of the HC bombs). This bomb was found to be unstable in flight even with a tubular tail, so a six-finned conventional-looking tail was required, giving the bomb an overall length of 196in. This bomb could only be carried in specially modified Lancasters with 'blown' bomb-bay doors which were enlarged to fit around the bomb, and were delivered to 617 Squadron from September 1943.

Following the Dams Raid, Harris had decided to retain 617 Squadron as a special operations squadron – during July the squadron (now partly re-equipped with standard Lancasters) mounted a conventional bombing attack on targets in northern Italy, then were unimpressed at being sent on several leaflet-dropping raids

RIGHT A Blockbuster showing the three charge sections and six-finned tail; two of the lugs were used to winch the bomb into the bomb bay where the large central lug engaged with the bomb slip. *(Crown Copyright via EOD TIC – BOE OP1665)*

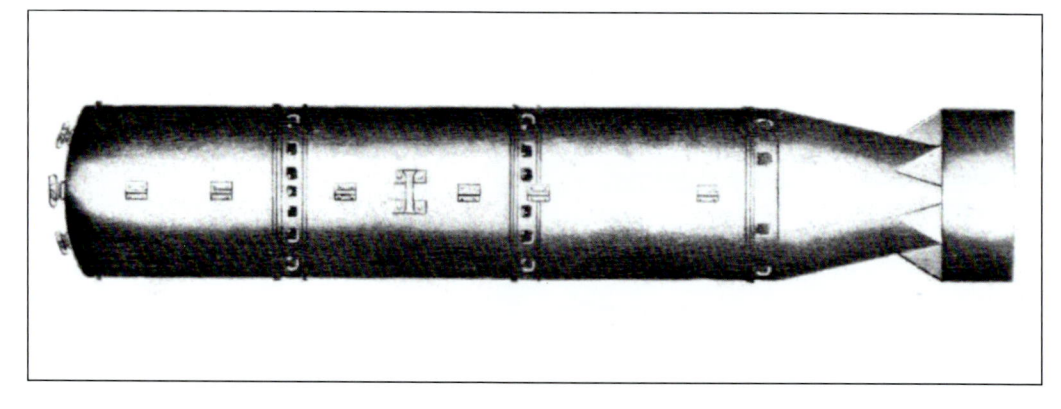

Key principles – target marking

Early in the war, when the decision was taken to concentrate effort on night bombing, the problem of target marking became an acute one – illumination of the target area was required, plus some method of visually identifying the aiming point on the ground.

Main Force raids generally used three types of markers (often laid by 8 Group 'The Pathfinders' latterly using Mosquitoes fitted with the Oboe navigation aid). These were: sky markers illuminating the path to the target area (codenamed 'Wanganui'), flares to illuminate the target from above ('Newhaven'), and target indicators ('Paramatta') which burned on the ground to give the bomb aimers an aiming point; the latter could be dropped visually by the light of the flares, or dropped 'blind' using H2S radar. TIs were colour coded, both to allow the Master Bomber (who orbited the target to guide the Main Force in) to tell the crews which TIs to aim for, and also to prevent the enemy from lighting decoy fires (as they would not know which colour to make them).

However, for 617's typical pinpoint targets, even the Pathfinders were not accurate enough, so Sqn Ldr Cheshire developed new marking techniques for the squadron. Further, as TIs could spread out over several hundred yards, they were not suitable for small targets, so coloured 'spot fires' were used instead; standard incendiary bombs could also be dropped to function as target markers. Markers only burned for a few minutes, so the bombers had only a short time to make their attacks, otherwise re-marking could be required. This might also be necessary if the bombing was so accurate that it landed on the markers and put them out.

617 used both low-level and medium-level marking as required, initially using Lancasters. For greater accuracy in placing the markers, they tried dive-bombing them into place. More agile aircraft were an obvious choice for this role, and Cheshire succeeded in persuading Harris to let the squadron have use of Mosquitoes. Subsequently, P-51 Mustangs were acquired by the squadron for marking duties, spot fires being carried on racks beneath the wings. Once the squadron switched to predominantly daylight attacks, the need for marking was removed altogether, as their targets were typically large and easily seen even from altitude.

(known as 'Nickels') to Italian cities. However, the 12,000lb HC was to become their distinctive weapon until the deep-penetration Tallboy became available some nine months later. On many operations, 617 Squadron operated on its own; on others (especially the Tallboy raids) they often worked with 9 Squadron, and on some raids they formed part of a Main Force attack (though often with a unique aiming point within the target area); their proficiency at marking for themselves assisted this partial autonomy.

On 1 September, the squadron moved to RAF Coningsby (which had hard runways) to allow Scampton's to be laid; the squadron's codes were changed from AJ to KC at this time (although the remaining Type 464 aircraft kept their AJ codes).

Official Air Publication 2852A Vol.1 Sect.5 Chapter 5 gives details of the procedure for assembling the Blockbuster:

- the 12,000lb HC bomb is supplied in three sections, and is to be assembled complete with suspension lug, hoisting brackets and tail unit prior to fuzing; each section has two brackets for use when hoisting the section, two of which are also used to hoist the complete bomb. The suspension lug and hoisting brackets are secured by four bolts to the casing reinforced by a steel pad on the inside of the casing; the suspension lug is at the bomb's centre of gravity
- bomb sections are supplied fitted with protective rings, and are to be placed on

RIGHT A special jig was required to assemble the three sections of the bomb with correct alignment. *(Crown Copyright via The National Archives – AP2852)*

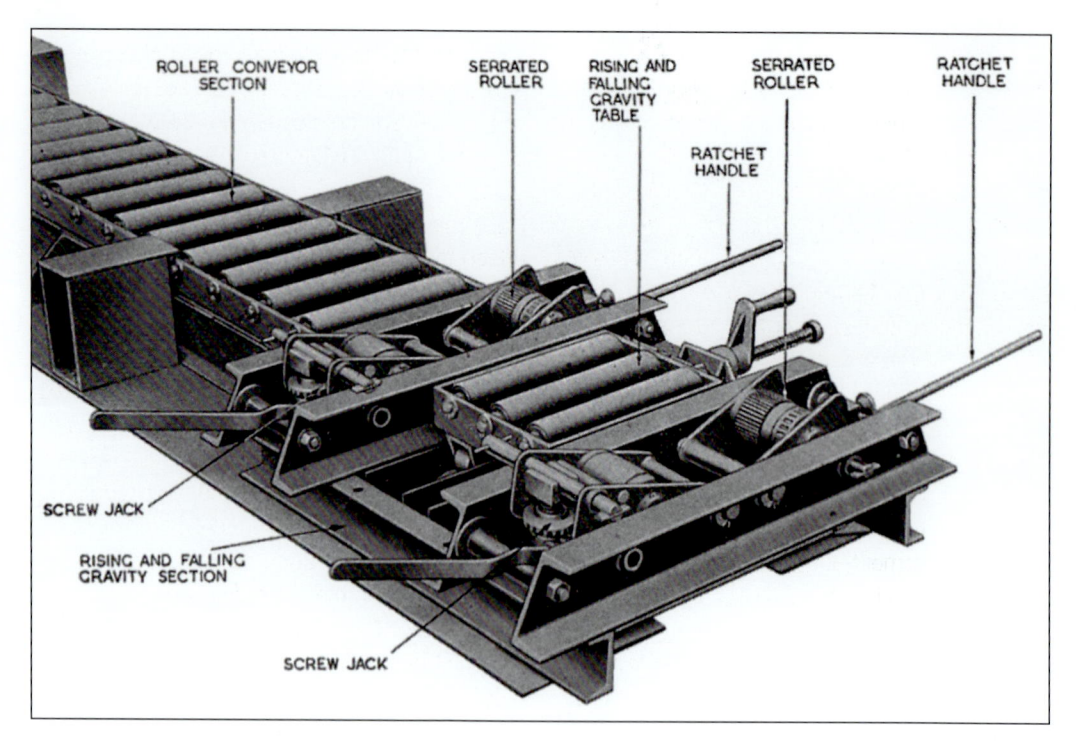

- battens with sufficient ground clearance for the removal of the rings by unscrewing and removing assembly bolts (to be retained for joining of sections); protective ring on rear section only to be removed when tail is about to be fitted
- assembly takes place on an assembly platform (see figure); roll one mid-section onto roller conveyor section so that assembly bolts are at rear end of bomb section, pushing it onto the gravity table; roll rear section onto conveyor, assembly bolts at rear, and push along until it almost meets rear of mid-section; using screw jacks to adjust height and ratchet handles to rotate mid-section until sections are in alignment, lever sections together (taking care not to damage bolts), replace nuts on assembly bolts and tighten (in diametrically opposite pairs)
- raise gravity table and lower screw jacks to allow bomb to be rolled clear of table; transfer nose section (with protecting ring removed) onto gravity table, then roll back mid-/rear sections and following same procedure for alignment, bolt on nose section; roll assembled bomb off platform
- roll bomb into position where suspension lug and hoisting bracket holes are accessible; remove cover plates and clean threads if required; position suspension lug and hoisting brackets and bolt onto body (two hoisting brackets are fitted, one at the forward position on the mid-section and one at the forward position on the rear section)
- remove protective ring from rear of bomb; remove tail unit from crate and offer up to rear of bomb, securing it with nuts from assembly bolts and tightening these with spanner inserted through the hand holes in the side of tail unit; bomb can now be stored until ready for fuzing.

Main particulars – Blockbuster

Type	12,000lb high-capacity blast bomb
Length overall	196in
Diameter (body and tail)	38in
Weight	11,936lb
Charge/weight ratio	70 per cent approx.
Casing thickness	0.5in
Filling	Amatex, Torpex or Minol
Tail type	No.33 Mk.I or No.52 Mk.I (six-fin ring tail)
Typical fuzing	three No.27, No.42 or No.44 impact pistols in the nose
Appearance	dark green overall with 1in green band and 1in red band around each bomb section
Number expended on operations	149 (80 by 617 Squadron and 69 by 9 Squadron, according to ORBs)

Fuzing

The Blockbuster was fitted with three exploder pockets in the nose, the middle one on the bomb's central axis and running the full length of the nose section. The other two were angled so that they came close to the central exploder, hence any one of the three pistols could initiate the central exploder which ran the length of all three sections, so that all of the sections would be initiated virtually simultaneously.

The No.27 nose pistol was typically used in these bombs. Its central striker was held in position by a shear wire and surmounted by a pressure plate, which was protected by a set of nose vanes, these being held fixed by a safety fork. At the moment of release, the fuzing wire attached to the aircraft pulled out the safety fork, allowing the airflow to spin the vanes, unscrewing them from the nose of the bomb and revealing the pressure plate. At impact, the force on the pressure plate caused the shear wire to fail, and the striker to impinge on the detonator cap, initiating the detonation chain. If the bomb was to be dropped safe, the fuzing wire was released from the aircraft, so the safety fork was not withdrawn and the vanes would not unscrew.

Modifications to the Lancaster

Although the 8,000 and 12,000lb HC bombs were carried in the same way as their smaller cousins, their girth was too large for the standard Lancaster bomb bay, and for carriage of these bombs, enlarged or 'blown' bomb doors had to be fitted. These doors had two sections with different radii – the hinge side was standard, but the opening side had an extra curved section to fit around the 38in diameter of the HC bombs. The extra size was washed into the fuselage profile at the forward end, but no attempt at fairing was done at the rear, the blown section simply coming to an abrupt end at the rear of the bomb bay. Special bomb slips and crutches were also fitted to carry the 12,000lb bomb.

Loading the Blockbuster

For ground handling, the large HC bombs were carried on a Type E trolley, a large trolley with the added refinement of steerable wheels at both ends to assist positioning of the bomb load beneath the aircraft; its only shortcoming was a ground clearance of less than six inches, which required some care to be taken when moving it around the airfield. The standard procedure for loading small bombs was to lower the bomb carrier down onto the bomb, attach the integral bomb slip to the lug on the bomb, then winch the carrier (with the bomb attached) back up into the aircraft, using a winch fitted above the bomb bay roof; once the carrier was secured to the roof, the winch could be removed from the aircraft. The HC bombs were also carried in the aircraft held in a single bomb slip, but the slip remained attached to the aircraft and two winches were used to lift them into the bomb bay. The bomb slip was positioned within the bomb bay roof structure; a Type F slip was used for the 4,000lb HC and a Type G (a modified Type F) was used for the 8,000 and 12,000lb HC. Once attached to

BELOW Sectional views of the forward and centre section of the Blockbuster in their transport frames; note the nose pistols and the main exploder which ran the full length of the core. (Crown Copyright via EOD TIC – BOE OP1665)

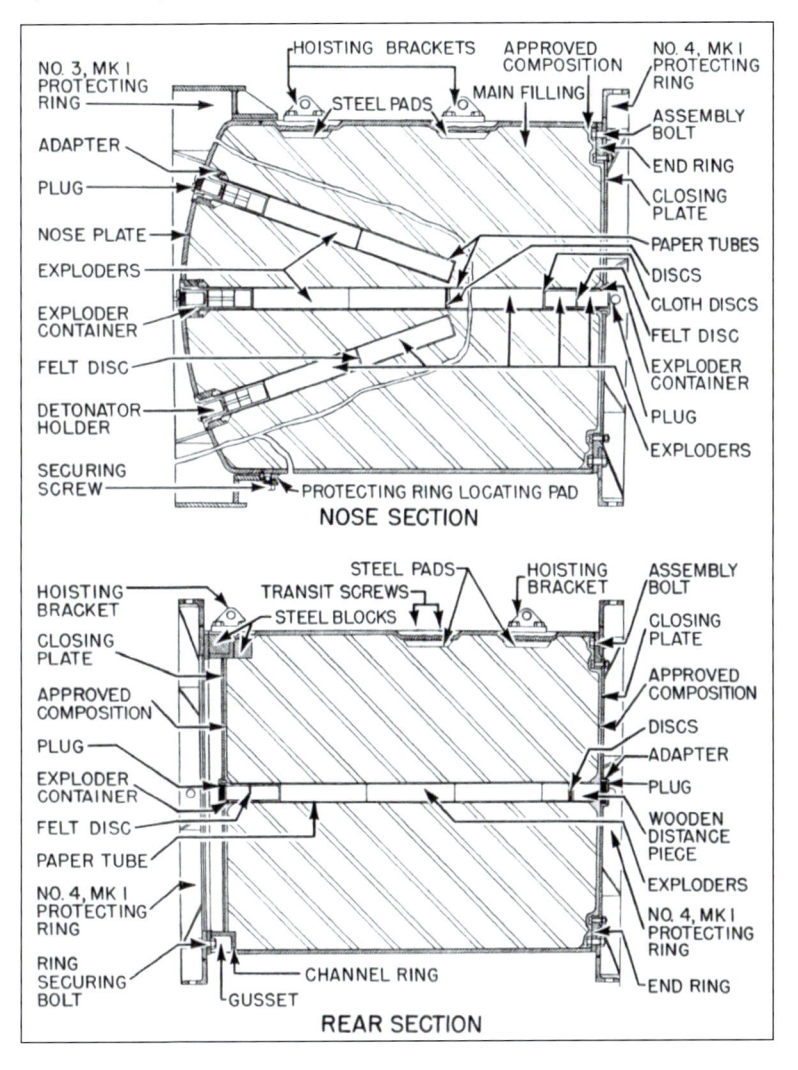

ABOVE A Blockbuster on a Type E trolley beneath Lancaster 'S for Sugar' at the RAF Museum, Hendon; the 'propellers' on the nose spun as the bomb fell to arm the impact pistols. *(Author)*

the slip, the winches were removed and four supporting crutches (two forward, two aft) were positioned using turnbuckles to hold the bomb steady within the bomb bay during flight.

Blockbuster targets

Upkeep had been mooted for use against canal banks and viaduct piers, but after poor results in trials, the Blockbuster was seen as a better alternative, following successful experimental drops into shallow water from low altitude.

One target of particular interest was the Dortmund–Ems Canal, one of the main transport links between the Ruhr and central Germany, and planners identified a stretch of the canal near Ladbergen where it was raised above the surrounding land and a breach in the banks would thus be devastating. 617 Squadron, carrying Blockbusters for the first time, set off for Ladbergen on 14 September 1943, but while still outbound, the raid was called off when a weather reconnaissance aircraft reported fog over the target. Turning back over the North Sea, Maltby's wing clipped the water, and the Lancaster spun in – there were no survivors from the crew that had breached the Möhne Dam. Eight aircraft set out again the following night, and although the target area was reached successfully, weather conditions were again poor. Some bombs were dropped close to the canal, but it was not breached. Enemy action and low-level collisions claimed five of the Lancasters, including those flown by Holden, the new squadron CO, and Knight, who had breached the Eder Dam – although he was able to hold his damaged aircraft in the air long enough for his crew to bail out.

The next night, six aircraft from 617 Squadron accompanied six from 619 to attack the viaduct at Anthéor in the south of France in an effort to break one of the key supply routes into Italy. The viaduct was attacked at low level using a mixture of 4,000lb HC and 1,000lb general-purpose bombs, but although the weather was clear and there was little opposition, no damage was caused to the target. On 11 November, the squadron tried again (alongside a Main Force attack on marshalling yards at Cannes), this time with ten aircraft each carrying a Blockbuster. This operation was the first time that the squadron used the SABS (see Chapter 7), and the bombs were to be dropped from 8,000 to 10,000ft. Some crews had difficulty locating the target (which now had searchlights and flak guns around it) and the closest bomb landed 60yd away. Again no damage was done, despite the size of the bombs and the great accuracy of the attack (60yd was a very small margin for a drop from this height). Due to the heavy bomb load and the distance to the target, the bombers flew on to land at Blida in Algeria to refuel for the return trip.

The bomb's next outing was on the night of 16–17 December, as part of a raid on V-1 flying bomb sites (codenamed 'Noball' targets) near Abbeville. Under its new CO, Leonard Cheshire, 617 was detailed to attack the site at Flixecourt, and eight Blockbusters were dropped accurately on the markers – these had been dropped by an Oboe Mosquito but were about 350yd away from the target, which consequently was undamaged. The same happened on 30 December when attacking another 'Noball' site with ten Blockbusters – accurate bombing on the markers, but these were 200yd from the target. Cheshire thus proposed that 617 should perform its own marking duties, and throughout January (following another move to the single-squadron station of RAF Woodhall Spa) as they continued to play a part in Main Force attacks on the 'Noball' sites, he carried out some experiments in placing markers from low and medium level, including dive-bombing them into position. This was put to the test on 8 February 1944 when the squadron attacked the Gnome et Rhône aero engine factory at Limoges; there was civilian housing nearby. Cheshire flew over the factory several times at low level to warn the factory workers to evacuate, before dropping his incendiaries and spot fires onto

TARGET PROFILE

Anthéor Viaduct

Type: double track 9-arch railway viaduct
Location: 43° 26' 15" N 6° 53' 31" E (near Agay, Var, France)
Built: 1860–3
Length: 175m
Attacked: 16 September 1943 (1,000 and 4,000lb bombs), 11 November 1943 (10 Blockbusters), 12 February 1944 (9 Blockbusters); also attacked by USAAF on seven occasions October 1943–June 1944; two arches demolished by final attack
Current status: repaired with temporary beams 1944, arches reinstated 1945, in use

The viaduct at Anthéor was the weakest link in the railway running along the Côte d'Azur. In autumn 1943, this line was being used to ferry men and supplies into Italy to repel the Allied invasion in the south, hence the viaduct being selected as a target. Tallboys were not yet available so conventional bombs were used, including Blockbusters, but despite some close near misses, the viaduct remained standing. In the face of ever-increasing defences around the viaduct, the USAAF also attacked it seven times, finally destroying two arches in June 1944.

LEFT Reconnaissance photo of the Anthéor Viaduct, showing it nestled into the coastal folds of the Côte d'Azur. *(Author's Collection)*

RIGHT The Anthéor Viaduct from a contemporary postcard; the problem of low-level marking on this target is evident. *(Author's Collection)*

the factory (he carried no other bombs). The rest of the squadron then dropped their loads, which included five Blockbusters, accurately onto the markers from 8,000 to 10,000ft and the factory was destroyed. The dropping of the incendiaries was captured by a cameraman who was flying in the rear of Cheshire's aircraft, and his dramatic photographs were heavily featured in the press.

Four nights later, they flew to Anthéor for the third time, using RAF Ford on the south coast as a forward operating base, allowing them to do a round trip with the Blockbusters. Cheshire, flying down the steep valley behind the viaduct at low level, dropped his red spot fires onto the beach beside the viaduct. Martin attempted to drop his backup markers, but the defences had been further increased since their last visit and as he made his approach his aircraft was hit in the nose and his bomb aimer (who had been the bombing leader on Operation Chastise) was killed – he broke off his attack and flew on to land in Sardinia. The other nine aircraft bombed from 9,000 to 12,000ft, and although hits were probably made within 15yd of the structure, it was still not brought down.

On 2 March, the BMW aero engine factory at Albert in northern France was given similar treatment to Limoges, although the markers were dropped from mid-level (heavy defences precluded low-level marking) by Munro (as Cheshire's bomb sight was unserviceable) followed up by Wilson; eleven Blockbusters followed them down, all but one landing close to the aiming point, and the factory was erased. A repeat of the low-level marking technique was made at La Ricamerie needle bearing factory near St Etienne on 10 March, although the target was awkwardly situated in a valley, and both Cheshire and Munro saw their markers bounce clear of the target before Kell got his on target. However, the bombing (which was all with incendiaries and 1,000lb bombs) caused limited damage to the target. The method was employed again on 16 March against the Michelin tyre factory at Clermont Ferrand in central France, with Cheshire again making three passes over the target to give the workers time to evacuate before he dropped his markers. Ten Lancasters then released Blockbusters from 10,000ft, one aircraft also trying a new tactic – a 1,000lb bomb was released just before the Blockbuster so that its explosion would cause sympathetic detonation of the big bomb just before impact, thus spreading the blast over a wider area. Post-raid reconnaissance demonstrated bombing precision once again – the factory was destroyed, but the staff canteen beside it was unscathed.

The Blockbuster's final use by 617 Squadron came two nights later when (along with incendiaries and some 1,000lb bombs) six were dropped on an explosives factory beside the River Dordogne at Bergerac, with marking from mid-level; once again the target was destroyed. The squadron then began to use 8,000lb HCs as their main weapon, a total of 55 being used on raids on an explosives factory at Angoulême (when the air-burst tactic using 1,000lb bombs was used by several aircraft), aircraft works at Lyons and Toulouse and a German signals centre at St Cyr. On the Toulouse raid, Cheshire flew operationally in a Mosquito for the first time, this aircraft being better suited to the task of low-level marking than the Lancaster. The squadron quickly became so proficient at marking that they were occasionally called upon to mark targets for the Main Force, even in preference to the Pathfinders (a move which caused some inter-Group friction).

On 26 November 1944, 9 Squadron flew their first operation with the 12,000lb HC bomb (they had been operating with Tallboy since September so their aircraft were already fitted with the enlarged bomb bay doors, hence minimal modification was required). This was a raid on the city of Munich, when fifteen aircraft dropped these bombs. Two raids in December delivered a total of twenty-one on marshalling yards at Heilbronn and on a return trip to Munich, some 8,000lb HCs were also dropped. During March 1945, Essen, Dortmund and Würzburg were the targets of raids during which a further thirty-two of the bombs were released, bringing 9 Squadron's tally with the bomb to a close.

Although they saw limited deployment during the war, the Blockbusters were able to produce outstanding results when they were used on the right sort of targets – but their reputation would be overshadowed by another 12,000lb bomb.

BELOW **Proof of outstanding accuracy with a remarkable weapon – impact craters from several Blockbusters are clearly visible in the ruins of the Michelin factory at Clermont Ferrand on 17 March 1944. The staff canteen (lower right) was not targeted and remains virtually undamaged.** *(Imperial War Museum C4209)*

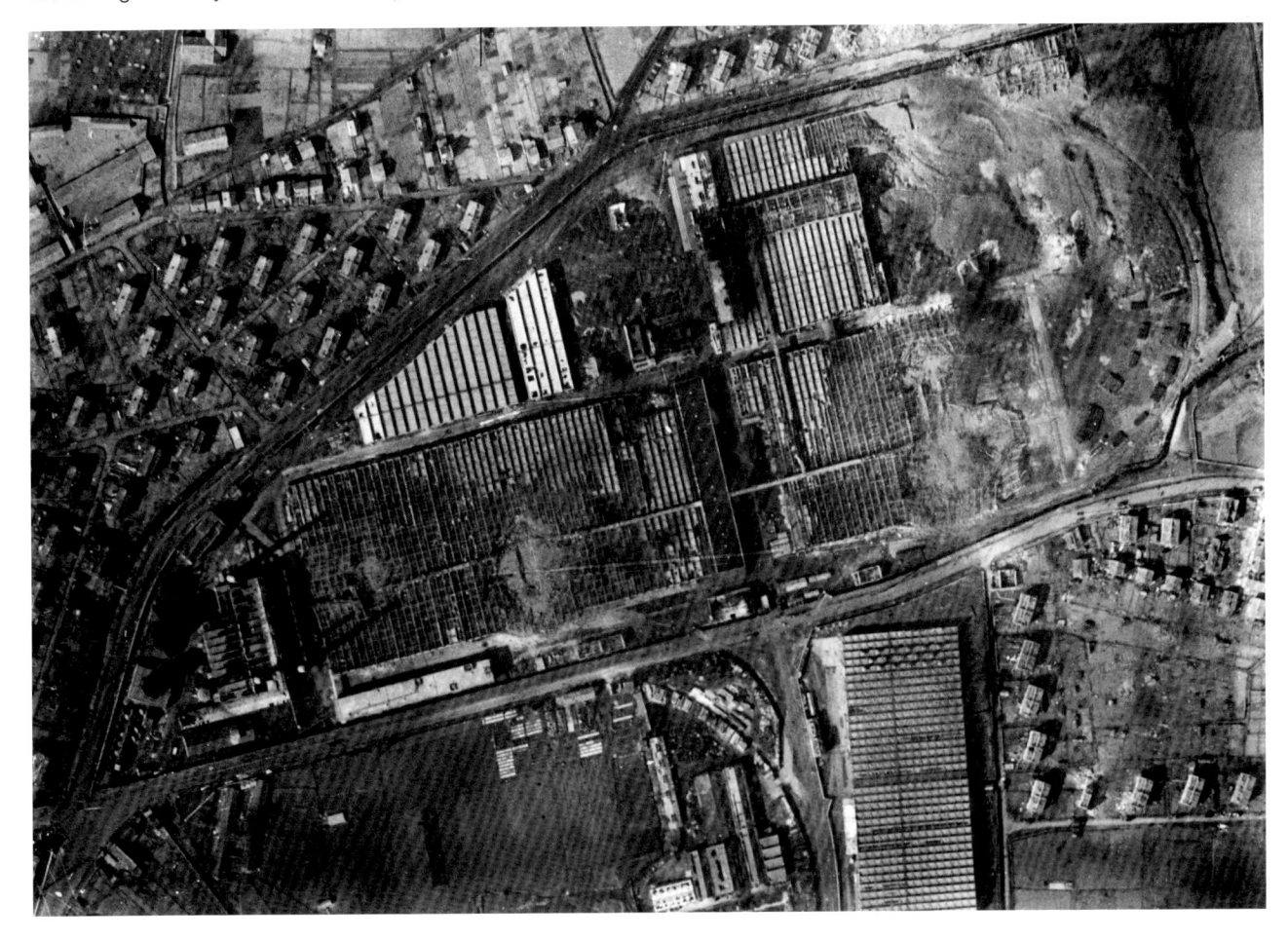

TORPEX

Chapter Five

Development of the Earthquake Bomb

Designed to penetrate the ground and destroy their target by creating a massive pressure wave, the earthquake bombs were another stroke of genius from Barnes Wallis.

OPPOSITE Ernest W. Weaver DFC, bomb aimer in Sayers' crew, poses with a Grand Slam – probably the one that he dropped on the Valentin U-boat factory at Farge on 27 March 1945, the only Grand Slam to have been dropped from above 19,000ft. *(Australian War Memorial UK3100)*

What is an 'Earthquake' bomb?

Wallis had already shown in his 'Note' of 1941 the expected efficacy of using large underground explosions to create shock waves and a gas bubble which could destroy a target, even if only a near miss was obtained. Although of a completely different design to the bomb described in the 'Note', Upkeep was based on the same principle and had proven that this effect could destroy a target as massive as a gravity dam – so another positive outcome of the Dams Raid was that it persuaded the Air Ministry to reconsider his plans for a ten-ton (22,000lb) deep-penetration bomb, the formal go-ahead being given in mid-July 1943 (initially these were referred to as DP (deep-penetration) bombs, but they were officially known as MC (medium-capacity) bombs, as the heavy casings meant that they had medium charge-to-weight ratios; the term 'earthquake' bombs, though widely used, is an unofficial one).

The requirements for the bomb were that it should:
- be aerodynamic, for maximum speed gain and more accurate bombing;
- be as heavy as practicable (to carry the largest possible charge to the target), and;
- have a casing strong enough to withstand ground penetration without deformation.

Although intended primarily for the destruction of underground facilities, it would also be used against other types of target, notably concrete bunkers, with some success. The cratering performance of the bomb was also notable, the large amount of material being thrown out being far more than that from smaller bombs of the same total weight; this meant that any craters would cause the enemy greater disruption, taking longer to make good.

Development and testing of Tallboy

Tallboy was conceived as a two-part weapon, a strong cast-metal pressure vessel in the nose section containing the charge and detonators which could penetrate the ground without breaking up, and a light alloy tail which would stabilise the bomb in flight then break away on impact.

The problem of creating a streamlined shape with the largest internal capacity was familiar to Wallis from his airship days, and he adopted the conventional ogival nose profile typically used in artillery shells. The nose of the bomb has a profile which is a circular section (with double the radius of the bomb) and the rear of the casing follows the same radius very briefly before the straight line of the tail continues the profile to the rear.

The details of the casing design, however, were more difficult. The casing had to be as thin as possible to allow the maximum charge to be carried, yet thick enough to withstand impact with the ground at supersonic speeds; too thin at the nose and the casing would mushroom, too thin at the rear and the impact forces would blow off the rear of the casing. To derive the dimensions which would satisfy these conflicting requirements, a series of 2in-diameter model casings were carefully machined with slightly varying thicknesses. These were then fired from a mortar into earth; those that were too thin split open (due to tensile failure), so the thinnest one which did not deform was the shape adopted for the full-size bomb. However, the casing was still so thick that the explosive content would be less than 45 per cent of the overall weight of the bomb, so they were designated as Medium Capacity (MC) bombs.

As well as the 22,000lb bomb, a six-ton (12,000lb) scaled-down version was to be developed at the same time, and a 4,000lb version was to be used for ballistic trials of the weapon. These were to be known as Tallboy Large, Medium and Small respectively. All were identical in shape, differing only in size – Tallboy Large (formally 'Bomb, MC, 22,000lb') was 25ft 5in long, the casing being 12ft 6in long and 46in in diameter, Medium (formally 'Bomb, MC, 12,000lb') was 21ft long, with the casing 10ft 4in long and 38in in diameter (the same diameter as the Blockbuster). One hundred each of the Large and Medium were ordered, plus eighteen of the Small.

The casing itself consisted of three main parts, a single large casting for the main body, a steel closing plate to hold the exploder pockets, which was attached onto the rear of the body

LEFT The only surviving example of the 4,000lb Tallboy Small is at Brooklands Museum, together with its 22,000lb big brother Grand Slam. *(Author)*

BELOW A Tallboy preserved at Brooklands Museum. *(Author)*

DEVELOPMENT OF THE EARTHQUAKE BOMB

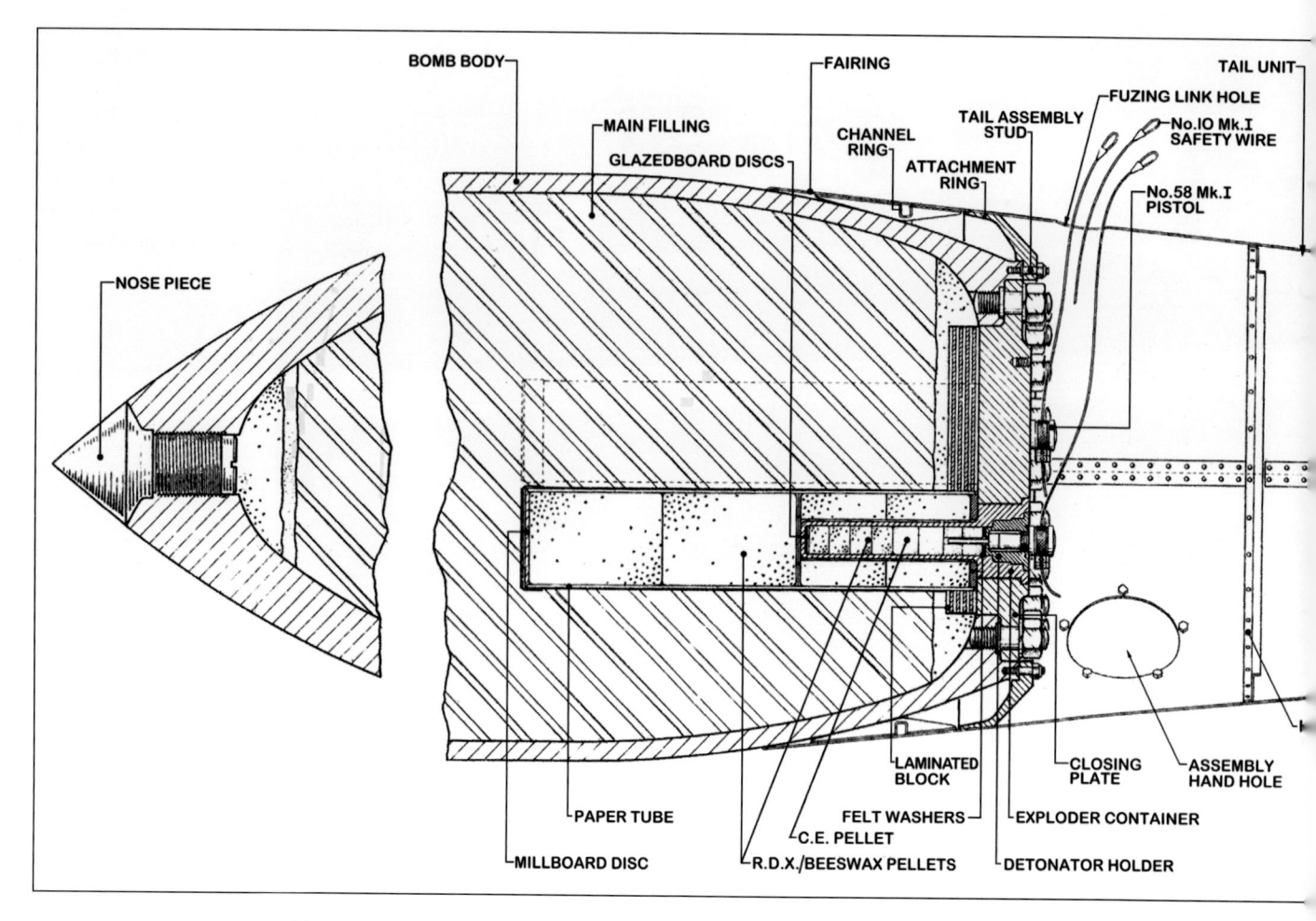

with twenty bolts, and a hardened nose plug which was screwed or cemented into a hole machined in the front of the main body; the combined body and nose plug were externally dressed on a lathe, so that the joint was rarely apparent. The casings were cast at several foundries, mostly in and around Sheffield; some were made from pearlitic manganese steel, others in chromium molybdenum steel, with machining done by several subcontractors near each site – it took the best part of a week to machine each of the casings, so the work had to be spread around the small number of companies tooled up to handle such large castings. The inside of the bomb was finished by hand, apprentices going inside the casings with an angle grinder to remove any surface imperfections; the inside was then coated with varnish to give a smooth finish (this was intended to prevent premature detonation due to friction with the filling at the moment of impact). Care had to be taken to achieve an even casing thickness as well as a smooth outer shape, as uneven thickness could lead to eccentricity as the bomb spun up; one bomb aimer reported seeing a Tallboy become so unbalanced that the tail was sheared off during its fall. A shallow recess 2in across was milled into one side of the casing in line with the bomb's centre of gravity (COG); this would engage a dowel in the roof of the bomb bay which held the bomb in position after loading. The finished casings were sent to ROF Woolwich for inert filling or to ROF Risley for HE filling, the latter being done by hand, pouring buckets of Torpex into the rear of the bomb, which was mounted on its nose.

The tail cones were made from light alloy by Short Bros at Rochester, with six internal circular ribs, and were attached to the casing by twelve assembly studs and Simmonds nuts; the aerodynamic profile of the bomb was maintained by a ring fairing which was fitted between the casing and the tail. Two hand holes in the tail gave access to the pistols, and a further hole carried the wires between the

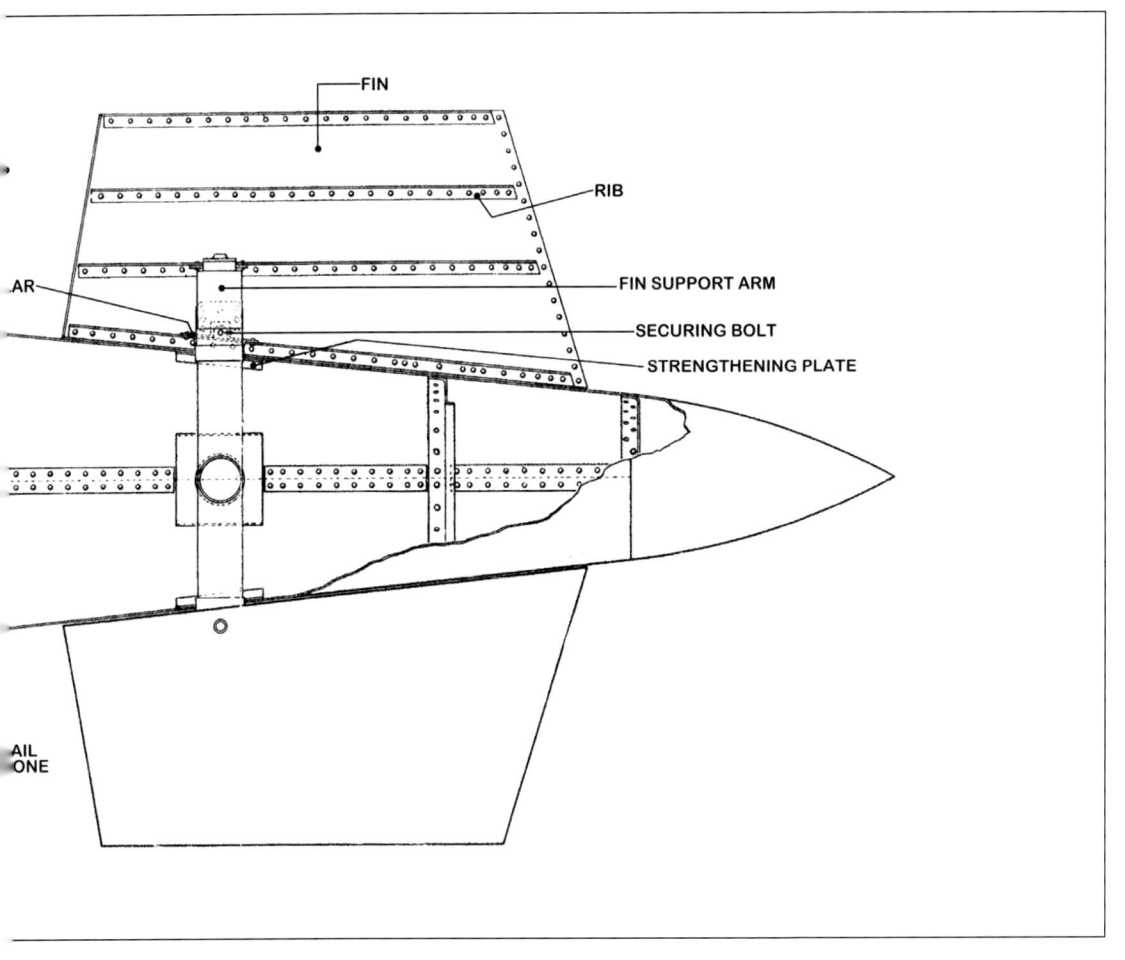

LEFT Tallboy cross-section showing the construction, casing thickness and details of the exploders. *(Crown Copyright via RAF Museum – AP 1661)*

LEFT Earthquake bombs being cast at the English Steel Corporation in Sheffield. *(USAF Museum)*

ABOVE A Tallboy on the lathe in the premises of the floorcovering manufacturers Michael Nairn & Co. Ltd in Kirkcaldy, one of the subcontractors who machined the casings; the nose fixture and base plate seating were machined first. *(Courtesy of Forbo Flooring UK Ltd)*

fuzing unit and the pistols, ready to be pulled out when the bomb was dropped. Four support arms projected from the tail near its apex, and these carried the fins. The bombs were normally stored without their tail cones, these being fitted in the bomb dump before loading.

Orders for the bomb casings were also placed with two companies in America (these being known as the Mk.II purely to differentiate its country of origin); one manufacturer cast the bombs using the method already described, but the other was unable to make such large

RIGHT Then the outside of the casing was dressed to remove surface imperfections. *(Courtesy of Forbo Flooring UK Ltd)*

ABOVE Fractures in the casings of early Tallboys led to the steel alloy being changed. *(BAE SYSTEMS via Brooklands Museum)*

LEFT This Tallboy at the Yorkshire Air Museum shows the 5° offset of the tail fins which imparted spin to the bomb as it fell, stabilising its flight through the transonic region. *(Author)*

castings, so constructed the bombs from smaller nose and tail castings plus three rolled plate sections for the straight part of the body, these five parts being welded together. The American casings were usually delivered without having been machined externally, sometimes having surface imperfections which led to problems when fitting the tails. They also used US standard bolts for fitting the rear plate and tail, which meant that different tool sets were required when working on these bombs.

After only a couple of months work, during which several prototype castings were made, it was decided to cancel Tallboy Large to concentrate resources on producing the Medium.

Meanwhile, the 2in mortar tests continued with numerous target materials being used to test penetration qualities – these included chalk, clay, sandstone, concrete and armour plate. The first ballistic tests of Tallboy Small took place in January 1944, revealing an instability which was cured by offsetting the fins by 5° to give the bombs spin as they fell, hence stabilising their path (an old archers' trick). Recovery of the casings revealed that they had failed, so harder steel was recommended for the larger bombs. Trials of the modified bombs in March gave satisfactory results. Trial loading of the Tallboy Medium prototype with a Lancaster took place in February at A&AEE, resulting in numerous guidelines being drawn up for the service installation of the bomb; this inert bomb was

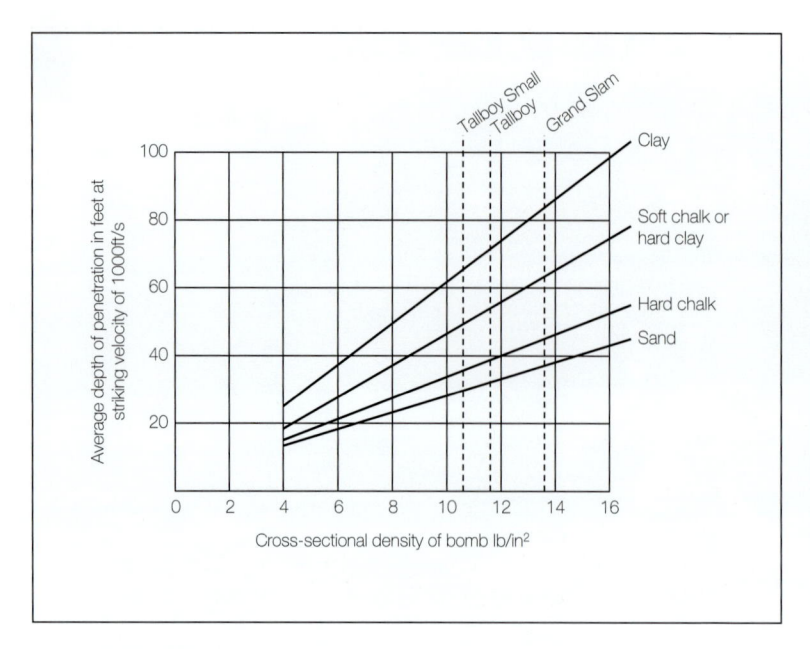

ABOVE The expected penetration of the earthquake bombs into different types of material. *(Author – based on drawing in Science Museum Wallis archive)*

dropped into chalk towards the end of March, and penetrated to 33ft. Live tests in April also showed satisfactory performance of the bomb, resulting in craters over 90ft in diameter.

The filling of the bombs also needed to be able to cope with the ground impact at high speed. Torpex with 5 per cent beeswax as a desensitiser was the filling adopted (although in operational use on hard targets, even this was found to detonate prematurely in some instances).

Ideally to be dropped from a height of 40,000ft, the Lancaster could get nowhere near this height carrying a Tallboy, but the achievable heights of around 15,000 to 18,000ft were deemed enough to give a sufficient degree of target penetration. Impact velocities of 1,000–1,500ft per second were achieved from this height, meaning that the bombs struck at speeds faster than sound; the terminal velocity of the bombs was calculated to be 3,800fps, so they were still accelerating as they struck.

Due to the manufacturing complexity of these bombs, Cochrane ordered that they were not to be dropped unless the bomb aimer could clearly see his target, and if a crew wished to jettison a bomb, they had to seek permission from the raid leader before doing so.

Official Air Publication 1661B Vol.1 Sect.10 Chapter 22 gives the full technical specification of 'Bombs, HE, Aircraft, MC 12,000lb Mk.I and II' (i.e. Tallboy) of which the following is a summary (see also accompanying diagrams) for the Mk.I:

- these bombs are designed for the attack of special targets where deep penetration into soil sub-strata is required; they have a streamline contour and can only be fuzed at the tail using either three No.58 or No.47 pistols.
- the bomb consists of a bomb body, filled with high explosive and provided with three tail fuzing positions and a No.78 tail unit which is secured to the bomb body by twelve assembly studs and Simmonds nuts; a fairing, held in position on the bomb body by three turnbuckles, is fitted to maintain continuous streamlining of the assembled bomb.
- the bomb body is manufactured of cast steel with a solid nose formed by a conical nose piece which is screwed and sealed into the nose of the bomb. The tail opening is covered by a closing plate which has three tapped holes for lifting purposes and is attached to the body by twenty studs with nuts and spring washers (usually stored in a box built into the transit cradle). The rear end of the body has twelve tapped holes to receive the tail assembly studs, which

Main particulars – Tallboy

Type	medium-capacity deep-penetration bomb
Length overall	252in (casing 124in, fairing 13in, tail 121in)
Diameter	38in (44.3in across fins)
Weight	11,855lb (of which charge 5,200lb, fairing 25lb, tail 150lb)
Charge/weight ratio	43.9 per cent
Casing thickness	variable
Tail type	No.78 hollow cone with four fins offset 5°
Filling	Torpex D.1 with desensitiser
Typical fuzing	three No.58 impact pistols or three No.47 delay pistols in the rear of the bomb body
Appearance	dark green body with pale green (anodised) tail; narrow red band and wider pale green band stencilled 'TORPEX D.1' around nose
Number expended on operations	877 (578 by 617 Squadron and 299 by 9 Squadron)*

*Different sources sometimes disagree on the numbers and types of bombs dropped; the figures used here are the best estimate from the available sources (usually the ORB), and include all bombs expended during raids, including those that missed or were jettisoned.

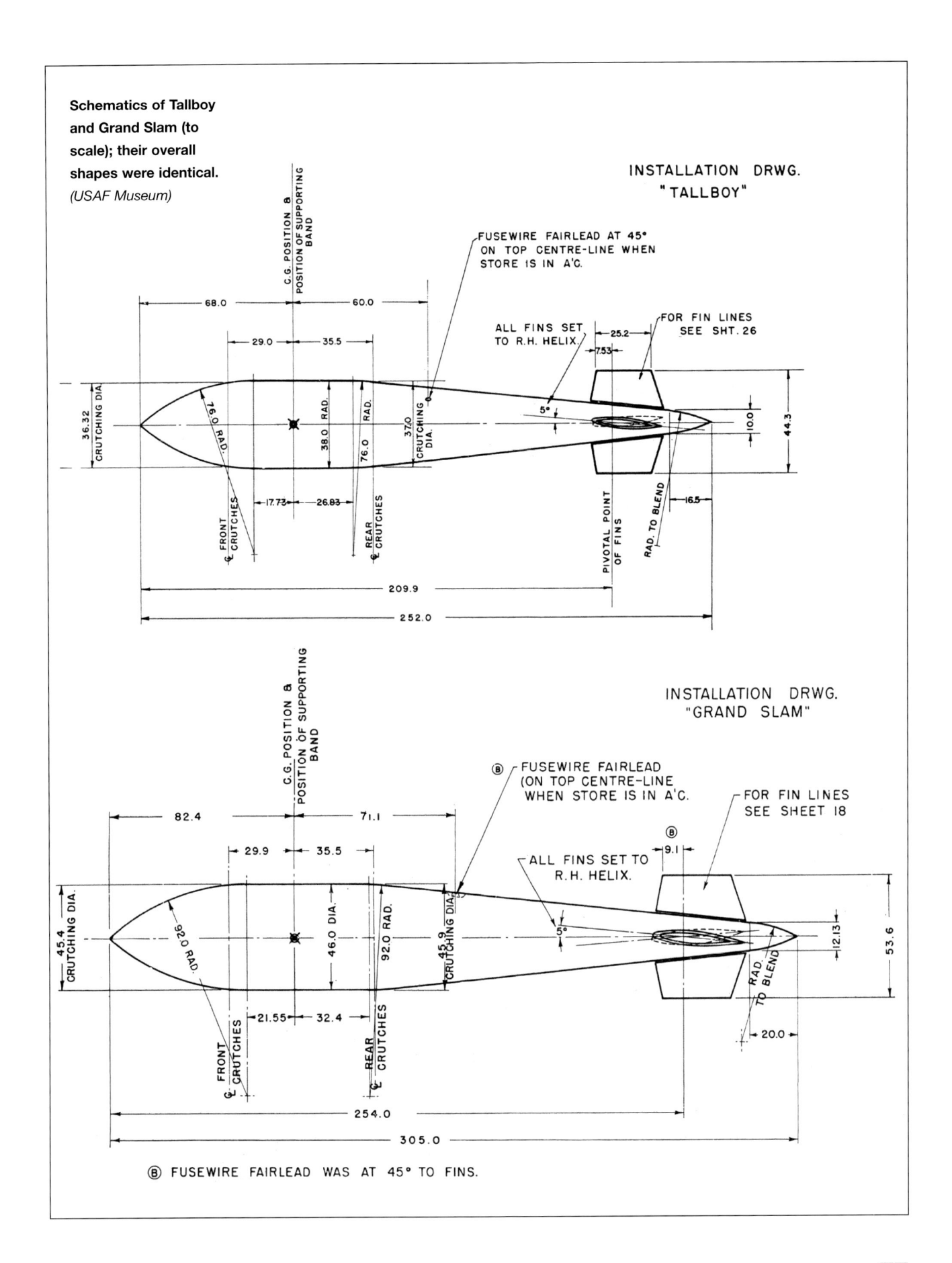

Schematics of Tallboy and Grand Slam (to scale); their overall shapes were identical.
(USAF Museum)

- are threaded at each end and have flanges which seat in the countersunk stud holes.
- screwed into the closing plate are three exploder containers, each of which holds an RDX/beeswax exploder and a CE exploder, covered by glazedboard discs and a felt washer respectively. A detonator holder is screwed into each container, which is inset in an RDX/beeswax exploder which is itself contained in a bakelised paper or cardboard tube.
- the bomb body is filled with Torpex D.1 and is sealed at the nose end with a layer of RD composition and TNT and at the rear end by RD composition or woodmeal wax and TNT; a laminated block composed of alternate layers of plywood and felt is recessed in the sealing compound.
- a recessed dowel hole is located almost midway along the length of the bomb body and serves to position the bomb correctly in the aircraft.
- the tail unit consists of a tail cone to which four fins of aerofoil section are attached, the fins being inclined at 5° to the axis so as to impart spin; the tail cone has a framework of six hoops covered by metal plating, adjoining sections being riveted either to a hoop or butt strap between hoops.
- towards the apex are four projecting support arms (to carry the fins) set at right angles, the casing being strengthened by a metal plate where each arm passes through. Each fin consists of a metal skin riveted to four elliptical plates bent over at the edges to form ribs. The largest rib is fitted with a flanged metal collar carried by two plates cast integral with the collar and riveted to the skin plating; a securing bolt passes through the collar and support arm.
- at the base of the tail cone is an attachment ring drilled with twelve holes to take the tail assembly studs. Two hand holes in the cone give access to the assembly studs and the fuzing positions after the tail has been fitted, these being covered by a panel when not in use. The fuzing link wires, which connect the pistols to the electro-magnetic fuzing unit in the aircraft, pass through a further hole in the tail. An arrow painted on the base of the tail is intended to facilitate lining up the fuzing link hole with the dowel hole on the bomb body.
- the fairing is formed from three curved panel sections which overlap slightly, the inside of each having a channel ring which connects to the other two via turnbuckles, these drawing the sections together when turned
- the Mk.II bomb is similar, being allocated a different number to indicate that it is of American manufacture; note that the tail assembly studs of this bomb are not interchangeable with the Mk.I.

Fuzing

Each Tallboy carried three identical pistols in the three exploder pockets set into the rear plate of the bomb casing. The Tallboys could be fitted with several types of pistols and detonators to give particular detonation delays after impact, but one of three common settings was typically used – 'instantaneous', 11 seconds and 30 minutes.

No.58 pistols were used when detonation on impact was required, and these were very simple and effective. The pistol consisted of a brass body which screwed into the end of the exploder pocket behind the detonator. Within the pistol was a solid metal rod carrying the striker on the forward end, the metal bar being supported within the pistol body by a light brass cross bolted to the rear. The cross was normally sufficient to hold the rod in place, but when the bomb impacted, the momentum of the rod was sufficient to deform the arms of the cross, allowing the rod with the striker to shoot forwards and strike the percussion cap. The head of the pistol was covered with a sealing cap. The pistol was provided with two safety pins which pegged the striker rod in place. One was removed by the armourers prior to flight, and the other was withdrawn (as the bomb was dropped) by a fuzing wire attached to the aircraft. If the bomb was to be dropped 'safe', the fuzing wire was released from the aircraft, and so stayed with the bomb and prevented the pistol from operating. In practice, impact fuzing was rarely used with Tallboys, as generally ground penetration was desired before detonation – a notable exception to this being shipping targets, such as the *Tirpitz*, where any delay to the detonation might have allowed the bomb to go right past (or through) the ship.

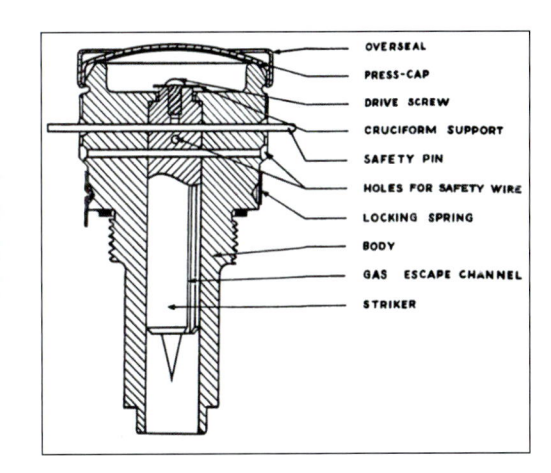

ABOVE The No.58 pistol operated instantaneously, the inertia of the striker bar pushing it forward into the detonator. The example on the left has been sectioned to show the strikers. *(Author)*

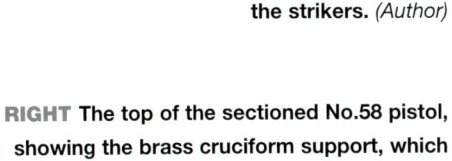

RIGHT The top of the sectioned No.58 pistol, showing the brass cruciform support, which holds the striker. *(Author)*

ABOVE Construction of the No.58 pistol. *(Crown Copyright via RAF Museum – AP 1661)*

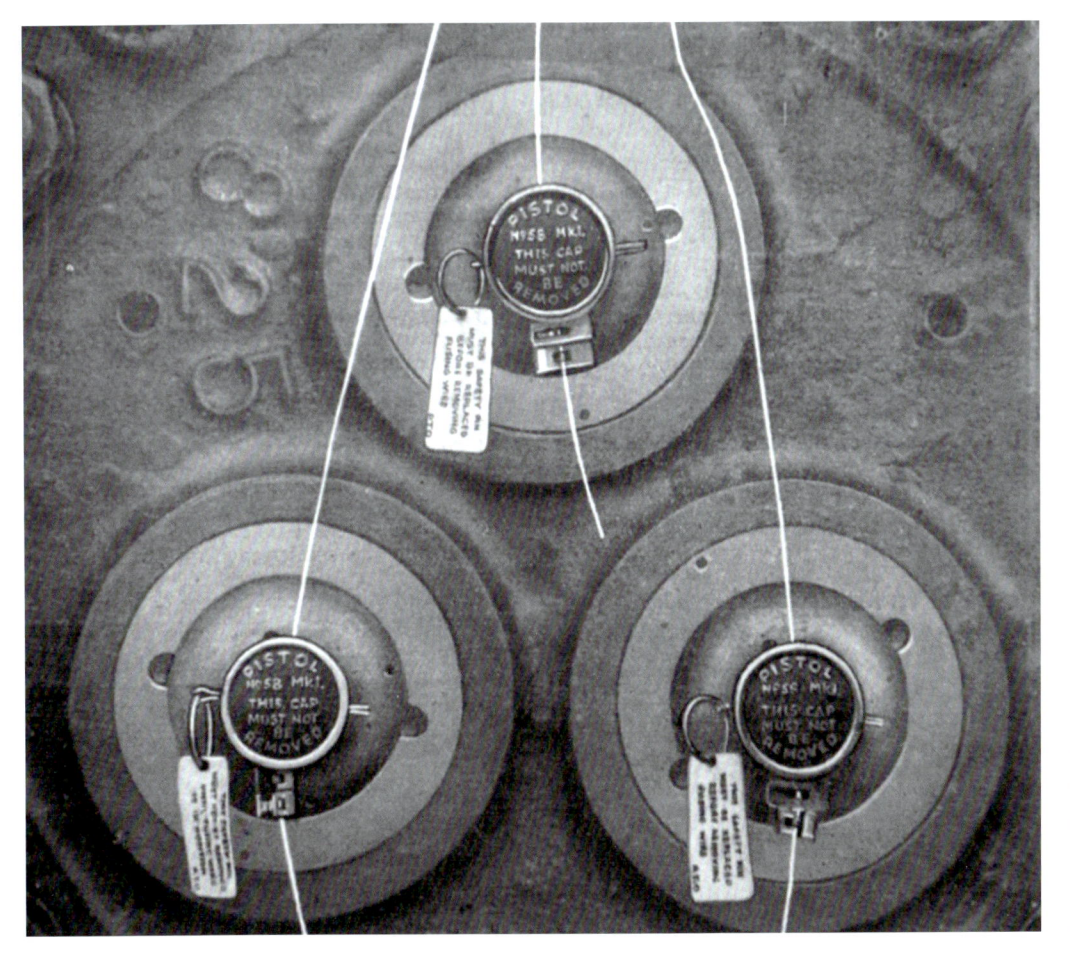

LEFT The rear of a Tallboy casing with three No.58 pistols in place with their arming wires. *(Crown Copyright via The National Archives – AP 2852)*

79

DEVELOPMENT OF THE EARTHQUAKE BOMB

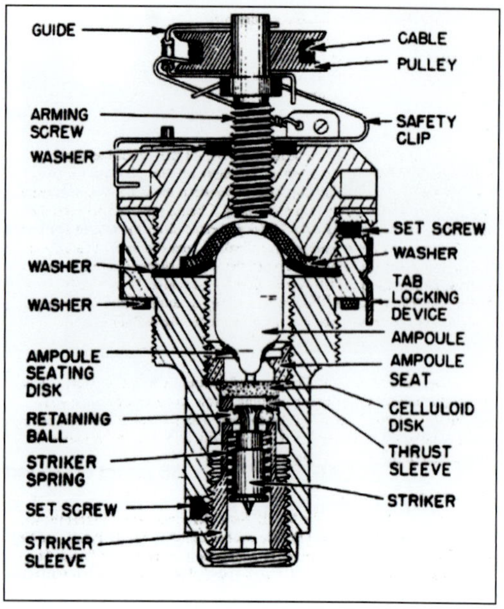

ABOVE The No.47 pistol gave a 30-minute delay, as the acetone in the glass ampule dissolved a disc holding the striker; the example on the left has been sectioned to show the mechanism. *(Author)*

ABOVE RIGHT Construction of the No.47 pistol; pulling the cable off the pulley screwed it into the ampule to start the sequence. *(Crown Copyright via RAF Museum – AP 1661)*

The use of an 11-second delay was more common, as this allowed the bomb to penetrate to maximum depth and come to rest, and also allow some fall back of earth behind the bomb, helping to tamp the explosion and transfer its energy to the surrounding earth. For this, the No.58 pistol was again used, but fitted with a No.35 delay detonator.

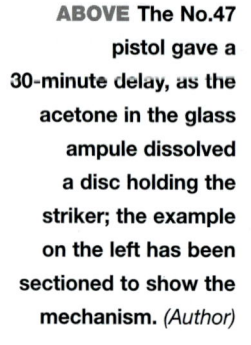

RIGHT The rear of a Tallboy casing with three No.47 pistols in place with their arming wires. *(Crown Copyright via The National Archives – AP 2852)*

For longer delays, the No.47 pistol was used. The striker in this pistol was spring loaded, but held back by a cellulose disc within the pistol body. On the other side of the disc was a glass ampule containing a mixture of acetone and alcohol. At the aft end of the pistol was a screw attached to a pulley, upon which a phosphor-bronze cable was wound. When the bomb was released from the aircraft, the wire caused the pulley to rotate, thus screwing the screw into the pistol body where it broke the glass ampule. This released the acetone mixture, which reacted with the cellulose disc, softening it over time. After around 30 minutes, the disc became so soft that it could no longer withstand the force of the spring, so the striker was released to initiate the detonator. In theory, this pistol could also be dropped 'safe', but in practice ground impact would usually break the ampule and hence start the detonation sequence anyway.

From time to time, all three pistols failed to operate, and this allowed the Germans to recover several intact Tallboys – the first at Wizernes within six weeks of their operational debut.

Modifications to the Lancaster

As the Tallboy had the same diameter as the Blockbuster, Lancasters with the 'blown' bomb bay doors were required to carry Tallboy. For aerodynamic reasons, the bomb was not fitted with a suspension lug, so a conventional bomb carrier could not be used. Instead, the bomb was carried in an ML sling which supported the bomb. This sling consisted of a series of links, each made up of two flat strips of steel interconnected by a bolt. The top ends of each half of the sling were connected to the bomb bay roof structure, and the bottom ends met in a heavy duty electromagnetic release unit (this unit would become the centre of investigation when a number of late releases were reported, though no specific fault was found).

LEFT Lancaster bomb bay fitted for Tallboy; the dowel pin is in the centre of the roof, with the cables to pull up the ends of the sling, the sling brackets are at the sides, and the crutches are at the four corners.
(USAF Museum)

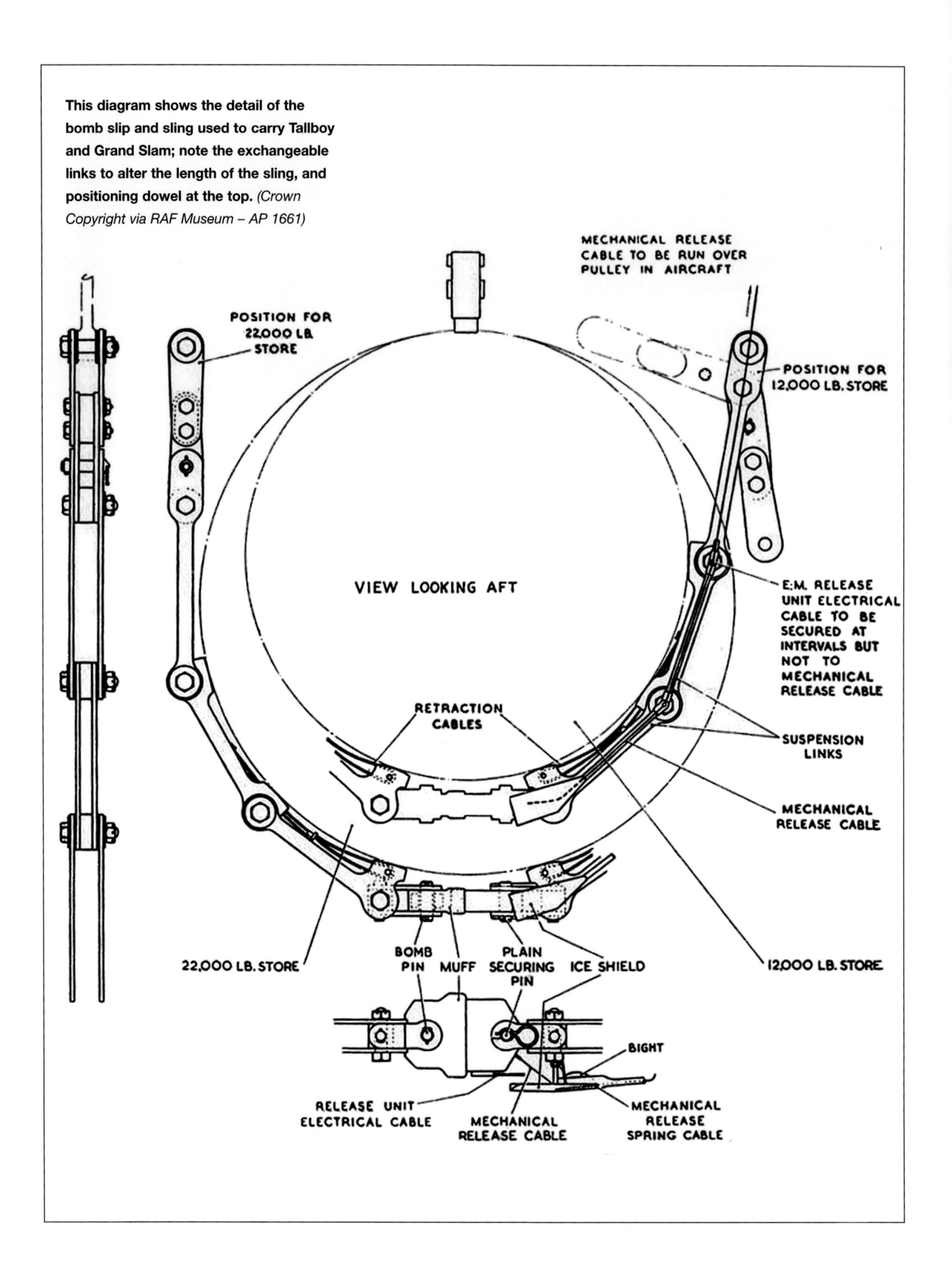

This diagram shows the detail of the bomb slip and sling used to carry Tallboy and Grand Slam; note the exchangeable links to alter the length of the sling, and positioning dowel at the top. *(Crown Copyright via RAF Museum – AP 1661)*

The electric release cable and another cable for manual release ran along the sling, passing through support eyes attached to each of the bolts. After release of the bomb, when closing the bomb bay doors, it was found that the sling hung down between the doors, leading to damage to the door edges as they were closed. To prevent this, ropes were attached to the ends of the sling and, after dropping the bomb, a member of the aircrew would use these to pull up the ends of the sling before the doors were closed (rubber bungees had been tried to pull up the ends automatically after release, but these did not work well).

Other changes included the addition of a manual release handle in the bomb aimer's compartment (used if the electric release mechanism failed), and the fitting of a spring-loaded steel dowel in the roof of the bomb bay. The dowel prevented the bomb from moving forward or back from its original position near the aircraft's centre of gravity, although on at least one occasion it was not engaged correctly, causing the bomb to slip and the aircraft to abort its sortie; the dowel was also fitted with an internal indicator to

ABOVE The RAF Museum holds this sling for the earthquake bombs, though this example does not include the bomb slip. *(Author)*

LEFT Detail of the construction of the sling. *(Author)*

LEFT The bomb slip, from another example held by the RAF Museum. *(RAF Museum)*

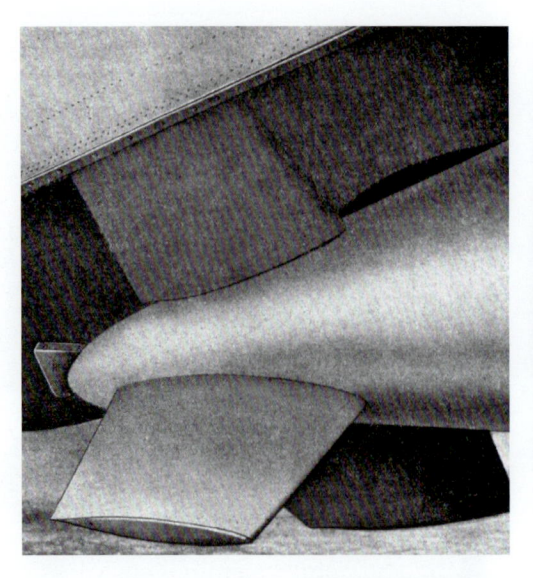

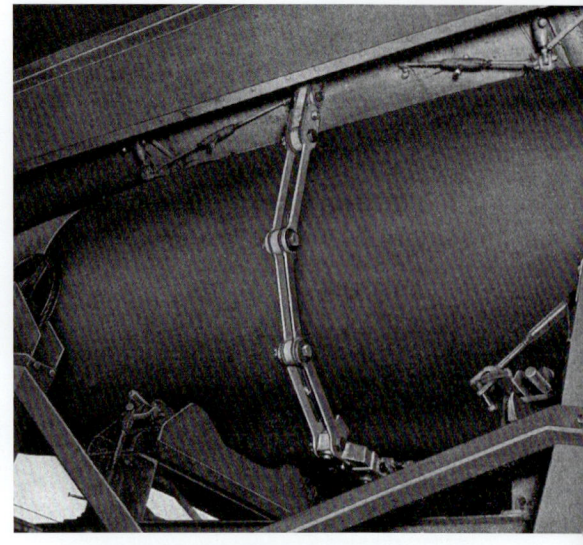

RIGHT Close-up of a Tallboy tail in the bomb bay; note the template which marks the location of the rear of the tail. *(Crown Copyright via RAF Museum – AP 1661)*

FAR RIGHT Tallboy winched up into the bomb bay and sling attached; two of the crutches are seen at the top. *(Crown Copyright via RAF Museum – AP 1661)*

show whether the bomb had been dropped. The four crutches fitted to hold the Blockbuster steady within the bomb bay were retained for the Tallboy.

Bomb trolley

Official Air Publication 2852A Vol.1 Sect.2 Chapter 9 gives details of the Type H bomb trolleys used for the Tallboy and Grand Slam bombs, and instructions for their use:

- the Type H chassis is similar in construction to the Type E, but the Type H is different from all other trolleys in that it contains the mechanism to raise the bombs into the aircraft; trolleys to be inspected before each use.
- tyre pressures (80lb/in^2) must be checked regularly; incorrect pressures or faulty brakes render the trolley unserviceable. Screw jacks are fitted near each wheel; if the trolley is left standing for an appreciable period, the weight on the tyres must be relieved by lowering the jacks to support the trolley (with wooden blocks beneath if the trolley is on soft ground).
- the rear wheels are steerable to reduce the turning circle when positioning the trolley during bombing-up, and a steering wheel

RIGHT This Grand Slam on its Type H trolley is in the RAF Museum, Hendon. *(Author)*

and seat are supplied for the operator; when moving along the road, the rear wheels must be locked straight.
- four standard 6,000lb bomb winches integral to the trolley (one in each corner post) are used to raise and lower the cradle carrying the bomb (by pulling on cables going over pulleys at the top of each post); the winches must be tested on a test rig before use.
- the bomb on the cradle is supported by two bearers, each of which incorporates a plain and serrated roller chock, which may be rotated either way by raising and lowering a handle. On the opposite side to the serrated roller chock is a traverse screw arrangement, enabling the bearers to be moved independently across the trolley to position the bomb laterally. The two forward posts on the trolley are 6in taller than those at the rear, allowing the bomb to be winched into a tail-down attitude to allow it to be easily mated with the bomb bay of the Lancaster when sitting on the ground.

Fitting the bomb tail unit

Official Air Publication 2852A Vol.1 Sect.5 Chapter 6 gives details of the procedure for fitting the tail to the Tallboy (and Grand Slam):
- when unloaded at the storage area, the bomb body should be positioned on storage battens or a cradle with the dowel hole uppermost and the rear of the body overhanging the rear batten by approx. 2ft.
- the tail units are to be fitted to the bomb bodies before fuzing, and will normally be done at the bomb storage area; before fitting, the twelve stud holes should be checked to be free from dirt and grease.
- a nut should be screwed onto the longer thread of each stud, then the shorter thread screwed into the hole in the rear of the bomb body so that the flange is well seated into the countersunk hole; once in position, the nut should be removed.
- the fairing and tail unit should be removed from their transit crate and inspected for damage; the panels covering the hand holes should be detached by undoing four of the five securing screws, pivoting the panel open on the fifth screw and replacing the four screws to prevent loss.
- the fairing turnbuckles should be slackened and the fairing placed loosely over the rear of the bomb body; the tail unit can then be offered up to the body so that the painted arrows on tail and body are aligned and the stud holes mate with the studs.
- ten nuts should then be screwed onto the studs; before fitting nuts on the top two, the fuze-setting control link shield is fitted on these studs. All nuts should then be tightened using an appropriate spanner, working in diametrically opposite pairs to ensure the tail unit is pulled evenly to the rear of the bomb body.
- the fairing can then be drawn back over the gap between the body and tail, and secured by tightening the three turnbuckles with a small tommy bar.

Some armourers would then check (using a wooden template) that the tail was fitted

ABOVE Grand Slam on the Type H trolley, showing the chains attaching it to the cradle and two of the winches. *(Crown Copyright)*

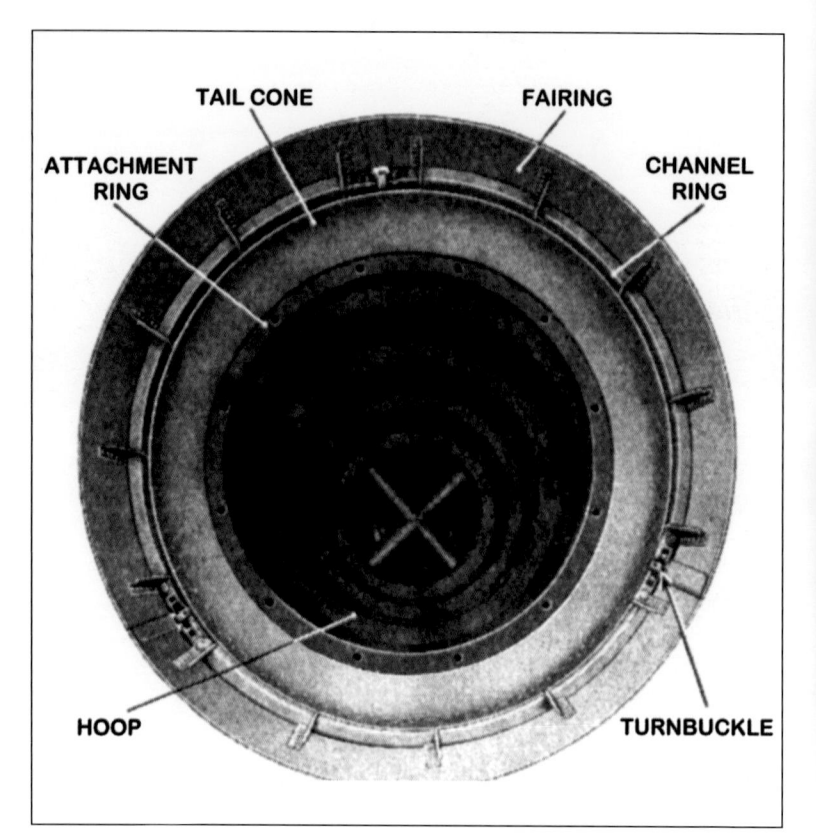

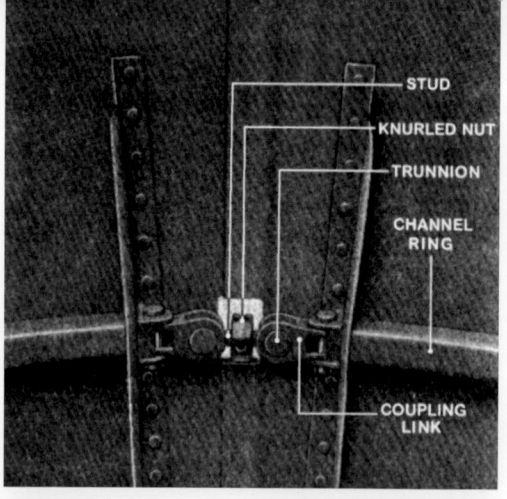

ABOVE View into the tail, showing the hoop structure and the struts holding the fins. *(Crown Copyright via RAF Museum – AP 1661)*

RIGHT, TOP The turnbuckle used to tighten the ring fairing onto the casing. *(Crown Copyright via RAF Museum – AP 1661)*

RIGHT, CENTRE The rear of a Tallboy awaiting a tail. The ring fairing and twelve studs have already been fitted, and transit plugs cover the exploder pockets. *(Crown Copyright via The National Archives – AP 2852)*

RIGHT A team of armourers fit a tail to a Tallboy. *(Crown Copyright)*

straight, hence ensuring balance when the bomb started to spin during its fall.

Loading Tallboy

The sequence for loading Tallboy onto the trolley at the bomb dump was as follows:

- ■ position the extra heavy crane to face the side of the bomb, with the head of the crane directly just above the bomb body; attach the Vickers sling, removing the quick-release pins which secure the free ends of the cables to the cross member of the sling; pass the cables around the bomb and re-secure the free ends to the cross member, ensuring the cables are equally disposed on each side of the dowel hole.
- ■ hoist the bomb just enough to clear the top of the trolley, and move the crane away from the bomb store (as short a distance as possible) to enable the trolley to be manoeuvred beneath the bomb, which must be prevented from swinging.
- ■ use a tractor to back the trolley slowly beneath the bomb, using front and rear steering, to position the bomb correctly above the bearers; apply trolley brakes; ensure bomb cradle is at lowest position and resting on bottom members.
- ■ lower bomb onto cradle, ensuring bomb does not foul hoisting pulleys and sling cables are on the outer side of each bearer; remove sling.
- ■ use ratchet handles of roller chocks to rotate bomb to bring dowel hole uppermost (approximately – final adjustment to be carried out at the aircraft); attach safety chains over bomb and tighten using turnbuckles.

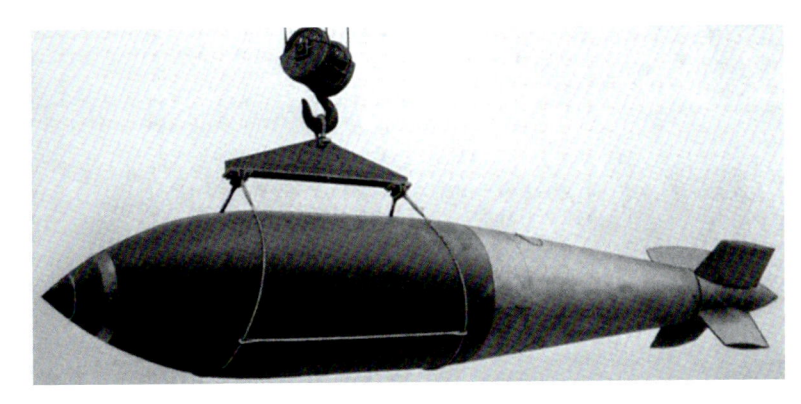

ABOVE A Grand Slam being lifted using the Vickers sling. *(Crown Copyright via The National Archives – AP 2852)*

LEFT A Tallboy being lifted from the bomb dump. *(Australian War Memorial SUK14438)*

- trolleys to be towed singly at no more than 5mph with as little jolting as possible; trolley to be escorted by armourer to operate rear wheel steering if required.
- if transportation at night is required, the tractor is to use headlights and the trolley is to have a rear light and frame sides painted white.

Trolleys were taken to the fuzing shed for fitting of the detonators and pistols; one bomb was completed before passing on to the next, as follows:

- the fuzing party comprises two men – an NCO or airman of the trade of fitter armourer (or similar) and an armament assistant; sufficient pistols and sensitive-type detonators to be drawn from stores and checked.
- check hand hole panels in tails are open; remove transit plugs from exploder containers.
- gauge all three detonator cavities and check that exploders are correctly in position.
- insert appropriate sensitive-type detonator into holder; screw one pistol into place by hand, checking that it is properly seated on its leather washer.
- for No.47 pistol – attach hooked end of fuze-setting control link to pistol safety clip/ for No.58 Pistol – pass end of safety wire through uppermost hole in pistol, fit two safety clips to wire.
- once all three pistols fitted, collect safety wires and pass them through fuzing link hole and position wood block to prevent wires falling back through; hand holes to be left uncovered.
- lettering to be stencilled 3in high on main circumference of bomb body near dowel hole ('L.D.47' for No.47 pistols or 'FZD' for No.58 pistols); detonator number to be stencilled at rear of bomb body above detonator holders.
- tow trolley to front of aircraft (about two trolley lengths away) and position for backing under bomb bay, with tractor and trolley as near as possible to fore-and-aft axis of aircraft; release pusher arms from stowage lugs on tow bar.

BELOW A row of Tallboys on their trolleys awaiting transport to RAF Bardney for loading. *(Australian War Memorial P04387-004)*

The loading crew at the aircraft consisted of an NCO and six men, one of whom stayed at the rear of the bomb at all times to ensure that it did not strike the aircraft. The following loading procedure was followed:

- ■ test operation of electromagnetic release unit and manual release cable (though armourers are not to interfere with bomb sight), check fuzing units, check dowel pin in roof has freedom of movement.
- ■ set position of links in sling appropriately for size of bomb carried; lower suspension sling from stowed position and slacken nuts; change length of manual release cable as required; front and rear crutches to be positioned as required; fit appropriate positioning template (which marks tail position) to bomb bay roof.
- ■ check store is in same attitude as aircraft; reverse tractor to push trolley under aircraft, steering with trolley rear wheels; slacken off safety chains attaching bomb to cradle and use tommy bar to rotate bomb until dowel hole aligns approximately with the dowel and top two fins are equidistant from roof [standard practice was to carry the bombs with the fins at 45° to vertical]; wind in all four winches evenly until bomb is ½in from dowel; using trolley traverse gear and tractor, move trolley to achieve precise alignment with dowel (crewman inside aircraft to check alignment); wind in all four winches ensuring that dowel is engaged, continuing until bomb is 1.5in from roof; remove safety chains; fit appropriate positioning template to rear of bomb bay with wing nuts; engage sling around bomb; cock electromagnetic release unit with manual release and check cocked by attempting to pull halves apart; take up any slack (equally) on suspension sling via screws inside fuselage; adjust crutches holding store to line up tail precisely with template, then lock them; tighten all nuts on sling; lower trolley cradle; check tip of the tail unit is in line with hole in template and about 1in away from it; make final adjustments with crutch turnbuckles if necessary; insert fuze-setting control links into fuzing unit and remove safety pins from pistols (these are then stored in the aircraft); replace and secure the panels covering the two hand- holes in the tail unit; remove positioning template from fuselage.

If an operation was cancelled, the whole procedure was reversed, the pistols and detonators being removed in the fuzing shed, then the bombs trolleyed back to the bomb dump (though the tails would not be removed).

Bombing tactics

During the attack run, it was desirable that the whole squadron pass over the target in as short a time as possible in order to minimise exposure to flak; if all the bombs were dropped in one pass it also allowed each aircraft to get a clear sight on the target, without the bombs of earlier aircraft obscuring markers (this was also one of the reasons for adopting delayed-action fuzing). 617 normally used a 'gaggle' formation (also used by some other Main Force squadrons) which packed a large number of aircraft into a small volume of sky, while separating the aircraft laterally, longitudinally and by height in order to minimise the risk of collisions between aircraft. This allowed the whole squadron to drop their bombs in as little as one minute. 9 Squadron

BELOW The gaggle formation used by 617 Squadron, which allowed all the aircraft to bomb within a short space of time, with little danger of collision. (Author)

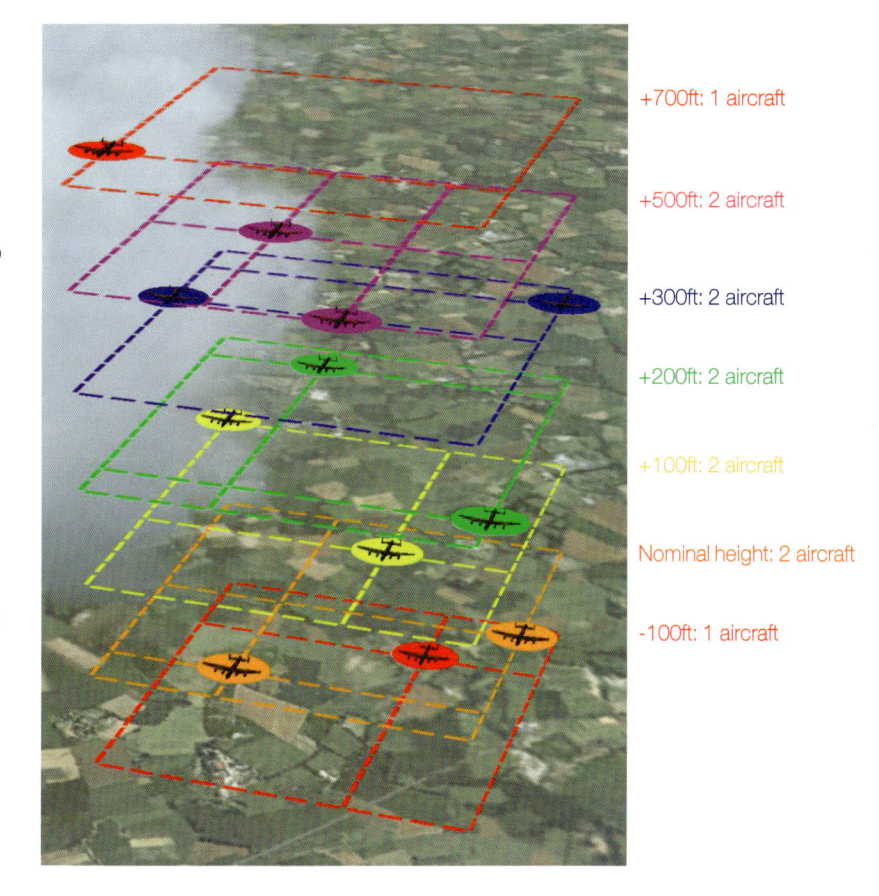

+700ft: 1 aircraft
+500ft: 2 aircraft
+300ft: 2 aircraft
+200ft: 2 aircraft
+100ft: 2 aircraft
Nominal height: 2 aircraft
-100ft: 1 aircraft

Main particulars – Grand Slam

Type	medium-capacity deep-penetration bomb
Length overall	308in (casing 148in, fairing 16in, tail 160in)
Diameter	46in (53.6in across fins)
Weight	21,500lb (of which charge 9,135lb, fairing 28lb, tail 160lb)
Charge/weight ratio	42.5 per cent
Casing thickness	variable
Tail type	No.82 hollow cone with four fins offset 5°
Filling	Torpex D.1 with desensitiser
Typical fuzing	three No.58 impact pistols or three No.47 delay pistols in the rear of the bomb body
Appearance	dark green body with pale green (anodised) tail; narrow red band and wider pale green band stencilled 'TORPEX D.1' around nose
Number expended on operations	41 (all by 617 Squadron); inconsistencies in the ORB mean that the actual total may be 42 or 43

favoured attacking in line astern, the wind finders going on ahead to perform their task, then falling in behind to join the rest of the squadron on the bombing run. For a variety of reasons (such as hang-ups and smoke), individual aircraft often made more than one run on the target, bomb aimers only dropping when they were fully satisfied with the bomb run. By 1945, another level of sophistication was used to minimise wastage of the expensive bombs – some of the aircraft would bomb first, then only if the target remained standing would the others then come in to bomb.

All of the earthquake bomb targets were covered by post-raid photo reconnaissance and bomb plots were compiled to examine the accuracy and spread of the bombing; the archives hold many of these plots, and most of the targets were also given detailed evaluation in the post-war bombing surveys.

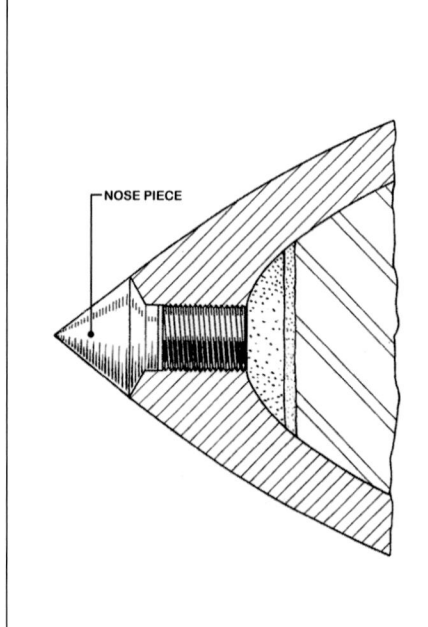

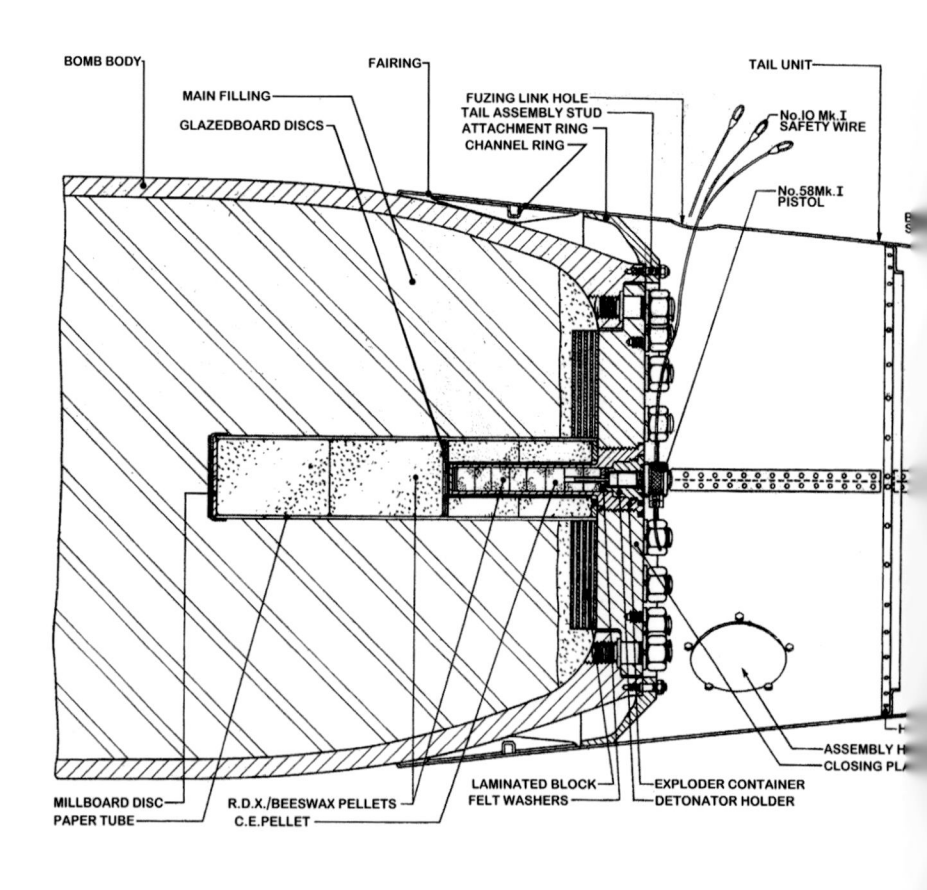

Grand Slam

Within a month of the operational deployment of Tallboy Medium, clearance had been given for work to restart on the Large version, which would become known as 'Grand Slam'; although the 'Tallboy' name appears to have been an official codename, the use of 'Grand Slam' for the ten-ton 'Bomb, MC, 22,000lb' received less official sanction, but was still as commonly used – though the ORB referred to it simply as a 'Special Store'. The bomb was constructed in exactly the same way as Tallboy of which it was essentially a scaled-up version, with the pistols remaining as before (although some versions have the exploder pockets in line, rather than 120° apart around the axis). Due to the charge-cubed law, although Grand Slam carried slightly less than double the charge of Tallboy, it was more than five times as powerful. As with Tallboy, the Mk.II designation was used for US-made bombs.

Official Air Publication 1661B Vol.1 Sect.10 Chapter 23 gives the full technical specification of 'Bombs, HE, Aircraft, MC 22,000lb Mk.I and II' (i.e. Grand Slam), which overall is very similar to the description of the Tallboy, with two exceptions: the tail unit is a No.82, and the closing plate has only two tapped holes for lifting purposes.

The bombing-up process was very similar to Tallboy, being covered by the same Air Publication 2852A. Most notably, the sling links had to be adjusted for the wider bomb casing, the positioning template moved to a new location, and the fuzing units moved aft (the crutch positions were unchanged).

The Lancaster B.I Special

Given the greater size and weight of Grand Slam, it was not practical to carry the bomb with a standard Lancaster, so the B.I Special variant was created – the requirement for a

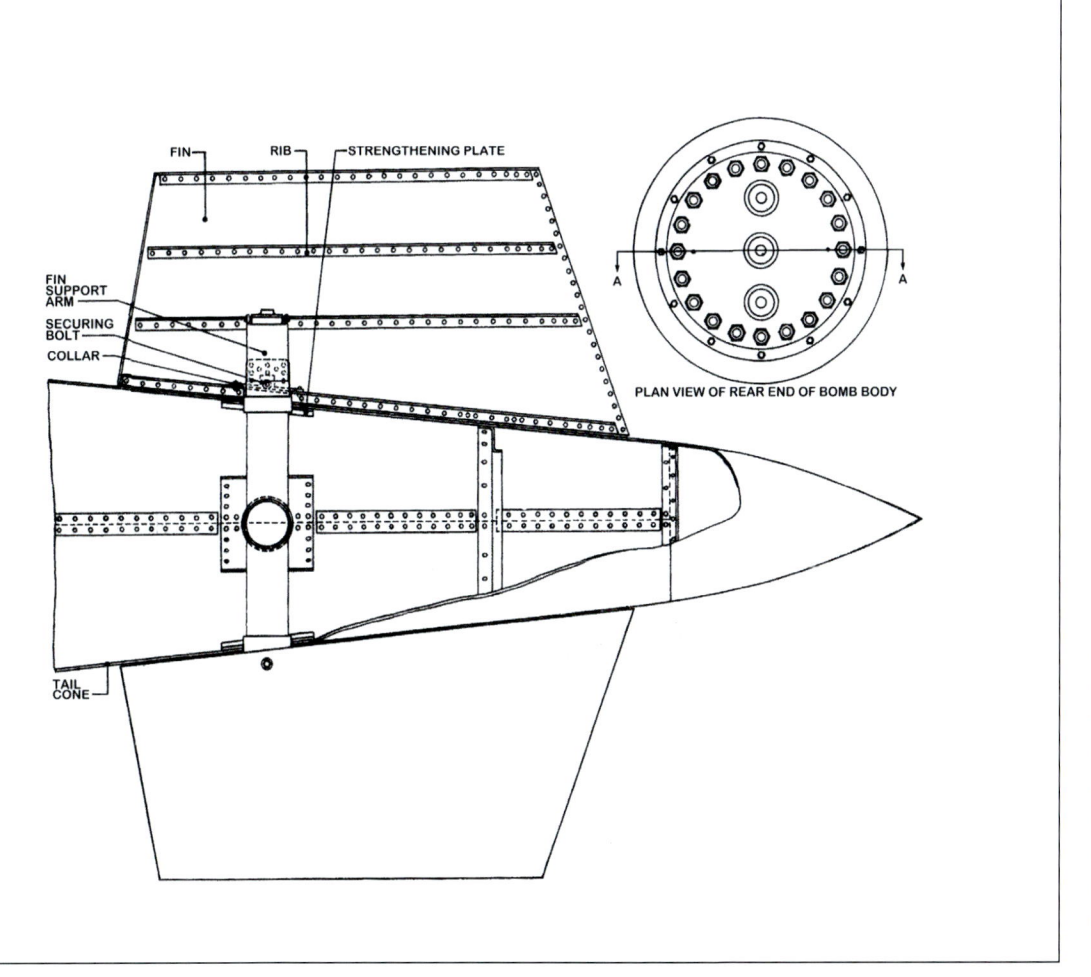

LEFT Grand Slam cross-section showing the construction, casing thickness and details of the exploders. Note the exploder pockets are shown in a line. *(Crown Copyright via RAF Museum – AP 1661)*

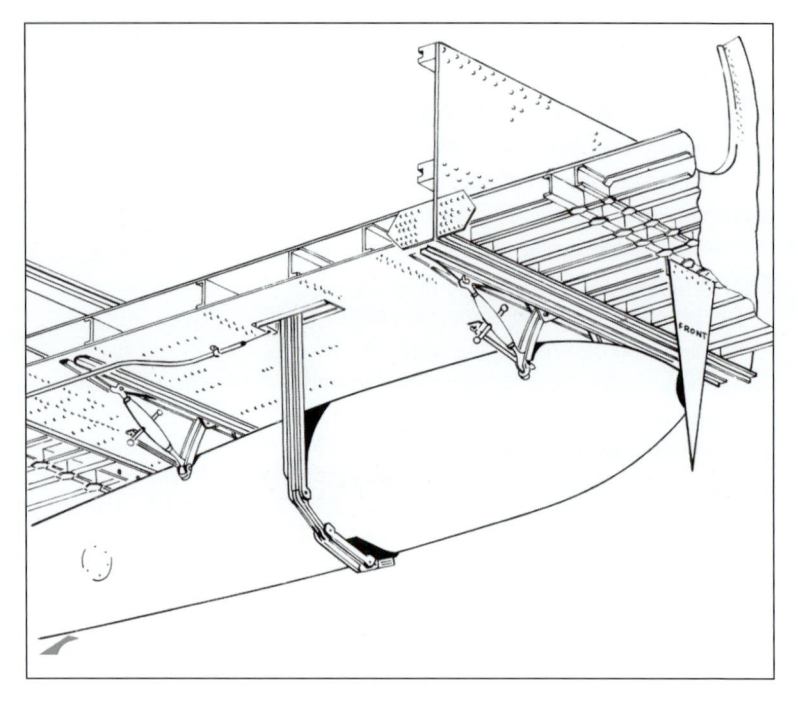

ABOVE Diagram of Grand Slam in the bomb bay, with position of crutches, sling and nose template shown. *(BAE SYSTEMS via Avro Heritage Centre)*

RIGHT Simulation of Lancaster B.I Special, PD129, carrying a Grand Slam. Note the crutches and sling holding the bomb, the aerodynamic fairing at the ends of the bomb bay and the deleted turrets. *(Author)*

OPPOSITE Lancaster B.I Special, PD119, of 617 Squadron, was one of 33 aircraft modified in February 1945 to carry the Grand Slam. *(Imperial War Museum MH30794)*

specialised aircraft had been one of the reasons for the initial cancelling of the Large version. This aircraft had the bomb bay doors removed entirely, and aerodynamic fairings were inserted at the front and rear of the bomb bay (the latter being flat, rather than the domed rear fairing used in the Type 464 Lancasters). To save weight, both front and mid-upper turrets were removed and faired over; some crew armour was also removed. In addition to the loss of the mid-upper gunner from the crew, no wireless operator was carried, hence the standard crew for these aircraft was only five men. Merlin 24 engines, each delivering 1,610hp, were fitted and the standard propellers were replaced with paddle-bladed propellers to give better purchase on the air at the altitudes required for dropping Grand Slam. The sling arrangement was the same as that on the earlier Tallboy aircraft, and the B.I could carry either a Tallboy or Grand Slam. As with Tallboy, drop heights of 12,000 to 15,000ft were typical, although drops of both bombs were made from up to 19,000ft. A total of thirty-three B.I Specials were built, although only twenty-two served with 617 Squadron (others went directly to 15 Squadron, to be joined by more from 617 (including some crews) when they adopted the Avro Lincoln as their primary aircraft); only one was ever lost in action. Details of all operations flown by B.I Specials are given in Appendix 3.

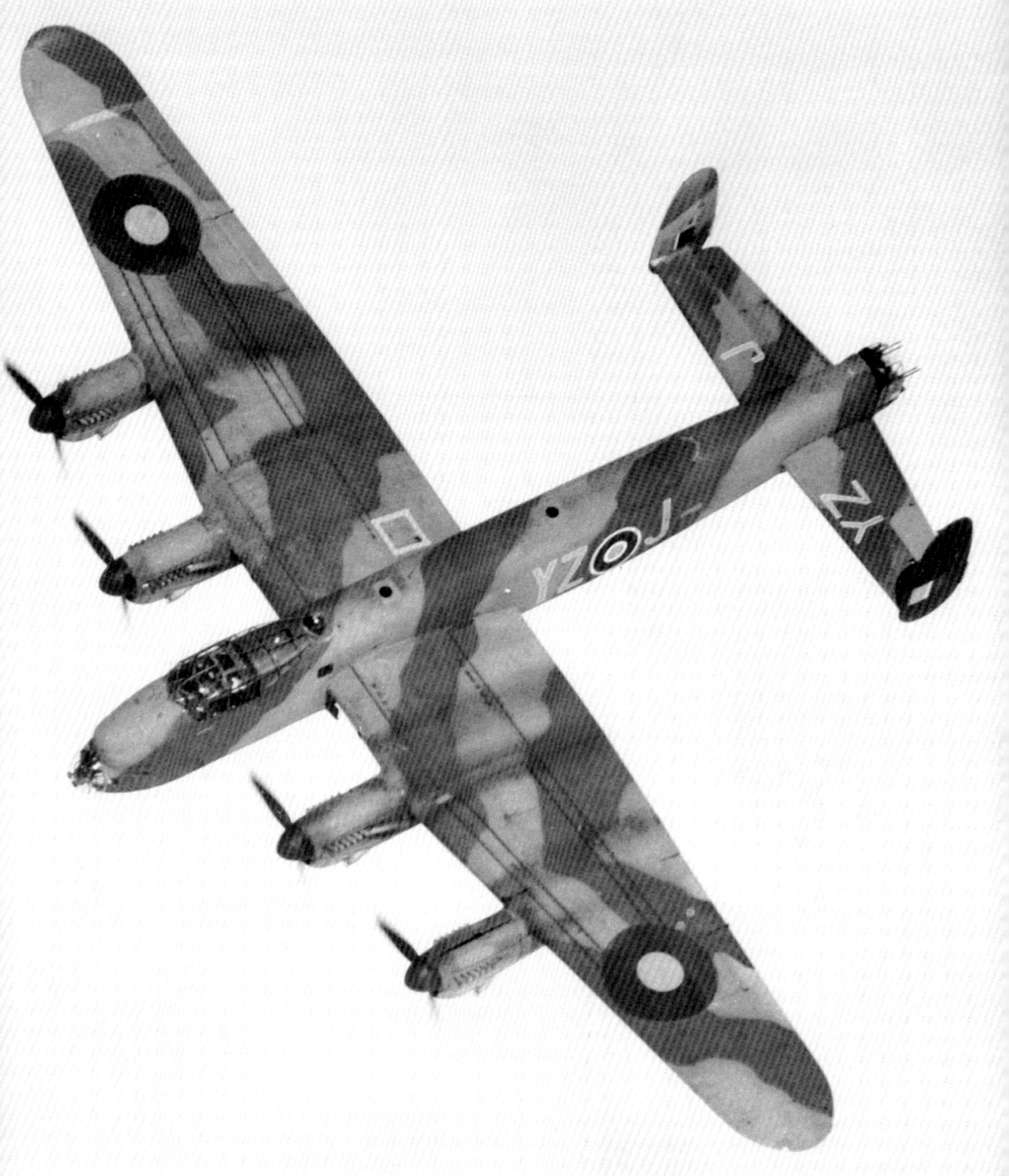
YZOJ
ZY
J

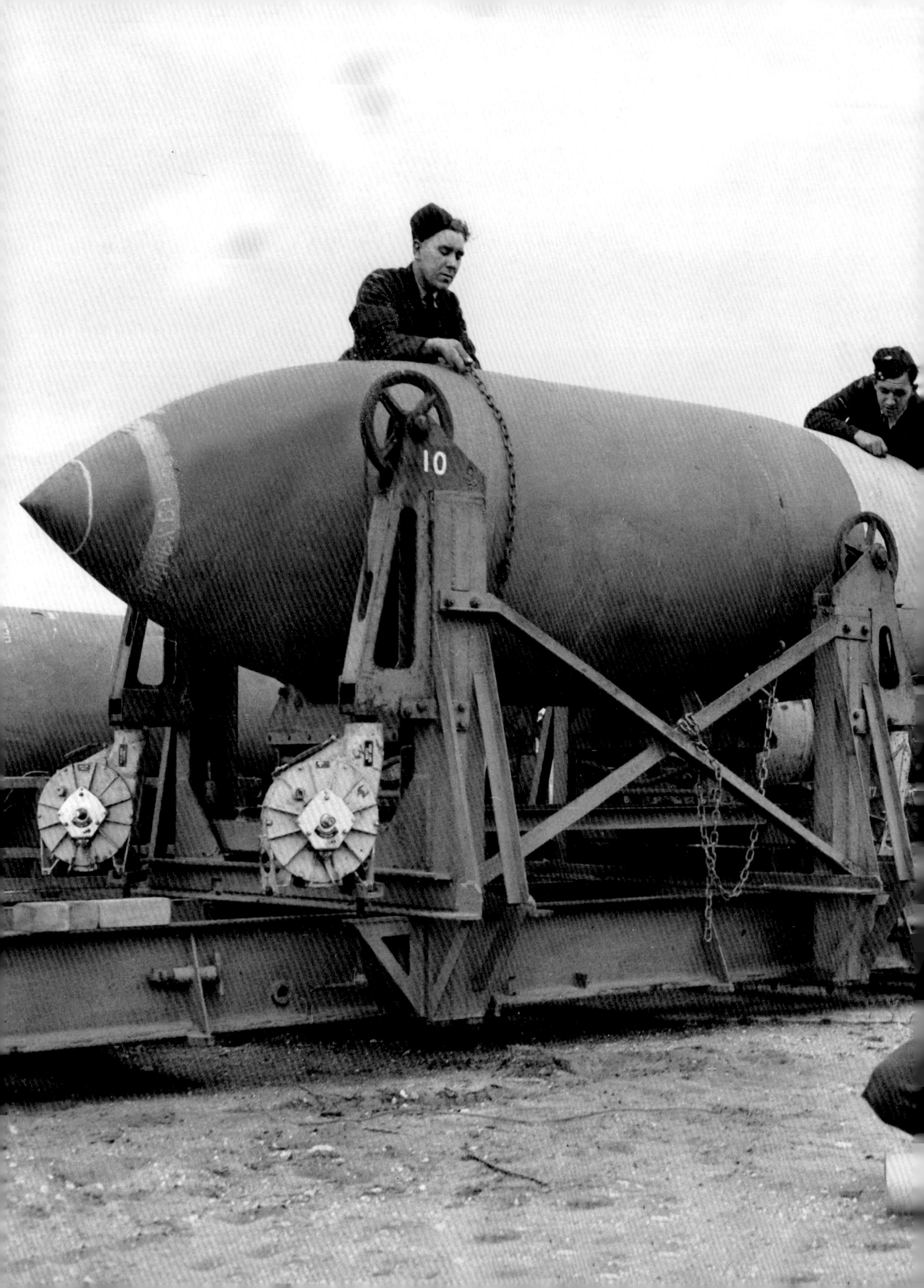
10

Chapter Six

The Earthquake Bomb Raids

The 'earthquake' bombs were deployed against a variety of targets, and they would prove to be probably the most effective conventional air-dropped weapons of the war.

OPPOSITE Leading Aircraftmen Davis and Dewberry with a 22,000lb Grand Slam (one man has his arm in the hole giving access to the pistols); Cpl Jeffries has a 40lb general-purpose bomb in the foreground for comparison, and the tail of a Blockbuster can be seen behind. *(Australian War Memorial SUK14593)*

Preparing for Tallboy

The deep-penetration bombs came to operational readiness at the same time as preparations for the D-Day invasion of Normandy. Their deployment was thus partly governed by the tactical considerations of the invasion and they also saw wide deployment against hardened concrete targets – targets for which they had not been intended, but for which they were the only weapon with any chance of success.

During most of May 1944, 617 were detailed for very few operations, and actually flew only one (marking for, and participating in, a Main Force raid on a military camp at Mailly). Most flying training during the month was for a very special operation, codenamed Operation Taxable, in support of the D-Day landings. On the night of the invasion, to make the Germans believe that an invasion was actually taking place in the Pas-de-Calais area, they flew a very accurate flight profile across the Channel towards Cap d'Antifer, repeatedly looping back on themselves while throwing out radar-reflective 'Window' strips at regular intervals, the effect on the German radar being the appearance of a large invasion fleet moving slowly across the Channel; Operation Glimmer was a complementary operation mounted by 218 Squadron further along the coast. The success of these operations was confirmed at dawn when German heavy artillery opened up on the non-existent fleet as the squadrons turned for home.

Tallboy arrives

Other than dams, Wallis's intended primary targets for his deep-penetration bombs were those buried underground – primarily oil storage tanks, tunnels and coal mines. A tunnel target presented itself as the first opportunity to use Tallboy – a German armoured column was known to be en route for the Normandy beachhead, and it would have to pass through the Saumur Tunnel and cross the adjacent

BELOW The chalky soil of Saumur shows up the Tallboy bomb craters, which are mostly around the mouth of the tunnel. The one to the right is behind the entrance and did most of the damage. *(Crown Copyright via The National Archives)*

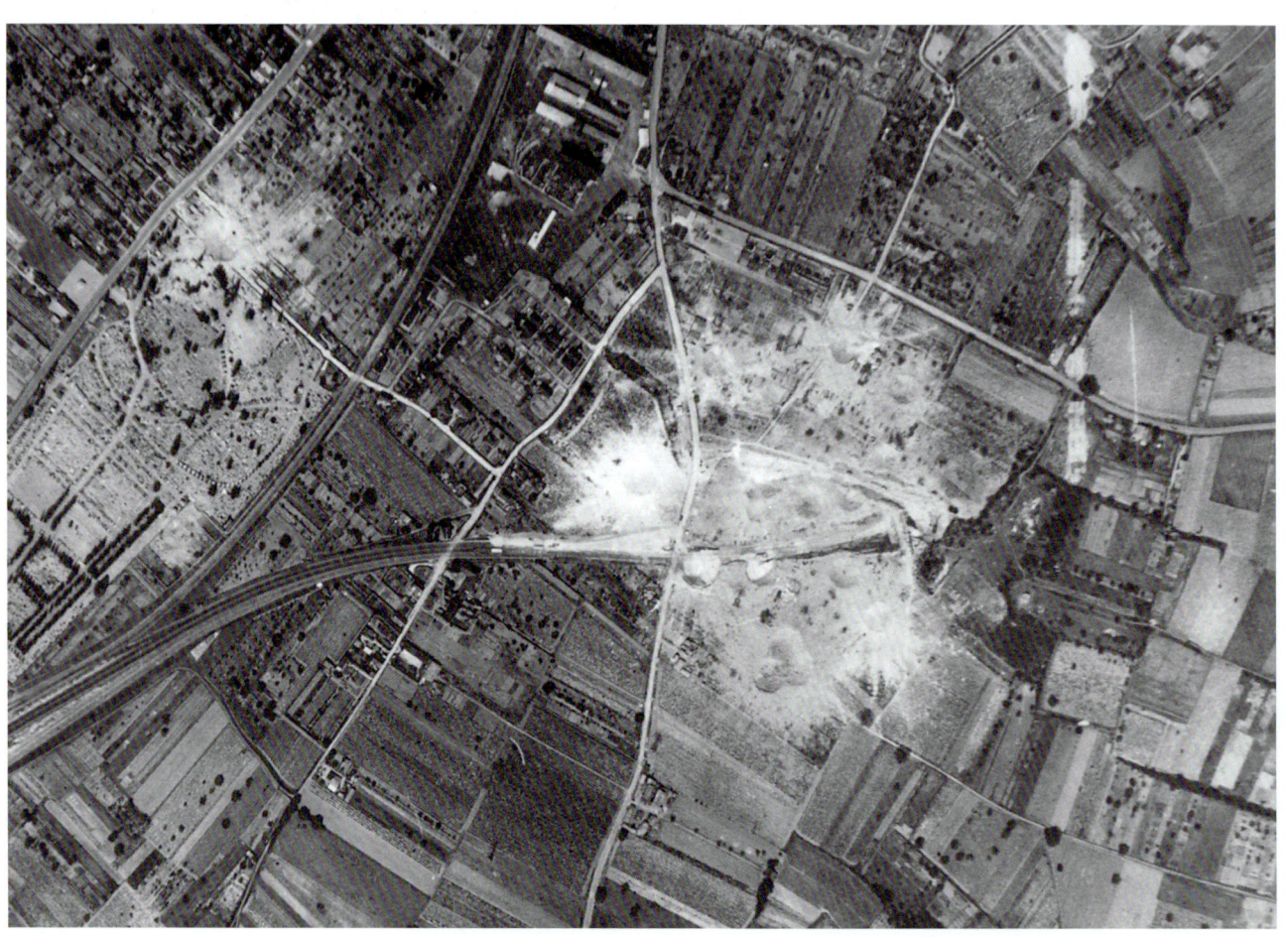

railway bridge over the Loire. As a result, on 8 June 617 squadron (along with 83 Squadron) was sent to destroy both using a combination of Tallboys and 1,000lb GP bombs. Although 617 were a little out of practice with SABS due to Taxable, the raid was a spectacular initiation for Tallboy. The south end of the tunnel was marked accurately by Cheshire, and the Tallboys, dropped from between 8,000 and 10,500ft, were so accurate that the debris from the first strikes obscured the spot fires periodically for the later aircraft. The north end was also marked, and one Tallboy and several loads of 1,000lb bombs were dropped there. The aircrews were disappointed by the Tallboys which, detonating underground, did not give such a spectacular show as the Blockbusters (despite instantaneous fuzing, which was not ideal for this type of target). However, this disappointment was swept away when post-raid reconnaissance photos were received. The track at the southern tunnel mouth had been broken in two places by large Tallboy craters,

TARGET PROFILE

Saumur Tunnel

Type: double-track railway tunnel
Location: between 47° 14' 37" N 0° 4' 1" W and 47° 15 5" N 0° 3' 35" W (near Saumur, Maine-et-Loire, France)
Built: 1886
Length: 1km
Attacked: 8–9 June 1944 (19 Tallboys), tunnel collapsed
Current status: repaired 1944, in use (now single track)

The railway bridge across the Loire at Saumur and the nearby tunnel were on a main route from central France towards the Normandy beachhead, so the decision to attack them was a tactical one to restrict reinforcements reaching the invasion defences. Bombed at both ends with Tallboys, the track at the south end was broken by two Tallboy craters (which were repaired within a couple of weeks and the track re-laid), but a third bomb struck the hill directly above the tunnel entrance and immediately proved Wallis's earthquake theory – burrowing deep into the soft chalk, over 15,000m³ of soil were brought down into the tunnel itself, and it had not been completely cleared by the time the area was liberated.

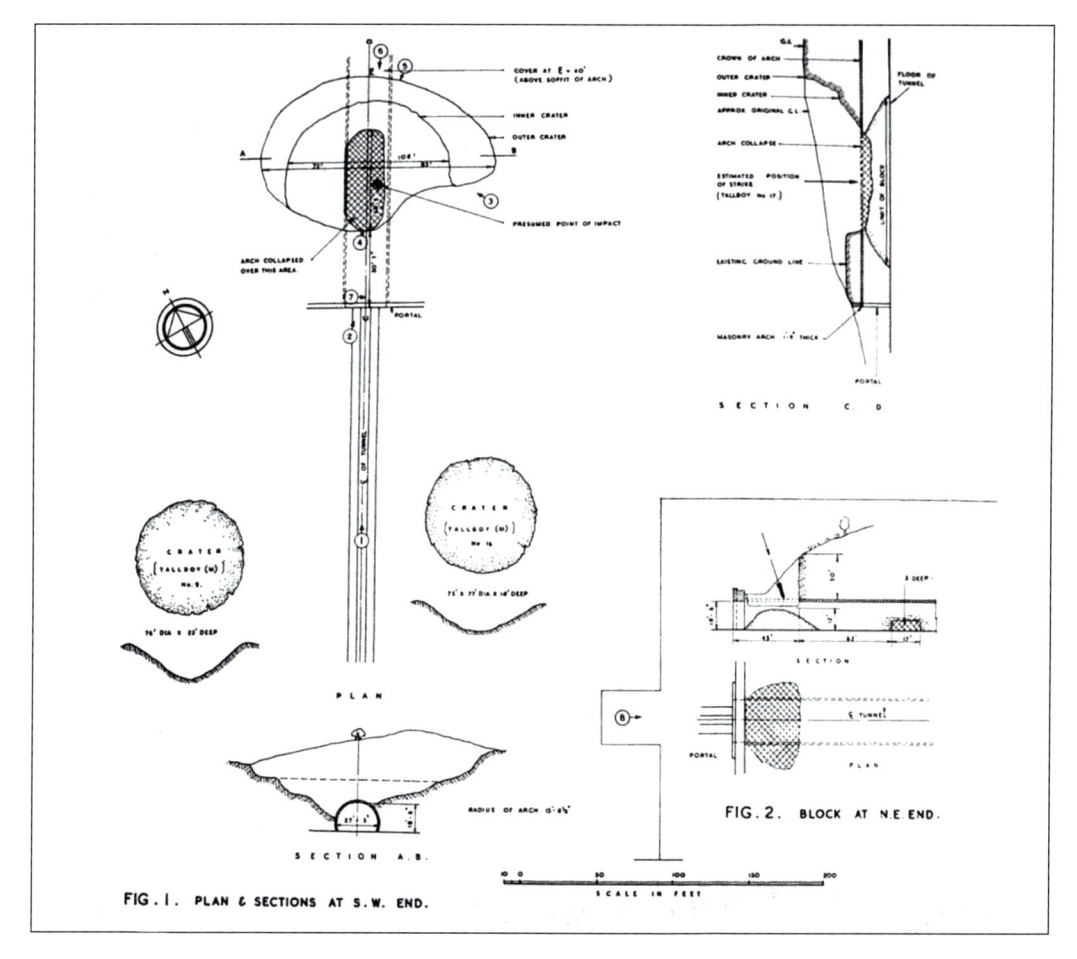

LEFT Post-liberation analysis of the results of the Saumur Tunnel attack. *(Crown Copyright via The National Archives)*

ABOVE View from inside the mouth of the tunnel looking back towards the crater, now cleared of debris.
(Crown Copyright via The National Archives)

and one bomb had hit the hill behind the tunnel mouth – this had brought a large section of the hill down into the tunnel and it remained blocked until the area was liberated.

The next missions for Tallboy were also in direct support of the invasion – German E-boats (fast motor torpedo boats) were harassing the invasion fleets with night attacks, and it was decided to hit two of their bases, at Le Havre and Boulogne. The E-boat pens were simple concrete garage structures – vertical walls with a flat roof – but both were very substantial to withstand bombing raids, the roofs typically being up to 11ft thick. Distinctive rectangular shapes, the pens were attacked at dusk, just as the E-boats were emerging ready for their night's work; both were hit and their roofs damaged. Other Tallboys which fell (as planned) into the water smashed the E-boats, hurling some of them up onto the quayside, and effectively ended the threat from these vessels – over 130 were sunk in the two raids, those that remained being pulled back to pens in the Netherlands (where they would meet Tallboy again). The attack on Le Havre saw twenty-two Tallboys dropped, a total that would remain unbeaten by any single squadron on a single raid. On the Boulogne raid, there were some overshoots attributed to delayed release problems, and although Wallis and other Vickers

TARGET PROFILES

E-boat pens

Name	Number of Pens	Location	Dimensions	Attacked using Earthquake Bombs	Current Status
Le Havre	8	49° 28' 23" N 0° 7' 48" E (in dock area, Le Havre, Seine-Maritime, France)	170 x 75m roof up to 3m	14 June 1944 (22 Tallboys), 2 hits, roof penetrated and many E-boats sunk	further damaged by French saboteurs and German demolition charges in 1944, demolished 1945
Boulogne	6	50° 43' 40" N 1° 35' 20" E (in dock area, Boulogne, Pas-de-Calais, France)	44 x 40m roof up to 4m	15 June 1944 (12 Tallboys), no hits but damaged by near misses and many E-boats sunk	partly demolished (one remaining pen in use as store)
IJmuiden	12	52° 27' 24" N 4° 35' 14" E (south-east end of herring harbour, IJmuiden, Netherlands)	146 x 64m roof 3m	24 August 1944 (8 Tallboys), 15 December 1944 (15 Tallboys), at least 4 hits, roof penetrated and walls damaged	demolished
IJmuiden	18	52° 27' 37" N 4° 34' 39" E (west end of herring harbour, IJmuiden, Netherlands)	215 x 100m roof up to 4m	3 February 1945 (17 Tallboys), 8 February 1945 (15 Tallboys), 2 hits and 2 near misses, roof heavily damaged	in use as a store
Waalhaven	16	51° 53' 13" N 4° 27' 25" E (east side of dock area, Waalhaven, Rotterdam, Netherlands)	50 x 25m roof up to 3m	29 December 1944 (16 Tallboys), roof damaged	demolished 1965

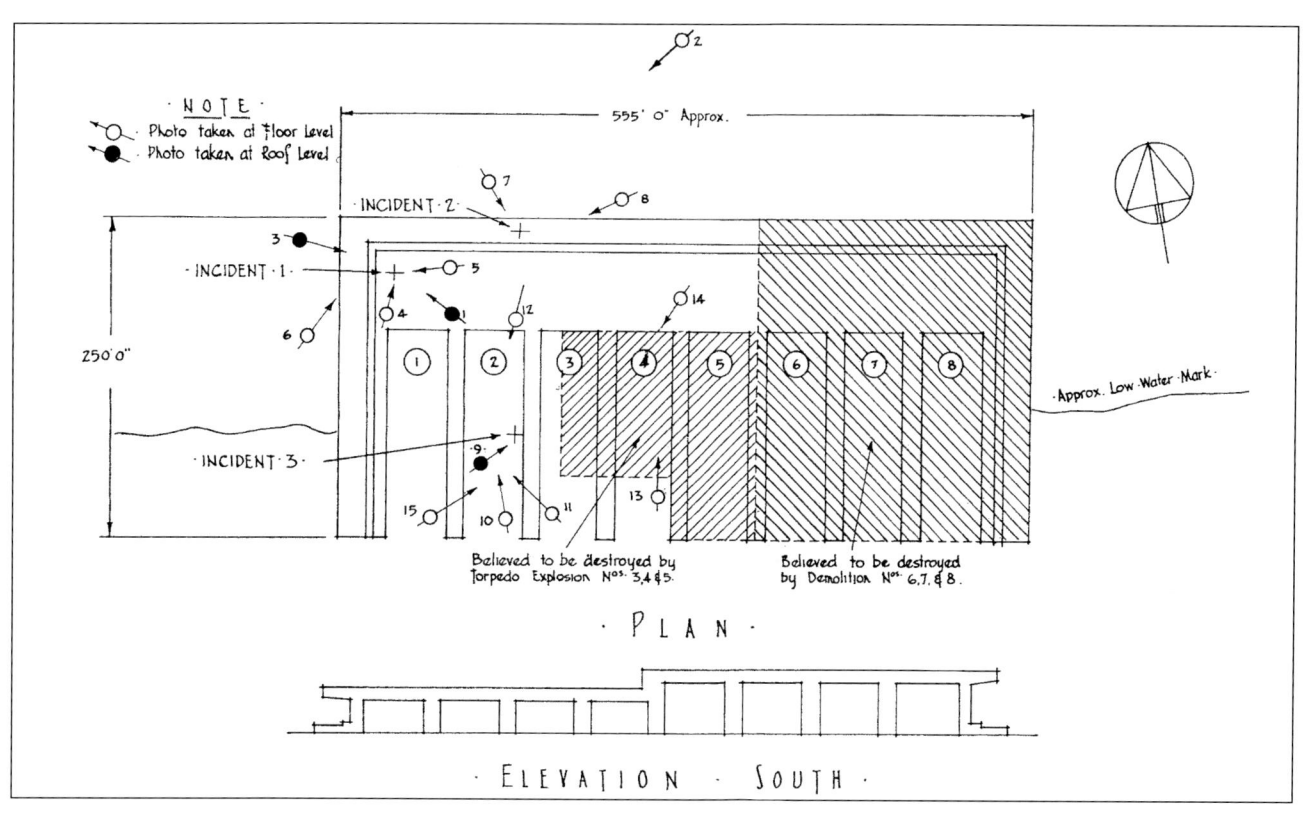

ABOVE Post-liberation analysis of the Tallboy attack on Le Havre's E-boat pens. The Tallboy hits are 'Incident 1' and 'Incident 2' on the north side. *(Crown Copyright via Zuckerman Archive, University of East Anglia)*

LEFT Aerial reconnaissance photo of the pens at Le Havre. Most of the damage was caused by sabotage and demolition charges. *(Crown Copyright via Zuckerman Archive, University of East Anglia)*

THE EARTHQUAKE BOMB RAIDS

LEFT The E-boat pens at Boulogne were damaged by several Tallboy near misses. *(Crown Copyright)*

staff, as well as technicians from A&AEE, put a lot of effort into tracing and rectifying these over the coming months, they were never entirely eliminated.

The V-weapon sites

Germany had been developing a series of revenge weapons for many years, and these programmes (known to the Allies as Crossbow) were now coming to operational readiness from a series of facilities constructed in the Pas-de-Calais area. By June 1944, Allied photo reconnaissance had already detected all of the sites and bombing attacks had been launched on many of them, even though their exact nature remained unknown. V-1 flying bombs, which began falling on London on 13 June, were being launched from a large number of small sites, and a large bunker under construction near the village of Siracourt was intended as a major launch site. The V-1s were stored in several underground locations, and these too were targeted. V-2 rockets were to be launched from a concrete blockhouse in the Fôret d'Éperlecques near Watten, but

ABOVE The smaller IJmuiden E-boat pen was at the south-eastern end of the harbour. Two roof penetrations are clear in this vertical reconnaissance photo. *(Imperial War Museum C4885)*

RIGHT The larger of the IJmuiden E-boat pens was on the south side of the harbour entrance. Note the Tallboy craters. *(Crown Copyright)*

TARGET PROFILE

V-weapon site, Fôret d'Éperlecques (contemporary documents refer to this site as Watten)

Type:	concrete blockhouse containing V-2 launch facility
Location:	50° 49' 43" N 2° 11' 2" E (in Fôret d'Éperlecques, near Watten, Pas-de-Calais, France)
Built:	1943–44
Dimensions:	70 x 43m (main block)
Attacked:	19 June 1944 (18 Tallboys)/25 July 1944 (15 Tallboys), roof damaged
Current status:	converted to Le Blockhaus museum

The Éperlecques blockhouse was a massive concrete structure for the launching of V-2 rockets – as many as fifty per day could have been launched from the site had it been completed. Designed to be road and rail transportable, the rockets would have arrived via a railway tunnel into a storage area on the north side of the site, then taken into the main blockhouse to be erected and fuelled. The liquid oxygen was produced by special plant in the blockhouse itself. Once fuelled, the rockets would be rolled out of massive doors in the south side of the blockhouse onto small launch pads and immediately launched, directed from a control room built into the side of the blockhouse. The site was attacked by the USAAF in 1943 when a substantial amount of fresh concrete had been poured, and this made such a mess of the rocket reception area that it was decided to abandon the site as a launch facility in favour of Wizernes, although the oxygen production plant would have remained at Éperlecques (the rocket doorways in the south wall were filled in). However, this was unknown to the Allies, and the site remained a target for both Tallboy and conventional bomb attacks. Only one Tallboy hit the blockhouse, damaging the edge of the roof; repairs to this were already in progress when the site was liberated by ground forces two months later. Parts for the Wizernes and Mimoyecques sites were also found in storage at Éperlecques. The site was used as a post-war target for Disney bombs (the few that hit caused little damage) and it is now used as a museum.

a USAAF raid in 1943 had so damaged the construction that it had been decided to move the launch facility to a site at nearby Wizernes. Most sinister of all was the V-3 site near Mimoyecques, which appeared only as a concrete slab flush with the surface of the ground. Deep beneath the slab were a series of fifteen angled pipes, each a large gun barrel capable of firing large finned shells all the way to London – many tens of tons of explosives per

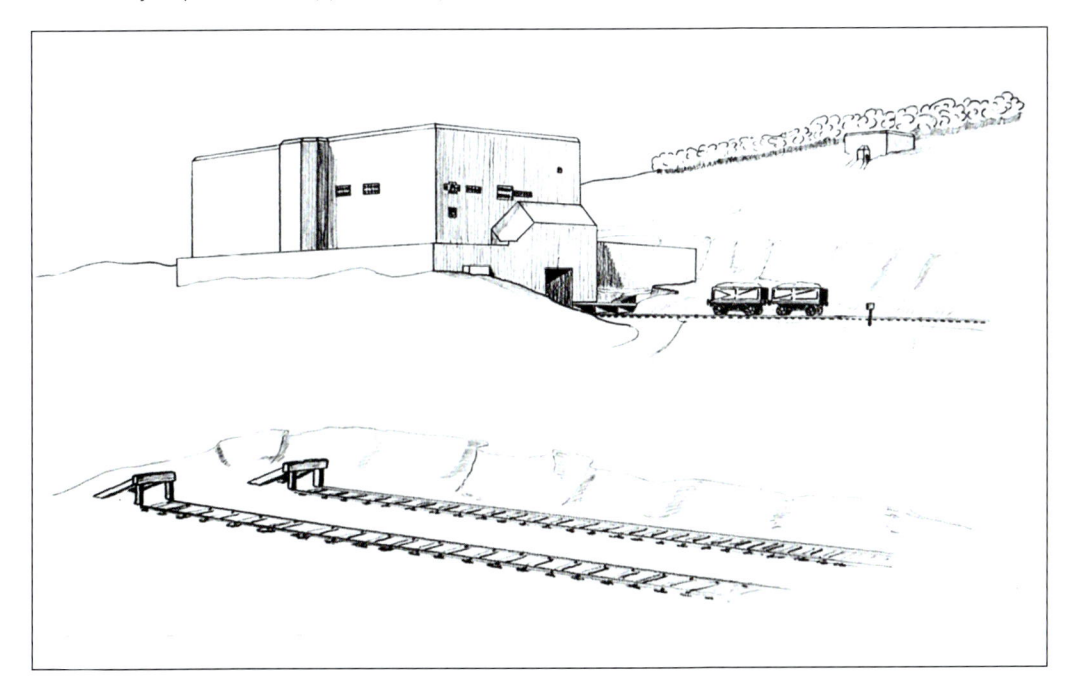

LEFT A post-liberation sketch of the V-2 launch bunker in the Éperlecques Forest. *(Crown Copyright via The National Archives)*

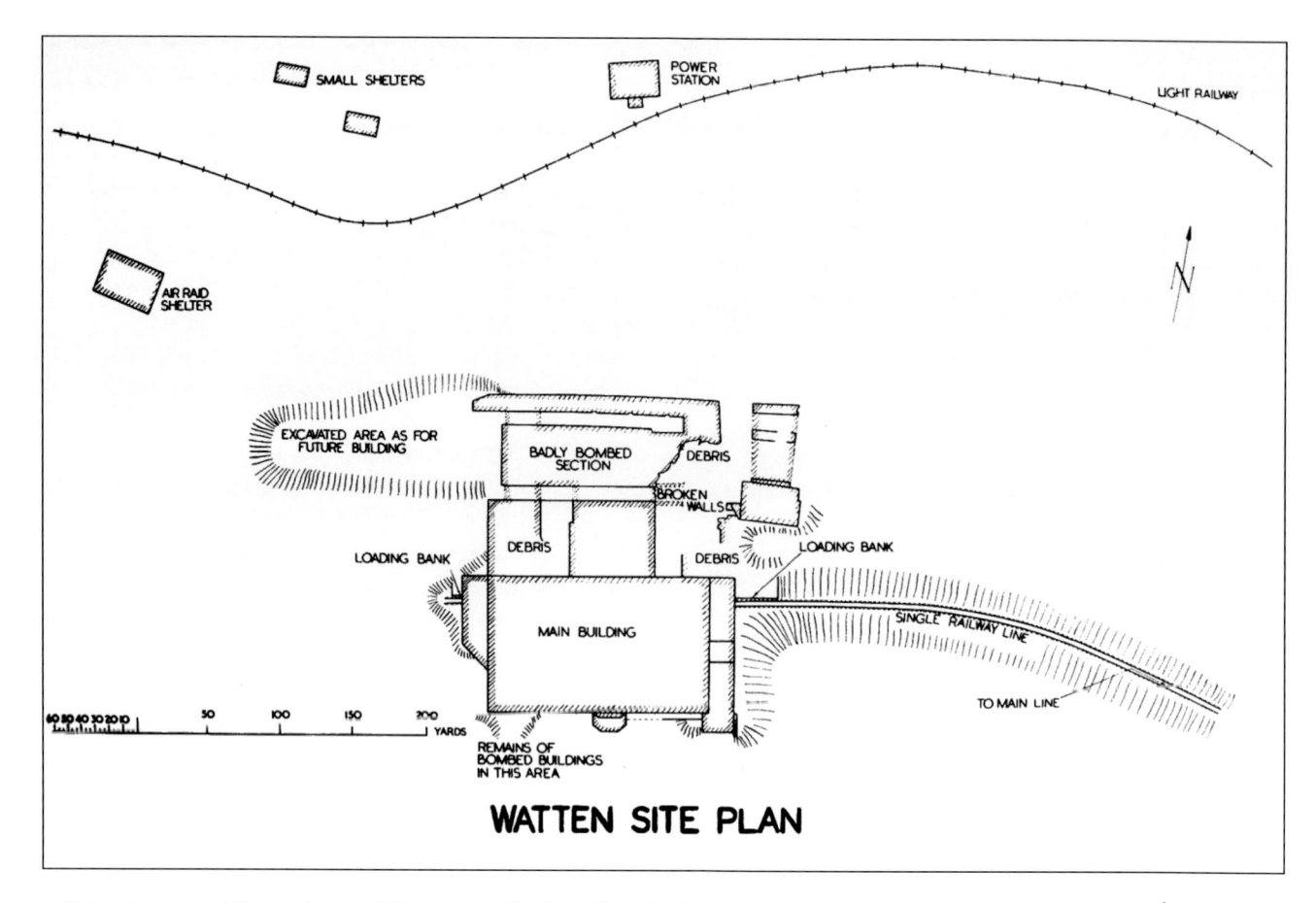

WATTEN SITE PLAN

ABOVE A plan of the Éperlecques bunker. *(Crown Copyright via The National Archives)*

day could have been fired had the site become operational. Post-war visits to the sites would reveal many of their secrets, but it was clear that they had to be attacked, which they were by Main Force and the USAAF in addition to the 617 precision attacks on the hardened targets (known as Heavy Crossbow sites). Following the success of the earlier attack at Éperlecques, the Germans had developed a new building technique known as *Verbunkerung* ('sheltering') or *Erdschalung* ('earth formwork'), which involved initially building the roof of a bunker on the ground, then either excavating a working chamber beneath it or jacking up the roof to

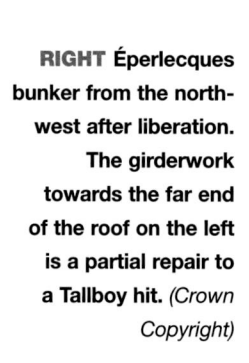

RIGHT Éperlecques bunker from the north-west after liberation. The girderwork towards the far end of the roof on the left is a partial repair to a Tallboy hit. *(Crown Copyright)*

create a space beneath – thus giving the enemy little that could be bombed effectively; Siracourt and Wizernes were both built in this way.

Although the Germans had abandoned the Éperlecques site as a launching complex, they continued to work on its oxygen production plant to support the new V-2 launch complex at Wizernes. Reconnaissance showed ongoing work at the original site, which led to the decision to attack it again, and 617 dropped a total of thirty-three Tallboys there during two raids in June and July. Several near misses made very little impression on the massive structure, but a large chunk of roof was blown off by a Tallboy which hit near the edge. A similar number of Tallboys were dropped on Wizernes over the same period; although the dome was not hit, several near misses caused the quarry face to slip, shifting the dome and blocking the tunnel entrances and many internal sections of tunnel. The V-1 bunker at Siracourt was then attacked with seventeen Tallboys, and its roof damaged. In mid-July, the V-3 complex at Marquise–Mimoyecques was hit by fourteen Tallboys, one blowing off the corner of the concrete slab and others collapsing the tunnels beneath. None of these V-weapon sites would ever become operational.

Two attacks were also made on V-1 storage facilities, the chalk cave complex at St Leu d'Esserent on the northern banks of the River Oise near Creil collapsing under twelve Tallboys augmented by Main Force bombs. At the end

TARGET PROFILE

V-weapon site, Wizernes

Type: concrete dome over tunnel complex containing V-2 launch facility
Location: 50° 42' 19" N 2° 14' 37" E (between Wizernes and Helfaut, Pas-de-Calais, France)
Built: 1943–44
Dome diameter: 90m
Attacked: 24 June 1944 (16 Tallboys)/17 July 1944 (16 Tallboys), tunnels collapsed, entrances blocked, dome undermined, site abandoned
Current status: converted to La Coupole museum

The Wizernes site was similar in concept to the Éperlecques blockhouse, but built into a hill above a quarry. It was dominated by a huge concrete dome built on the hill, beneath which a complex of tunnels was dug to store V-2 rockets delivered by railway, and a large chamber was excavated beneath the dome for the erection of the rockets. The completed rockets would then have been rolled out through giant doors onto two launch pads within the quarry for launch, controlled from a bunker alongside the dome. The site was bombed conventionally on many occasions by the RAF and USAAF with little result. As at Saumur, the chalky soil was ideal for penetration by Tallboy, and the attacks by 617 Squadron caused the face of the cliff beneath the dome to collapse, blocking the entrances and undermining the dome, as well as collapsing the tunnels deep underground. The site was abandoned by the Germans, although it was re-excavated in the 1990s to become a museum dedicated to the history of rocketry and the effects of the war on the Pas-de-Calais area.

LEFT This model shows how Wizernes would have looked when operational. V-2s would have been delivered by rail, erected beneath the dome and rolled out through doors in the wall of the quarry for immediate launch towards London. *(Author)*

RIGHT A post-liberation sectional sketch of the V-2 complex at Wizernes. *(Crown Copyright via The National Archives)*

BELOW A plan of Wizernes showing the network of tunnels for storing the V-2s, the octagonal fuelling area, and the two launch pads. *(Crown Copyright via The National Archives)*

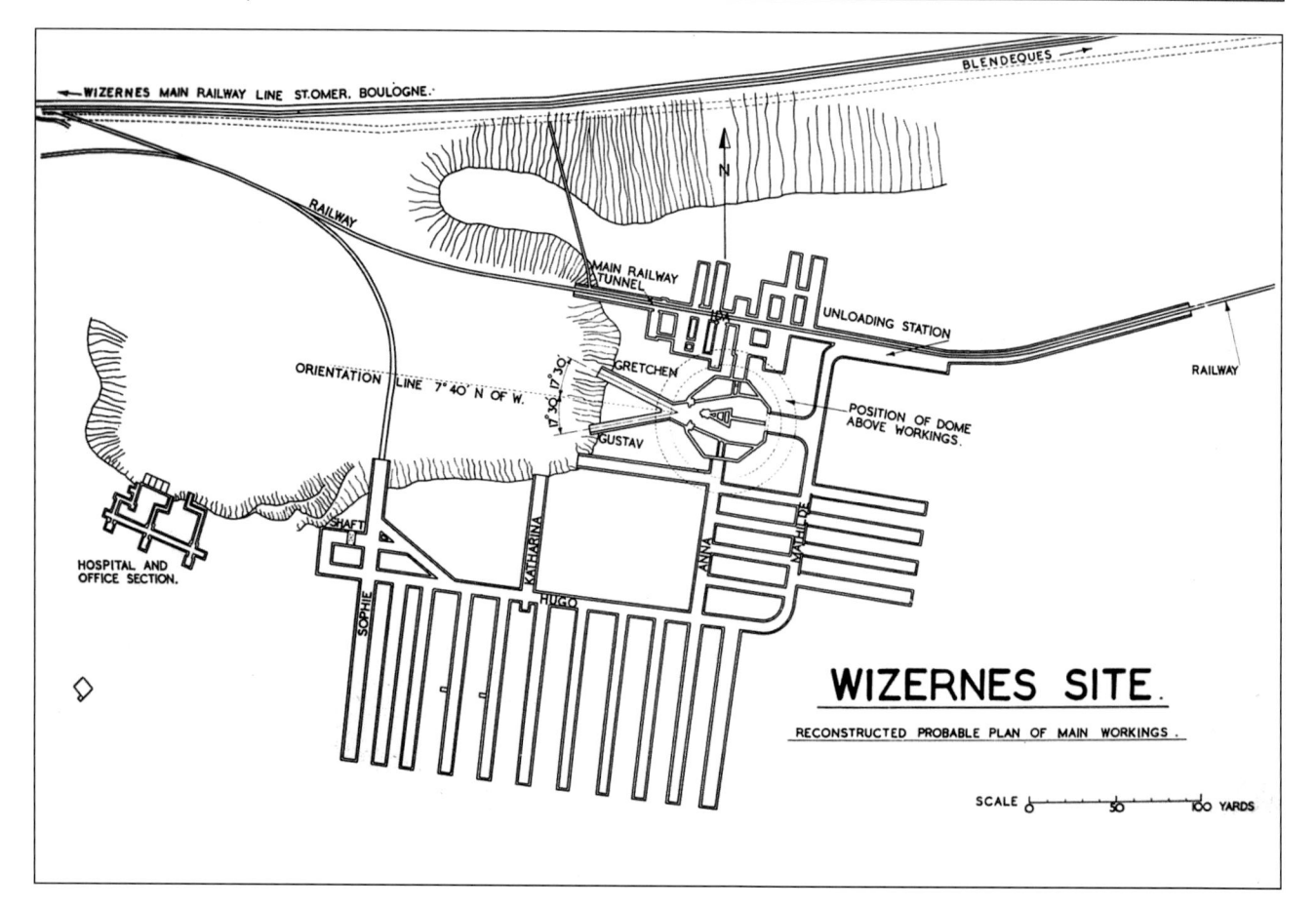

LEFT Aerial reconnaissance image of the heavily bombed Wizernes site. The dome was not hit by any Tallboys, but the workings beneath were collapsed. *(Crown Copyright)*

BELOW The dome as it looks today, showing some of the collapsed foundations. The building on the left was the launch control bunker. *(Author)*

TARGET PROFILE

V-weapon site, Siracourt

Type:	V-1 launch bunker
Location:	50° 22' 27" N 2° 16' 5" E (near Siracourt, Pas-de-Calais, France)
Built:	1943–44
Dimensions:	212 x 36 x 10m
Roof thickness:	up to 5m
Attacked:	25 June 1943 (17 Tallboys), large section of roof broken away, other damage
Current status:	extant in damaged condition

To launch V-1 cruise missiles towards London, a large number of small sites had been constructed around the Pas-de-Calais area, each consisting of an assembly building and a launch ramp. As these sites were open to bombing (and indeed were heavily bombed), it was decided to supplement these dispersed sites with two hardened launch bunkers constructed at Siracourt and Lottinghen (plus other sites on the Cotentin peninsula), although only the Siracourt bunker progressed far enough to be worthy of substantial attack. It consisted of a massive concrete roof built on the ground, underneath which a working area was to be excavated, served by a railway to deliver the V-1s. At right angles to the long axis of the roof, a ramp would have been constructed, from which a continuous stream of V-1s could have been launched. The key Tallboy hit was just above the exit to the ramp, which brought down a large section of the roof; another cratered the centreline of the roof.

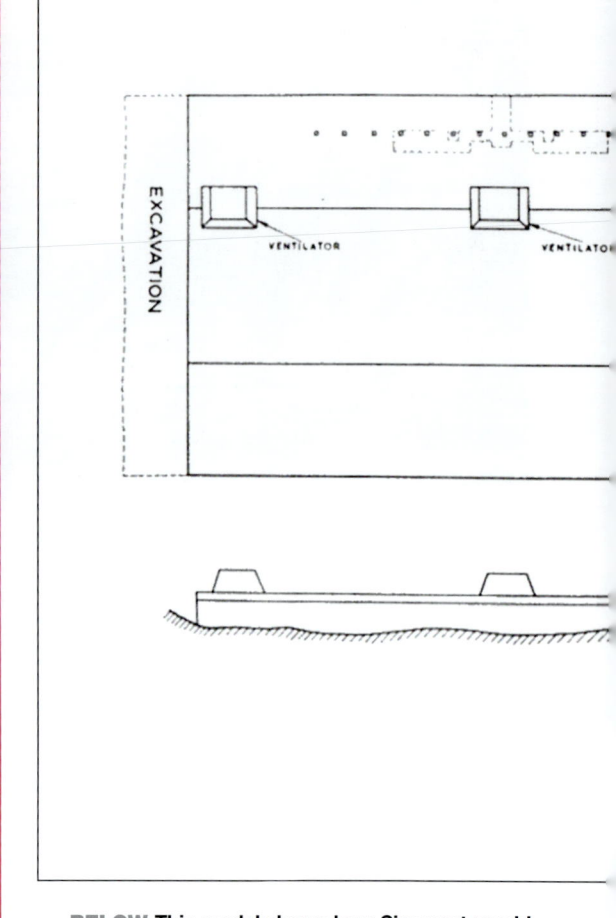

BELOW This model shows how Siracourt would have looked when operational. V-1s would have been delivered by rail and fired via the launch ramp. *(Author)*

106
DAM BUSTERS MANUAL

SIRACOURT.
MAIN BUILDINGS.

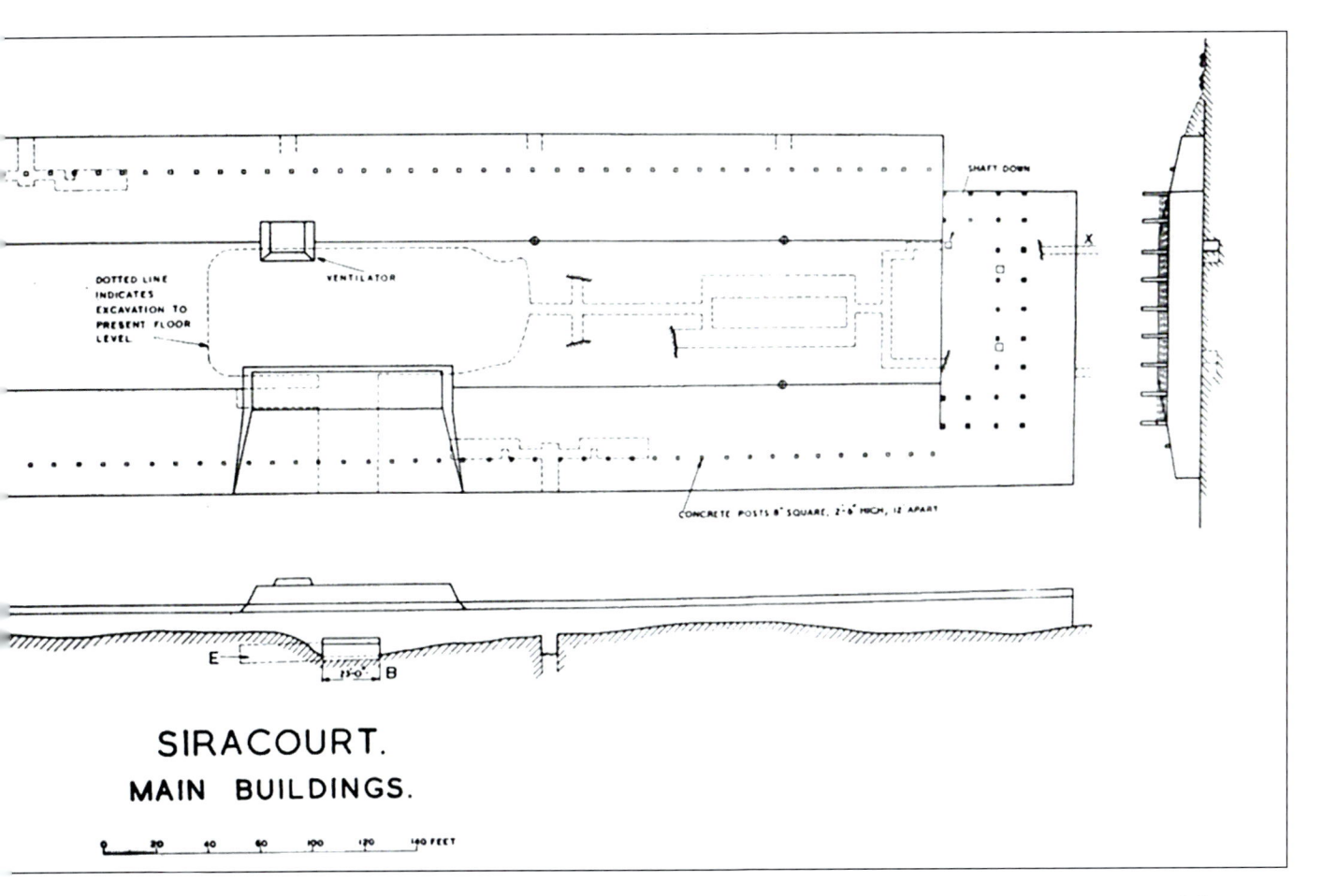

BELOW Layout of the Siracourt site. *(Crown Copyright via The National Archives)*

ABOVE The massive roof of the Siracourt bunker was built on the ground and the working area beneath had only been partly excavated when the site was overrun. *(Crown Copyright via The National Archives)*

BELOW The overhanging roof above the door was brought down by a Tallboy hit. *(Crown Copyright via The National Archives)*

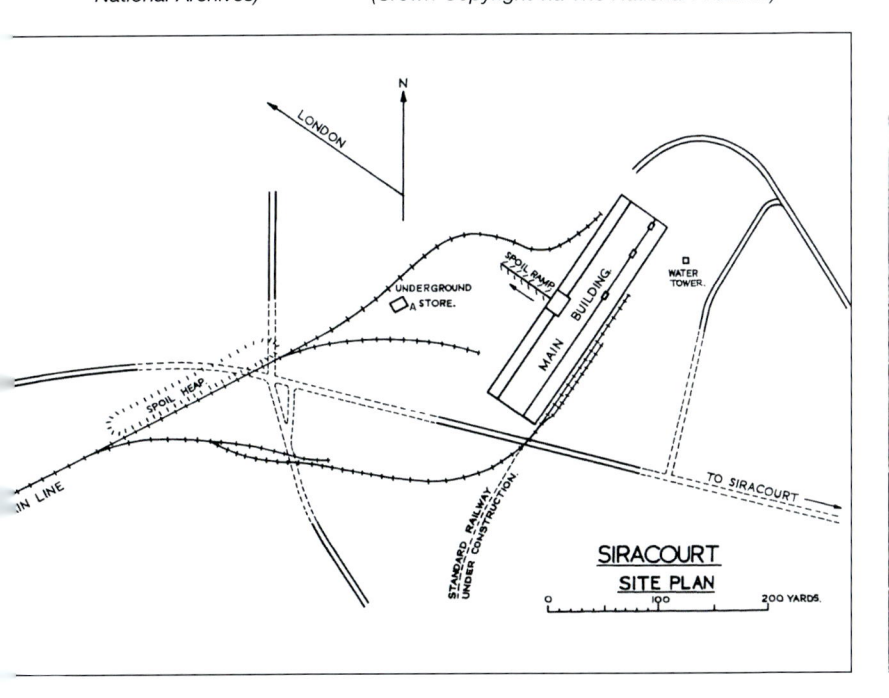

SIRACOURT SITE PLAN

107
THE EARTHQUAKE BOMB RAIDS

TARGET PROFILE

V-3 long-range gun complex, Marquise–Mimoyecques

Type: concrete slab over tunnel complex containing V-3 long-range guns
Location: 50° 51' 17" N 1° 45' 30" E (near Mimoyecques, Pas-de-Calais, France)
Built: 1943–44
Dimensions: 70 x 30 x 5.5m (cover slab)
Attacked: 6 July 1944 (14 Tallboys), slab damaged, tunnels collapsed
Current status: re-excavated, converted to La Forteresse de Mimoyecques museum

Photo interpreters easily spotted the works being built north-west of the village of Mimoyecques, but Allied Intelligence had no real idea of what the site was for; even when near completion, all that was visible was a plain concrete slab on the ground, with three small openings covered by steel plates. Concealed beneath the ground was a new design of missile launcher, consisting of three sets of five parallel tubes 150m in length, angled at 50° to the horizontal. Each of these was in effect a gun barrel with many side openings, each of which contained a propellant charge. The missile inside would be fired up the tube and as each side opening was passed, the charge there would fire, thus continually accelerating the missile up the pipe, until it emerged with sufficient muzzle velocity to carry it to London some 95 miles away. With so many barrels available, a high rate of fire would have been achievable, and with little visible to attack at the site, it was reckoned to be impregnable, and numerous conventional bombing raids had little effect on the site. However, Tallboy was perfect for this type of target, not only damaging the slab but also penetrating deep into the chalk to collapse the underground tunnels; this may have been Tallboy's most significant target of the war. The site was further demolished by the Royal Engineers after the war, but the site has been partly re-excavated and turned into a museum.

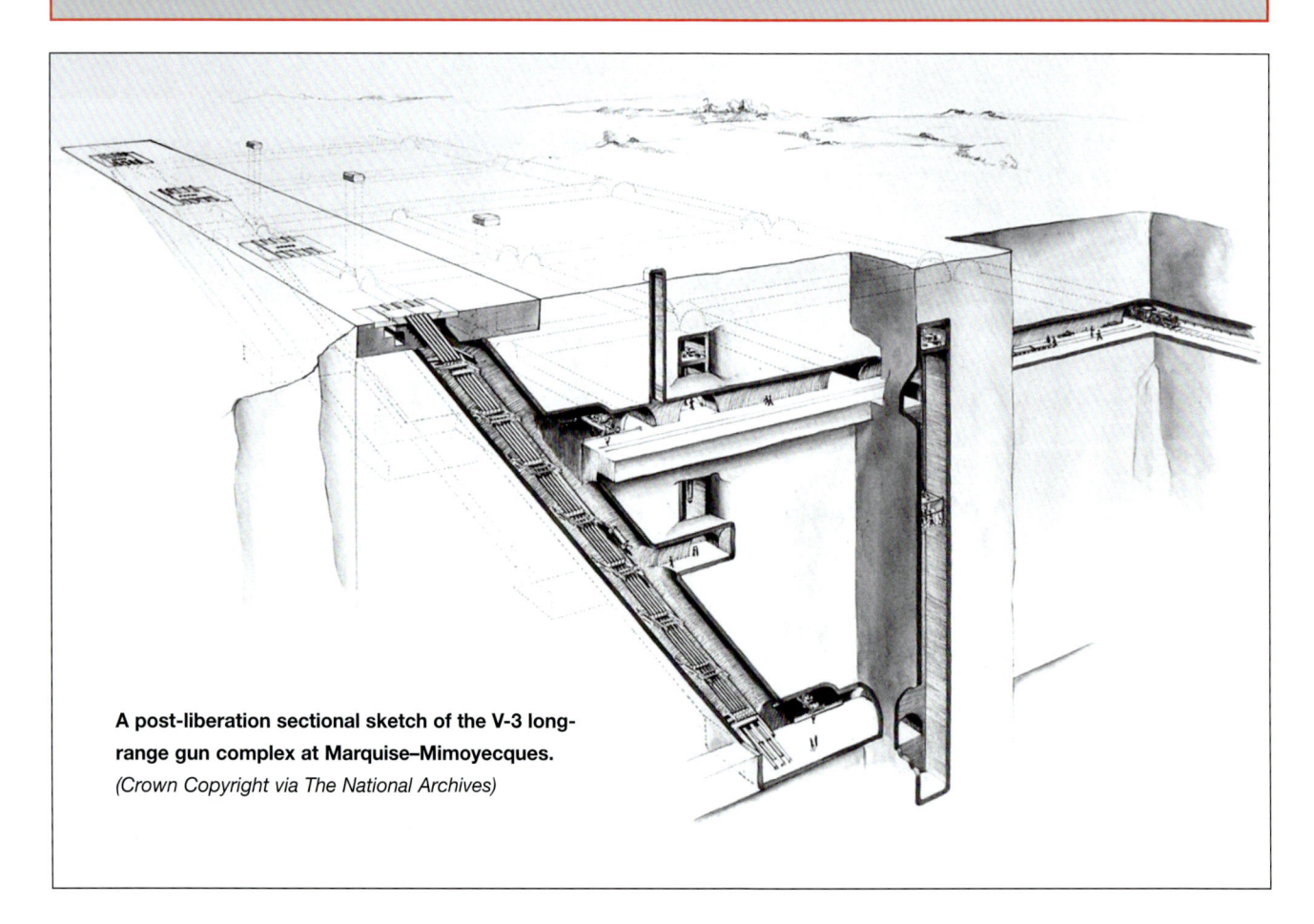

A post-liberation sectional sketch of the V-3 long-range gun complex at Marquise–Mimoyecques.
(Crown Copyright via The National Archives)

LEFT Aerial reconnaissance image of the Mimoyecques site, showing the Tallboy hit on the corner of the cover slab and the three slots through which the guns would have fired. *(Crown Copyright)*

TARGET PROFILE

V-weapon storage site, St Leu d'Esserent

Type:	caves used to store V-1s
Location:	49° 13' 41" N 2° 25' 43" E (near St Leu d'Esserent, Oise, France)
Built:	1943–44
Dimensions:	500 x 500m approx
Attacked:	4 July 1943 (12 Tallboys), 2 hits, roof collapsed
Current status:	land returned to agricultural use

This site consisted of caves and connecting tunnels within a chalk ridge, with the thickness of the ground above the caves being around 30ft. Used before the war for growing mushrooms, the caves had armoured doors fitted by the Germans. The bombing (which included GP bombs as well as the Tallboys) caused large roof falls inside the caves which effectively put them beyond use, as well as trapping many Germans who were sheltering in the caves when the attack came.

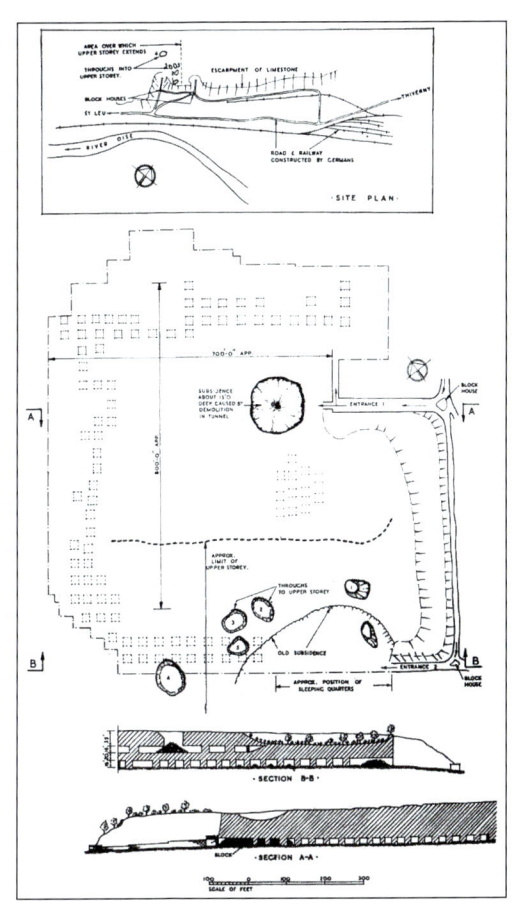

LEFT A plan of the St Leu d'Esserent site showing the bomb damage. *(Crown Copyright via The National Archives)*

109

THE EARTHQUAKE BOMB RAIDS

> **TARGET PROFILE**
>
> **V-weapon storage site, Rilly-la-Montagne**
>
> Type: railway tunnel used to store V-1s
> Location: between 49° 9' 49" N 4° 2' 21" E and 49° 8' 5" N 4° 1' 27" E (near Rilly-la-Montagne, Marne, France)
> Length: 5km
> Attacked: 31 July 1944 (12 Tallboys), cuttings cratered
> Current status: in use
>
> This V-1 storage site was a double-track railway tunnel running under a forested hill. Both ends of the tunnel were targeted, and the tracks were cratered by the Tallboys, putting the site out of use.

of July, a railway tunnel at Rilly-la-Montagne, also used as a V-1 store, was blocked at both ends by twelve Tallboys.

617 were next called upon to bomb a railway bridge across the River Canche at Étaples in the Pas-de-Calais; Tallboy supplies were being eaten away so only 1,000lb GP bombs were dropped, to little effect – Tallboy would have to wait for its first use against bridges.

The U-boat pens

As soon as the Germans had taken control of the French ports, they began to use them for the operation of U-boats, as they were closer to their Atlantic hunting grounds than

> **TARGET PROFILES**
>
> **U-boat Pens**
>
> | Name | Number of Pens | Location | Built | Dimensions | Attacked using Earthquake Bombs | Current Status |
> |---|---|---|---|---|---|---|
> | Brest | 15 | 48° 22' 0" N 4° 31" 19" W (Brest, France) | 1941–42 | 333 x 192 x 17m roof up to 6m, with *Fangrost* in places | 5 August 1944 (14 Tallboys), 12 August 1944 (9 Tallboys), 13 August 1944 (5 Tallboys), 9 hits, 5 penetrations | in use |
> | Keroman I, II and III | 5 + 7 + 7 | 47° 43" 45" N 3° 22' 12" W (Lorient, France) | 1941–43 | Keroman I – 120 x 85 x 18m, roof up to 3m Keroman II – 138 x 120 x 18m, roof up to 3m Keroman III – 170 x 135 x 20m, roof up to 7m), with *Fangrost* in places | 6 August 1944 (12 Tallboys), 3 hits | in use up to 1997; now derelict, partly open to the public |
> | La Pallice | 9 | 46° 9' 32" N 1° 12' 32" W (La Pallice, France) | 1941–42 | 195 x 165 x 14m roof over 7m, with *Fangrost* in places | 9 August 1944 (12 Tallboys), 18 August 1944 (6 Tallboys), 6 hits | derelict |
> | Bruno | 7 | 60° 23' 30" N 5° 17' 14" E (Bergen, Norway) | 1942–43 | 130 x 143m roof up to 6m | 12 January 1945 (27 Tallboys), 3 hits on roof – extensive internal damage, although roof not penetrated | partly demolished; two remaining pens in use as store/workshop |
> | Finkenwerder | 5 | 53° 32' 29" N 9° 51' 15" E (Hamburg, Germany) | 1941–44 | 153 x 139m roof up to 3.6m | 9 April 1945 (15 Tallboys and 2 Grand Slams), 6 hits, roof penetrated, several U-boats damaged | Demolished; foundations extant in grounds of Hamburg-Finkenwerder Airport |

bases in Germany. They immediately began a programme of building concrete pens for the U-boats in all of the major Biscay ports, and by 1944 these were all completed and in use. Obvious targets for Allied bombs (many of which they received during the course of the war), they were massively constructed with roofs up to 21ft thick, many with air gaps within the structure to prevent bombs penetrating through the roof. With the advent of Tallboy,

ABOVE **A modern photo of the Brest U-boat pens, still in use; the light bars on the roof are the incomplete** *Fangrost* **bomb traps, and the large building behind is the French Naval Academy.** *(Marine Nationale via l'Office de Tourisme de Brest Métropole Océane)*

BELOW **Post-war survey analysis of the roof thickness of the Brest U-boat pens. The nine Tallboy hits are marked.** *(USAF Museum)*

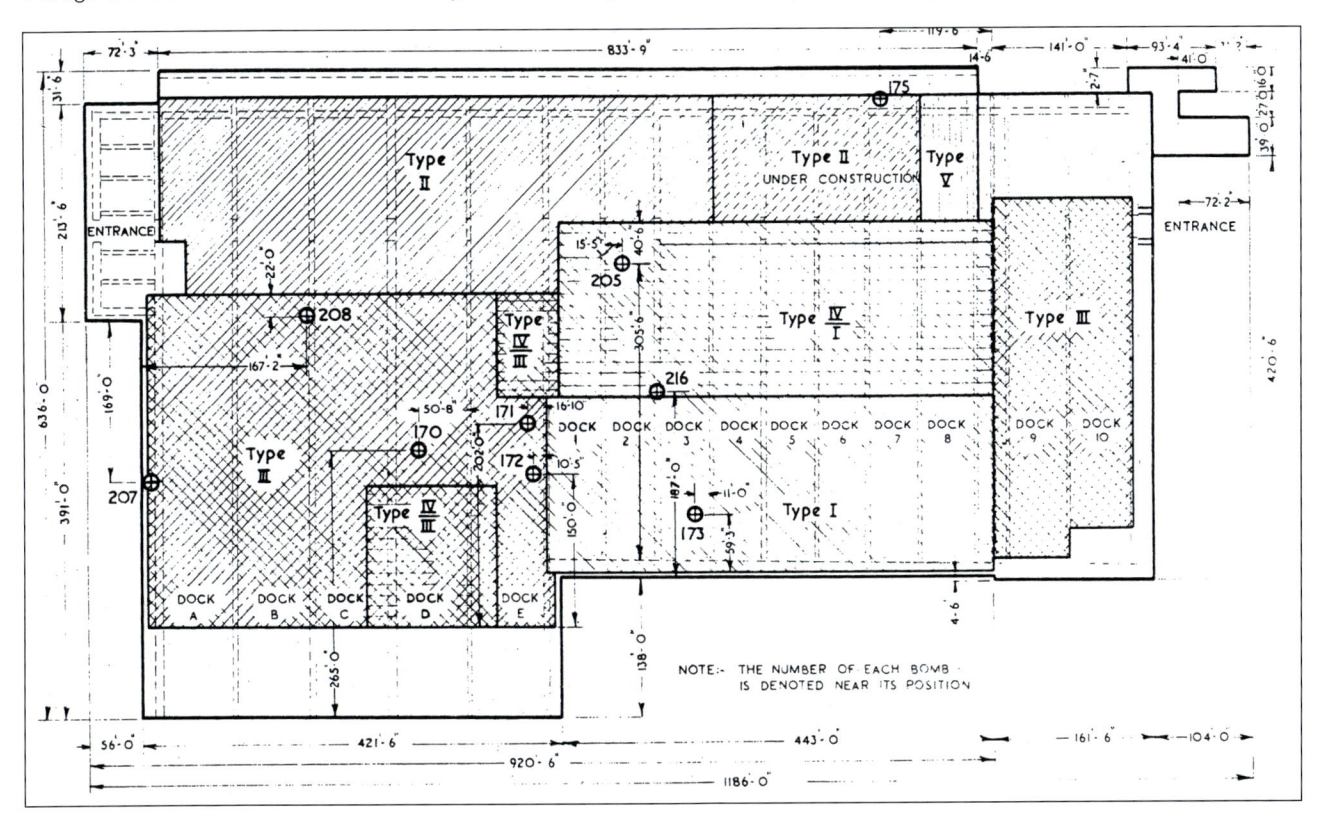

THE EARTHQUAKE BOMB RAIDS

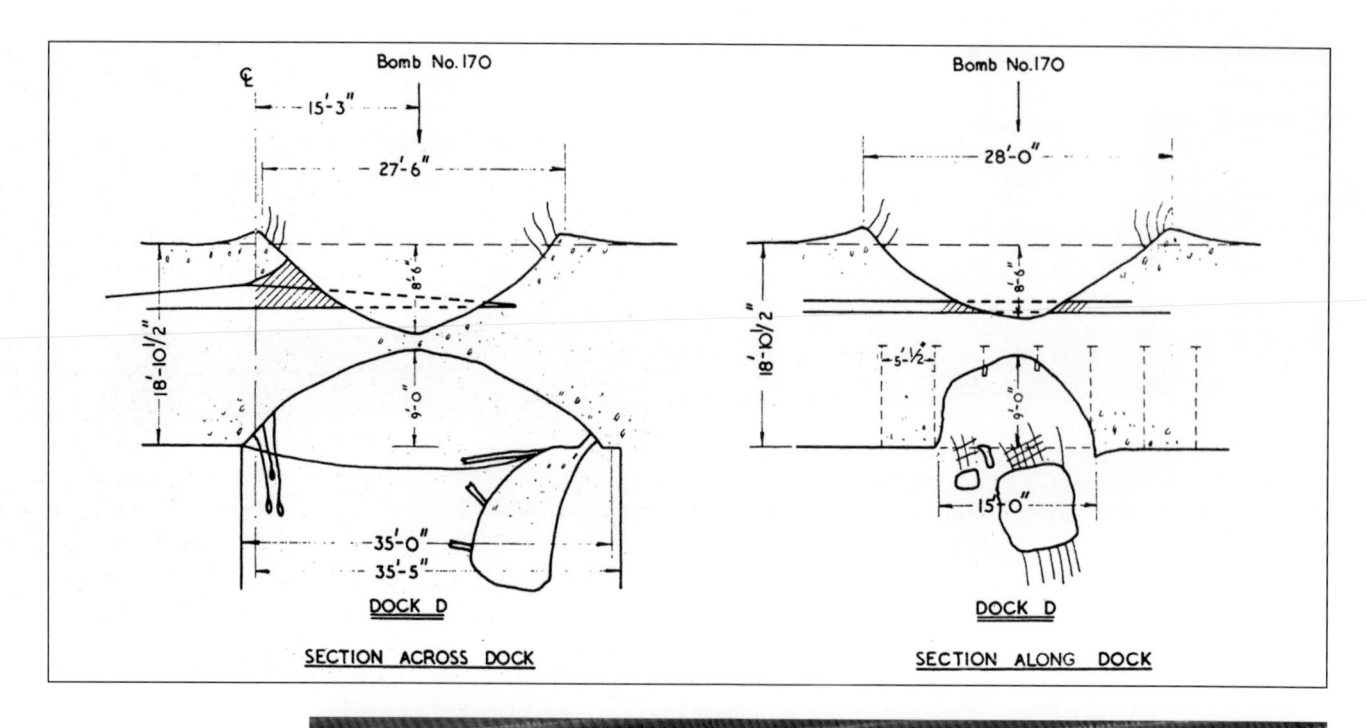

ABOVE Survey sketch of one of the Tallboy craters on the roof at Brest. Diagrams such as this were produced for many of the craters to record the efficacy of the bomb. *(USAF Museum)*

RIGHT A view inside one of the Brest pens (drained), showing the roof penetration by two Tallboys. *(Australian War Memorial R277925)*

112
DAM BUSTERS MANUAL

it was realised that this might not be enough, so some pens had further layers of concrete added, and many were to be fitted with *Fangrost* – this consisted of a series of beams laid parallel across the roof, with a further layer of half-rounded beams laid at right angles across the top. It was hoped that any bomb hitting the *Fangrost* would be deflected and lose some of its energy and thus have less likelihood of penetrating the roof beneath. It is likely that it would have been quite effective, but although several pens with partially installed *Fangrost* were struck by Tallboys, none hit the areas of the roof where the *Fangrost* had been installed. Several of the pens had their roofs penetrated by Tallboys, although all are believed to have detonated within the roof, achieving penetration by blowing concrete out above and below the point of detonation.

The offensive against the pens began on 5 August, and over the next three weeks, five attacks would be made by 617 against the Brest pens and a ship in the harbour (only three using Tallboys due to limited supply), three against La Pallice (two with Tallboys) and one against the largest pen complex, situated at Lorient. An attack was also made on another E-boat pen at IJmuiden in the Netherlands. There were many hits on the roofs of the pens, and several penetrations were achieved, although there was also evidence of premature detonation of some bombs. Once US-made Tallboys began to arrive, it became possible to implement the planned deployment to another squadron, 9 Squadron at Bardney under the command of Wg Cdr J.M. Bazin being chosen due to their excellent bombing record – theirs was to be a baptism of fire with the weapon.

LEFT The Bruno U-boat pens in the harbour at Bergen, Norway. *(Crown Copyright via The Science Museum)*

Main particulars – Johnny Walker (JW) mine

Type	JW (oscillating) mine
Length overall	72in
Diameter	20in
Weight	500lb approx. (of which charge 100lb)
Filling	Torpex D.1 with aluminium
Typical fuzing	impact
Number expended on operations	144 (48 dropped by 617 Squadron and 24 dropped by 9 Squadron, remainder jettisoned)

RIGHT **The JW mine – its only operational use was on Operation Paravane against the *Tirpitz*.** *(Author)*

BELOW ***Tirpitz* spent most of her career hidden away in the Norwegian fjords, where the terrain made a low-level attack almost impossible.** *(Imperial War Museum C4126)*

Tirpitz

The greatest of Germany's battleships, the *Tirpitz* had spent most of her operational career at anchor in the Norwegian fjords, where her mere presence forced major Allied warships to guard convoys to Russia, and an excursion into the Atlantic in the footsteps of her ill-fated sister *Bismarck* also remained a possibility. Despite many bombing raids, torpedo strikes and a successful attack by X-craft submarines in September 1943, she remained afloat and a threat.

In 1942, the Director of Armament Development had initiated development of a new anti-shipping weapon, the 'Johnny Walker' mine, and although Bomber Command had had supplies for over a year, it had not yet seen operational use. The JW was dropped by parachute into water, where an internal buoyancy tank was filled to bring it back towards the surface – hopefully it would then strike the bottom of a ship and detonate on this unarmoured part of the hull. If it failed to strike, the mine would sink again while propelling itself forward, then rise up again – it would continue this oscillating 'walking' motion until it struck a target, or the buoyancy gas was exhausted, whereupon the mine would self-destruct. Weighing 500lb, a Lancaster had the capacity to carry twelve of them.

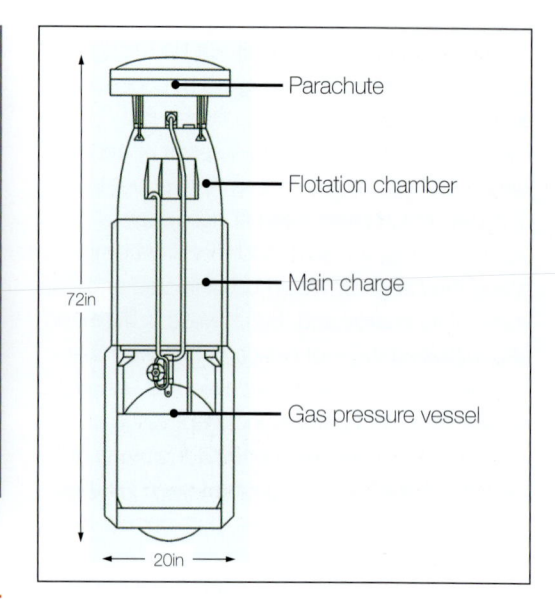

In September 1944, *Tirpitz* was in Kå Fjord near Alta, which was beyond the range of fully laden Lancasters from the UK, even with overload tanks and a northern departure airfield. A plan was conceived to fly the aircraft over Norway and Sweden to Russia and mount the attack from there, and on 11 September twenty 617 Squadron Lancasters (now under the command of J.B. 'Willie' Tait) and eighteen 9 Squadron Lancasters departed for Yagodnik; six aircraft of each squadron carried JW mines, the rest carried Tallboys with instantaneous pistols. Poor weather, poor radio communication and extreme range meant that some of the Lancasters did not manage to land at Yagodnik, some being severely damaged landing on unprepared ground with their fuel almost exhausted. Once all the serviceable aircraft were gathered and repaired, only twenty-seven were available for the attack (six with JW mines and twenty-one with Tallboys), and when a favourable weather report was finally received on 15 September, Operation Paravane was approved and they set off for Kå Fjord. The Tallboy force at 15,000 to 18,000ft came in along the line of the fjord (also the fore-and-aft line of the target) while the JW aircraft flew a dog leg to come in at 90° at around 12,000ft. As well as guns on the ship itself, there were many guns positioned around the fjord, but the main problem was the smoke generators deployed on the ship and along the shore. When an air-raid warning was received, these could submerge the ship beneath a blanket of smoke in minutes, which is exactly what happened. Consequently, the later aircraft had trouble seeing the ship, with some aiming for mastheads or gun flashes beneath the smoke; others decided to bring their bombs back. No results were observed from the air, but one Tallboy had penetrated the fo'c's'le and there had been several near misses – there is no record of any strikes by the JW mines and this weapon has largely been forgotten. The damage was enough to end *Tirpitz*'s ability to put to sea, but she otherwise remained operational, so it was decided to move her to shallow water near Tromsø to act as a gun battery for the expected invasion of Norway. Crucially, this was one hundred miles closer to the UK, so with two hundred miles shaved off a round trip, an attack from the UK became feasible. Even so, this required the Lancasters to

TARGET PROFILE

Tirpitz

Type: battleship
Location: 69° 56' 24" N 23° 3' 37" E (Kå Fjord, near Alta, Norway – September 1944 attack)/69° 38' 59" N 18° 49' 57" E (Tromsø Fjord, near Håkøy Island, Norway – October and November 1944 attacks)
Built: 1936–41
Dimensions: 254 x 36m
Attacked: 15 September 1944 (17 Tallboys +72 JW mines), 29 October 1944 (34 Tallboys), 12 November 1944 (29 Tallboys), sunk
Current status: dismantled for scrap

With the loss of the battleship *Bismarck* in 1941, her sister *Tirpitz* became the most important ship in the German Navy. The ship occupied the thoughts of Churchill on many occasions – he called her 'The Beast' and said 'No other target is comparable to it' – and many attacks were made on the ship by the RAF and Fleet Air Arm, with little success. The smaller 'bouncing bomb' Highball was designed primarily to attack *Tirpitz*, though it lost out operationally to the X-craft midget submarines which succeeded in crippling the ship in September 1943. When Tallboy became available, it was realised that this weapon had a chance to sink the ship, hence the remarkable lengths taken to facilitate an attack on her northern anchorage. Disabled by a Tallboy hit on her fo'c's'le on Operation Paravane, she was hit decisively on Operation Catechism and rolled over, trapping many crewmen within the upturned hull. After the war, the hull was cut up for scrap, and many pieces remain around the site and in museums.

LEFT The view from Sáhkkobátni down into Kå Fjord, showing two Tallboy craters on the foregound spit and another across the fjord. The blue outline shows the *Tirpitz*'s position when attacked by X-craft submarines in September 1943, the red outline is her position during Operation Paravane in September 1944.
(Kjell Sørensen)

Sections of ship at propeller shafts and amidships

SECTION at A-B (Aft)
- Starboard Shaft
- Centre Shaft
- Water
- Port Shaft
- Upper Deck

SECTION P-Q (Amidships)
- Starboard Bilge Keel
- Flat Bottom
- Water
- Upper Deck
- Superstructure (Control Tower, Funnel etc)

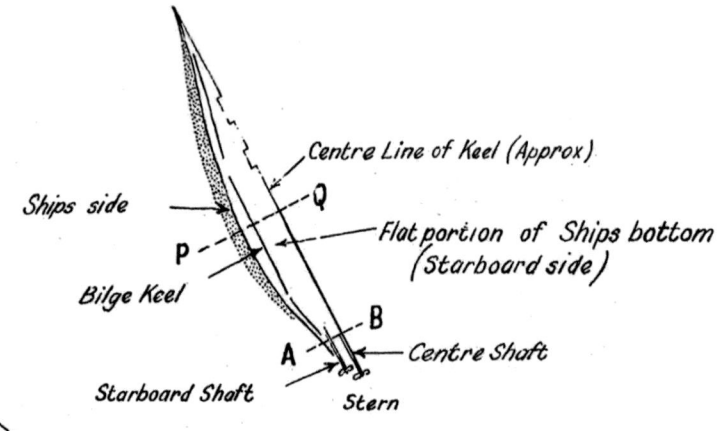

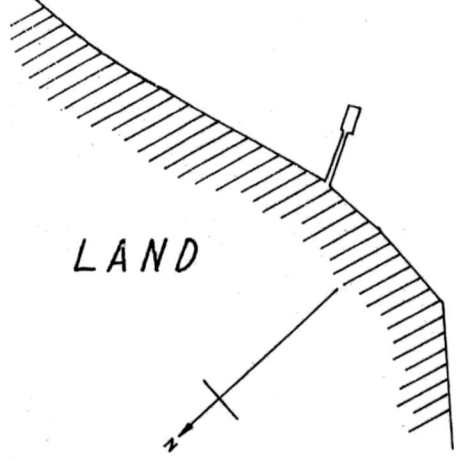

- Centre Line of Keel (Approx)
- Ships side
- Q
- Flat portion of Ships bottom (Starboard side)
- P
- Bilge Keel
- B
- A
- Centre Shaft
- Starboard Shaft
- Stern

LAND

Diagrams of
TIRPITZ
capsized at Tromso on 12-11-44

Interpretation Report N° K3361
Neg N° 46827 R

N.B :— These plans are diagramatic and NOT TO SCALE.

OPPOSITE Post-raid analysis enabled photo interpreters to draw this diagram of the *Tirpitz* in her capsized condition. *(USAF Museum)*

LEFT Aerial reconnaissance photo of the Dortmund–Ems Canal on 2 October 1944 shows the effect of the raid a week earlier, the banks breached by Tallboy craters and the outflow of water visible. *(Imperial War Museum C4667)*

be modified: the mid-upper turret was removed, two overload fuel tanks (one from a Wellington and one from a Mosquito) were fitted into the fuselage (a process requiring the removal and refitting of the rear turret), and all aircraft were fitted with the Merlin 24, the most powerful Merlin available, these being 'scrounged' from other squadrons across 5 Group.

The two squadrons left from RAF Lossiemouth for Operation Obviate on 11 September, crossing the North Sea and dog-legging through a known gap in the Norwegian coastal radar, to fly north over Sweden and approach the *Tirpitz* from the south-east. The smoke apparatus was not yet installed at the new location, but nature provided her own, a sheet of cloud rolling in below the bombers as they made their target runs. Most would still drop their bombs, but there were no hits on the ship this time. Operation Catechism was a repeat attempt on 12 November, and this time their luck held – at least three Tallboys struck the battleship, detonating a magazine and causing her to roll over, coming to rest when the superstructure hit the bottom of the fjord. The *Tirpitz* attacks are probably the most famous RAF raids of the war (after the Dams Raid itself) and a total of eighty Tallboys had been dropped over the three missions. Whose bomb had inflicted the fatal wound was a matter of contention, and rival claims by 9 and 617 have

TARGET PROFILE

Dortmund–Ems Canal

Type:	canal (two parallel branches, each crossing an aqueduct)
Location:	52° 2' 30" N 7° 40' 41" E (between Münster and Ladbergen, Germany)
Built:	1899
Attacked:	15 September 1943 (8 Blockbusters), 23 September 1944 (9 Tallboys), 3 March 1945 (18 Tallboys), banks of both canal branches breached by both Tallboy raids
Current status:	northern branch in use, southern branch now disused

The Dortmund–Ems Canal was the most important waterway in Germany, and a primary transport route for the movement of raw materials and goods between the industrial Ruhr and the rest of Germany. One weak point in the canal was near Ladbergen where the double branch of the canal crossed the River Glane on two aqueducts and the canal itself was above the level of the surrounding land. Considered for attack by rolling Upkeeps over land to drop into the canal, it saw the first operational use of the Blockbuster, but without success. Also attacked by Main Force aircraft with conventional bombs, the Tallboy attack in September 1944 successfully breached the banks and emptied the canal. Once repaired, it was attacked again six months later with the same result. After the war, the whole canal was widened, and the southern branch at this point was closed.

RIGHT The Dortmund–Ems Canal from ground level following the raid in March 1944, the water gone and barges grounded. *(Author's collection)*

continued over the years. Either way, Tallboy had found a new application and finally dealt with the festering problem of the *Tirpitz*.

Between the September and October visits to Norway, both squadrons had flown two other operations, one together as part of a Main Force attack on the Dortmund–Ems Canal near Ladbergen, and one operating independently against a dam. Several Tallboy strikes on the canal banks caused at least three breaches, and the waters flowed out over the surrounding countryside, grounding barges for miles.

TARGET PROFILE

Kembs Barrage

Type:	river barrage
Location:	47° 37' 9" N 7° 34' 20" E (near Kembs, France)
Built:	1928–32
Length:	165m
Height:	12m
Attacked:	7 October 1944 (13 Tallboys), sluice gate breached
Current status:	repaired, in use

Kembs Barrage on the Rhine was one of many such barrages on the river, used to maintain water levels to keep the river navigable while also housing a hydroelectric power station. One of the six bombs dropped from low level destroyed one of the sluices, releasing the water.

Dams again

As Allied forces pushed east towards the Rhine through the Belfort Gap, there were concerns that the Germans could sabotage the Kembs Barrage (as they had done with the Rurberg Dam) to flood them out with water from the Rhine, so it was decided to pre-empt such a move by destroying the barrage in advance using Tallboys, dropped from both high and low level. Upkeep would have been ideal for this attack (although the structure above the main barrage would have necessitated a sharp pull-up) but insufficient Type 464 Lancasters were available, and there was not enough time for adequate training (none of the Chastise crews were still with the squadron). It was thus decided to attack the barrage with Tallboys, seven aircraft being detailed to drop conventionally from 8,000ft or above, with six more approaching below 600ft. The 'low force' were fitted with Mk.III low-level 'angular velocity' bombsights: this sight had first been deployed in Bostons in 1943 and was mostly used by Coastal Command for attacking submarines – this was the only time the sight was ever fitted to heavy bombers. It had a sighting head similar to the Mk.XIV/T.1 (see Chapter 7), but as many of the complications handled by the standard sight were not significant at low level, the 'computor' for the Mk.III was a simple roller device for entering height and airspeed.

LEFT Aiming point photo from the attack on the Kembs Barrage. *(Crown Copyright via 617 Squadron)*

BELOW Post-raid photo at Kembs showing the outflow through the damaged sluice. *(Crown Copyright via 617 Squadron)*

TARGET PROFILE

Urft Dam

Type:	walled gravity dam
Location:	50° 36' 8" N 6° 25' 8" E (in Eifel National Park, Germany)
Built:	1900–05
Length:	226m
Height:	58m
Reservoir capacity:	45 million m³
Attacked:	8 December 1944 (4 Tallboys), 11 December 1944 (35 Tallboys), wall and spillway damaged
Current status:	repaired 1945–48, in use

The Urft Dam also became a target in December 1944 in order to prevent its use to flood approaching troops (although it had been considered previously as a potential Upkeep target, even progressing to model tests). Its location meant that a breach would probably have destroyed the Rurberg (Paulushof) and Roer (Schwammenauel) Dams which were just a few miles downstream. Despite two attacks and hits on the dam and spillway, the dam was not breached, but the Germans lowered the water level to prevent calamity, so the aim was largely achieved.

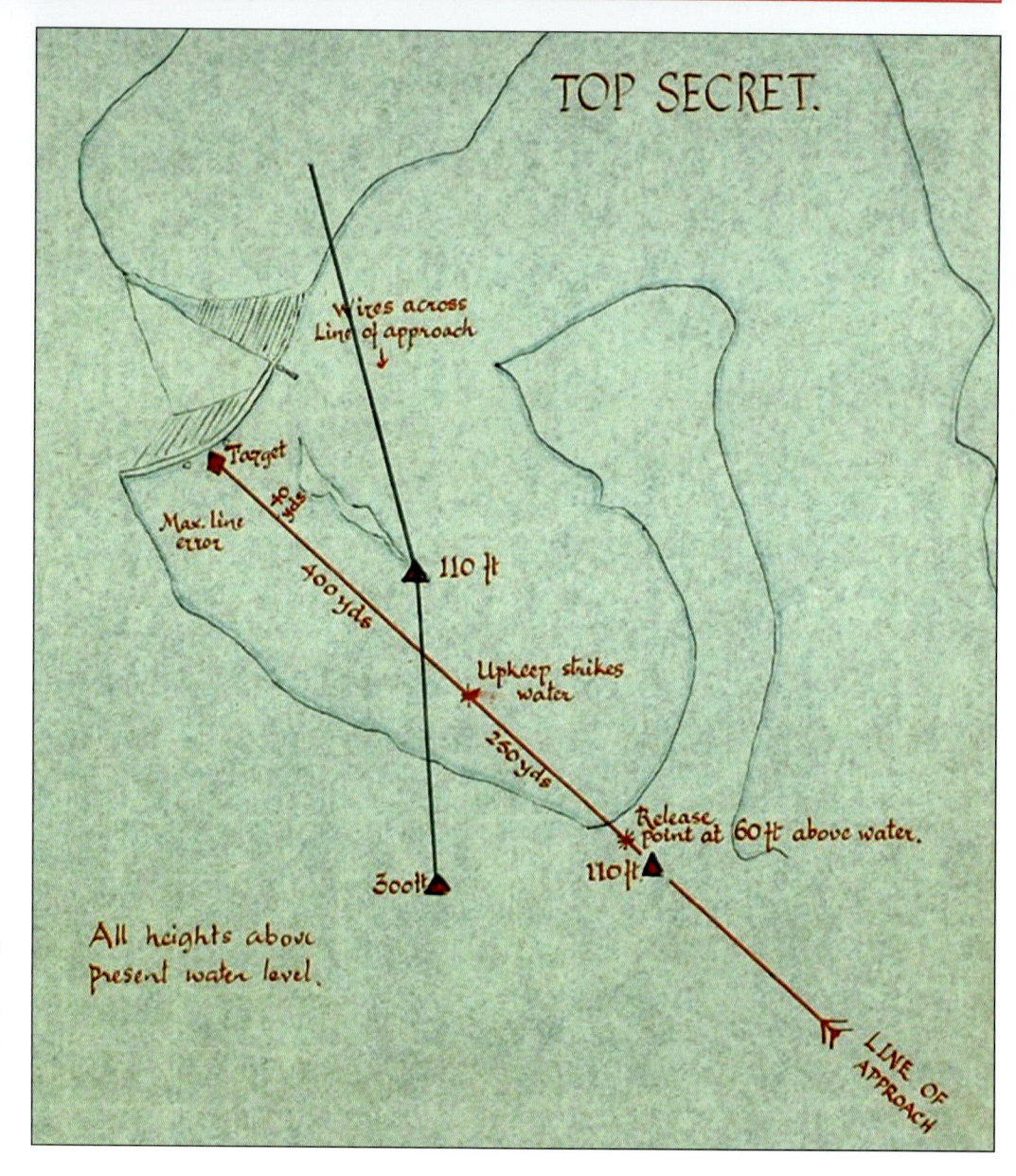

RIGHT Plans to attack the Urft Dam with Upkeep were foiled by the position of the hills and wires suspended across the flight path.
(Crown Copyright via The National Archives)

Release slip problems meant that none of the 'high force' bombs landed near the target, and two of the 'low force' were hit on their bombing runs and lost with their crews, but three Tallboys landed close to the barrage. These bombs had 30-minute delay pistols, and an observation Mosquito saw these detonate and carry away one of the sluices – the water poured through and water levels fell for many miles upstream.

Eight days later, 9 Squadron got their chance at being 'dam busters', using Tallboys on the Sorpe Dam. The dam was now protected by barrage balloons and numerous flak guns, and although the reservoir water level was being kept lower than it had been at the time of the earlier raid, it was hoped that Tallboys dropped on the upper part of the air side and the crest would damage the concrete core and lead to leakage via the craters, this outflow naturally building to a torrent that would breach the dam completely. The squadron were to attack from the direction of the air side in (as was this squadron's normal practice) line astern, and two Tallboys made direct hits on the crest, with three on the air side and more in the water. Despite this excellent result, the craters were not sufficient to cause any escape of water, so the dam remained intact. Some of the bombs did not detonate, three having to be defuzed when low water uncovered them in 1958.

Following the two *Tirpitz* operations, 9 Squadron participated in two Main Force raids on railway targets at Munich and Heilbronn, dropping a total of nineteen Blockbusters. 9 and 617 next joined a Main Force raid on 8 December to the Urft Dam – as at Kembs, breaching this dam was to prevent the Germans from using it to flood approaching troops. However, poor weather over the target meant that hardly any Tallboys were dropped, and the raid was repeated three days later. This time some hits were scored on the spillway and on the crest of the dam, but it was not breached. Thus Tallboy, a weapon conceived mainly to attack dams, paradoxically failed to breach either of the two dams upon which it was dropped.

Miscellaneous targets

The remainder of the month saw the two squadrons attacking a variety of targets. On 17 December, 9 Squadron dropped seventeen Blockbusters as part of a Main Force raid on Munich; two days earlier, 617 had paid a return visit to IJmuiden, damaging the roof, before participating in a Main Force raid into Poland to attack a synthetic oil plant at Pölitz (now Police) on 21 December. Tallboys were carried on this raid and although the plant was severely damaged, it was above ground and so it would probably have been more effectively damaged if Blockbusters had been used. E-boat pens at Rotterdam were attacked on 29 December and several hits scored, then on New Year's Eve the squadron, under its new CO Gp Capt Johnnie Fauquier attacked the cruisers *Emden* and *Köln* in Oslo Fjord together with sixteen bombers from two other squadrons, following up three Main Force raids on the area in the weeks

ABOVE LEFT Aerial reconnaissance image of the Urft Dam and its spillway before the attack. *(Crown Copyright via The National Archives)*

ABOVE The Urft Dam following the attacks, with several chunks of masonry missing from the top of the dam. *(Crown Copyright)*

TARGET PROFILE

Midget submarine base, Poortershaven

Type: wharf and dockside buildings (not hardened)
Location: 51° 56' 12" N 4° 12' 50" E (Rotterdam, Netherlands)
Attacked: 3 February 1945 (18 Tallboys), 8 hits, site completely destroyed
Current status: site redeveloped

Although often grouped with the E-boat and U-boat pens, the Poortershaven site was a commercial wharf with dockside buildings which had been modified for use as a midget submarine base. The buildings were not reinforced, and the Tallboy attack completely destroyed the site.

before. This was the only time that Tallboys were dropped on moving targets, and with the squadron bombing from 8,000ft, the ships had time to take avoiding action and only *Köln* received any damage.

9 and 617 were reunited on 12 January for a return to Norway, this time to attack the U-boat pens and shipping at Bergen. Despite having a fighter escort, German fighters fell onto the bombers, one 9 Squadron Lancaster and two from 617 failing to return, several members of another crew bailing out in error; however, the pens were damaged. On 3 February, the squadrons flew separately to the Netherlands, 9 Squadron revisiting the IJmuiden pens and 617 attacking a dock at Poortershaven; this was a commercial wharf which had been taken over by the Germans for use as a base for midget submarines. It was not hardened, and the Tallboys made short work of the whole site. 617 had another go at the IJmuiden pens on 8 February.

Bridges

As part of a campaign to cripple the German transport network, 22 February saw the first of a long series of attacks by both squadrons on railway viaducts, often as part of a larger Main Force attack though typically against separate targets. They started with the two assessed as the most important bridges in the Reich, 617 making their first trip to Bielefeld – still operational after many conventional bombing attacks. They dropped eighteen Tallboys

LEFT The quay and small harbour at Poortershaven were used by midget submarines; the buildings were not reinforced and the Tallboy attack destroyed the whole site. *(Crown Copyright)*

OPPOSITE LEFT The Bielefeld Viaduct following the first Tallboy attack; two spans of the nearest viaduct are down, but the other viaduct remains intact. *(Australian War Memorial SUK14014)*

OPPOSITE RIGHT The Bielefeld Viaduct three weeks later, now with a Grand Slam crater alongside and several spans of both viaducts down. *(Imperial War Museum C5086)*

TARGET PROFILES

German railway viaducts

Name	Location	Type	Length	Attacked Using Earthquake Bombs
Altenbeken Viaduct	51° 45' 49" N 8° 55' 37" E (W of Altenbeken)	Double track, 24 masonry arches (built 1851–53)	482m	22 February 1945 (16 Tallboys), one span destroyed by direct hit
Bielefeld Viaduct (Schildesche Viaduct)	52° 3' 18" N 8° 34' 12" E (NE of Bielefeld)	two viaducts, each double track, 28 masonry arches (built 1847 and 1917)	360m	22 February 1945 (18 Tallboys), 14 March 1945 (13 Tallboys and 1 Grand Slam), two piers of one viaduct destroyed by February raid, five piers of both viaducts destroyed by March raid
Arnsberg Viaduct	51° 24' 13" N 8° 3' 29" E (NW of Arnsberg)	double track, 7 masonry arches (built 1868–70)	125m	13 March 1945 (3 Tallboys), 14 March 1945 (17 Tallboys), 15 March 1945 (11 Tallboys and 1 Grand Slam), 19 March 1945 (12 Tallboys plus 6 Grand Slams), two arches destroyed and other damage to railway approaches
Vlotho Bridge	52° 9' 59" N 8° 53' 24" E (E of Vlotho)	single track, 4-span girder	300m	19 March 1945 (15 Tallboys), damaged by near miss
Arbergen Bridge	52° 9' 59" N 8° 53' 24" E (between Arbergen/ Dreye)	double track, 3-span girder	185m	21 March 1945 (19 Tallboys and 1 Grand Slam), two piers destroyed
Nienburg Bridge	52° 40' 5" N 9° 10' 52" E (NW of Nienburg)	single track, 3-span girder	240m	22 March 1945 (12 Tallboys and 5 Grand Slams), all spans destroyed or blown off piers
Bremen Bridge	53° 4' 49" N 8° 47" 20" E (Bremen)	double track, 5-span girder	220m	22 March 1945 (15 Tallboys), 23 March 1945 (11 Tallboys and 6 Grand Slams), one span collapsed and other damage
Bad Oeynhausen Bridge	52° 12' 44" N 8° 51' 0" E (E of Bad Oeynhausen)	two bridges, each single track, 3-span beam	200m	23 March 1945 (11 Tallboys), spans collapsed by near miss

All bridges are currently in use; Bielefeld Viaduct reopened with temporary spans in 1947, one viaduct reopened with concrete beam spans in 1965, second viaduct reopened with concrete beam spans in 1983; Bremen Bridge is now a 2-span bridge.

123

THE EARTHQUAKE BOMB RAIDS

RIGHT Map showing the Nienburg and Arbergen bridges; the exact location of Nienburg Bridge has been added at (1), as have the locations of Bremen Railway Bridge (2), Bad Oeynhausen (3), Vlotho (4) and Bielefeld (5). *(RAF Museum B3253)*

BELOW Analysis of the crater that felled the Bielefeld Viaduct; the reference to 'Tallboy Medium' should be 'Large'. *(BAE SYSTEMS via The Science Museum)*

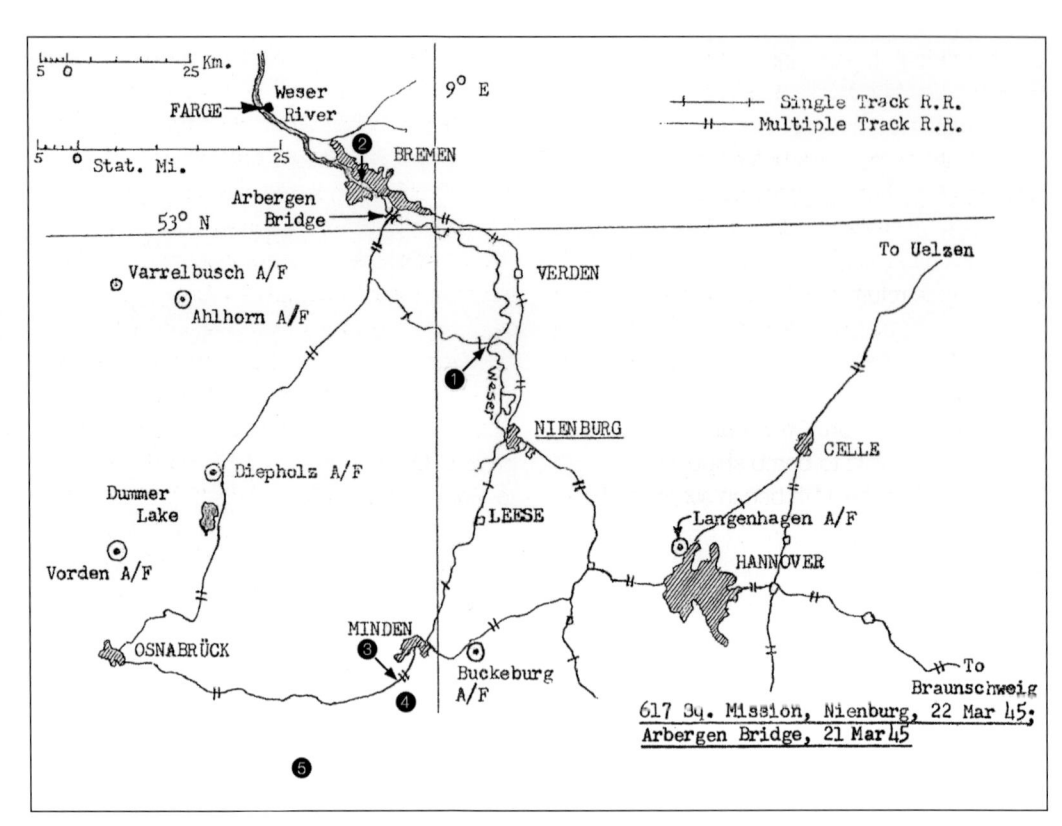

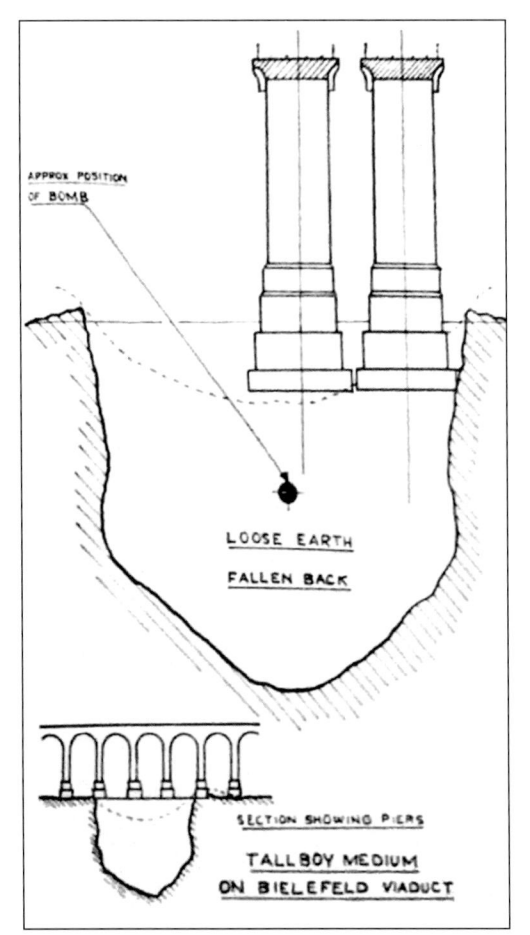

BELOW The last moments of the Arbergen Bridge on 19 March 1945; the aircraft is Lancaster B.1 Special PD114 (the first painted in 'day' camouflage) flown by Sqn Ldr Cockshott. *(Crown Copyright)*

124
DAM BUSTERS MANUAL

which took out three spans of one of the two viaducts. Meanwhile, 9 Squadron went to Altenbeken (having lost one aircraft on an aborted attack the week before) breaking the viaduct, which had recently been repaired after previous USAAF raids. On 3 March, 9 Squadron formed the Tallboy element of a Main Force return to the Dortmund–Ems Canal, which had been repaired after the breach six months before. This raid was also successful, both branches of the double canal being breached again. On 6 March, 9 took Tallboys to Sassnitz to bomb shipping in the harbour, and on the 11th began six days of back-to-back operations taking Blockbusters to Essen, then to Dortmund on the 12th, all as part of Main Force attacks, the latter two raids successively breaking the record for the largest number of aircraft deployed against a single target. The next three days saw Tallboy attacks on the Arnsberg Viaduct, the first seeing only three dropped due to poor weather over the target, made up for by seventeen the next day and eleven on the third, but this target proved to be elusive for the moment. 9 Squadron completed this run by contributing six Blockbusters to a Main Force raid on Würzburg on the 16th.

Grand Slam arrives

Meanwhile, 617 Squadron had received the first of the ten-ton Grand Slam bombs. On 13 March, the prototype had been dropped by an A&AEE pilot at the Ashley Walk range, making a crater over 120ft in diameter and 30ft deep. Two had immediately been cleared for use on another trip to Bielefeld the same day, but bad weather meant that none of the nineteen aircraft dropped their bombs, and Fauquier and Calder brought their cargoes back, landing on the long runway at RAF Carnaby. They were to repeat the trip the following day, but Fauquier's Lancaster developed a fault as the engines were run up – he ran to take over the other aircraft but Calder saw him coming and gunned his engines! Joined en route by fourteen other aircraft with their Tallboys, the squadron headed for Bielefeld, and the Grand Slam was dropped alongside the viaduct. When the smoke cleared, more than four hundred feet of both viaducts had gone – it is estimated that over three thousand tons of bombs had been dropped on the viaduct, but it was the last ten in the Grand Slam which had done the job.

Next day, two 617 Lancasters with Grand Slams joined the 9 Squadron force to Arnsberg, but haze meant that Calder brought his bomb back, and the other one didn't land close enough to bring down the viaduct. They tried again on 19 March, twelve Tallboys and six Grand Slams leaving two spans of the bridge in ruins. On the same day, 9 Squadron went to Vlotho, fifteen Tallboys knocking one span out of alignment. Two days later, 617 went to Arbergen, Calder dropping a single Grand Slam alongside the nineteen Tallboys from the rest of the squadron; although not destroyed, some spans were blown from their supports and the approaches were cratered, so the bridge was out of action.

On 22 March, 9 dropped fifteen Tallboys on the railway bridge at Bremen without

BELOW The prototype Grand Slam, painted white and black for visibility, falls away from Lancaster B.1 Special PB592 over the River Avon heading towards the Ashley Walk range. *(USAF Museum)*

result, while 617 dropped twelve Tallboys and five Grand Slams at Nienburg, breaking or dislodging every span. More bombs were now available, but such good results were being achieved that some bombs were being deliberately held back in case the earlier ones were enough – which they were on this occasion. The next day was 617's turn at Bremen, one span being dislodged by the six Grand Slams and eleven Tallboys. Meanwhile, 9 Squadron dropped eleven Tallboys on another bridge at Bad Oeynhausen; this time they got it at the first attempt, spans of both tracks being brought down. These raids marked the end of the transport attacks.

The last raids

On 27 March, both squadrons set off for the town of Farge, about fifteen miles down the River Weser from Bremen, although they would be attacking two different – and unique – targets. 617 were to attack the massive Valentin U-boat facility on the banks of the river, and would use more Grand Slams here than on any other target, thirteen outweighing the five Tallboys also dropped. Only two Grand Slams appear to have struck the roof, penetrating partway before detonating – this damaged the roof and some of the equipment inside. Repairs meant that the facility was not completed by the end of the war.

9 Squadron's target was in a forest about two miles north-east of the Valentin facility, and was an underground oil storage area, one of the largest in Germany, able to supply a number of piers on the Weser. Fifteen Tallboys were dropped, all with 30-minute delays, so no results were seen. This target appears to have been disregarded by post-war bombing surveys, so the effects of this attack are unknown, which is unfortunate as underground storage tanks were one of Wallis's primary targets for his deep-penetration weapons.

On 7 April, 617 went once more to IJmuiden, this time to sink a vessel that might have been used by the Germans to block the harbour. The following day, 9 bombed the Lutzkendorf oil refinery at Hamburg, which had escaped damage in a Main Force raid the day before; seventeen Tallboys were dropped on this target. The day after that, 617 also went to Hamburg, to attack the Finkenwerder U-boat pens which had not yet had the big-bomb treatment; fifteen Tallboys and two

TARGET PROFILE

Valentin U-boat facility, Farge

Type:	concrete U-boat construction facility
Location:	53° 13' 2" N 8° 30' 13" E (NW of Farge, Germany)
Built:	1943–45
Dimensions:	426 x 97 x 22m
Roof thickness:	up to 7m
Attacked:	27 March 1945 (5 Tallboys and 13 Grand Slams), several hits, roof penetrated in 2 places
Current status:	western end derelict, eastern end in use as a store

The huge Valentin facility near Farge (about fifteen miles NW of Bremen) was not a conventional U-boat pen, but an enclosed U-boat construction facility for the completion of U-boats assembled from prefabricated sections built around Germany. The site included a wet dock, into which components could be delivered by barge, an internal crane lifting them onto the production line, which filled the rest of the building. Once a U-boat was completed, it would have been lowered into the same dock, and would have sailed away into the River Weser under its own power. An obvious target, the building was massively constructed, with a roof made of heavy reinforced concrete trusses with further reinforced concrete on top making the roof up to 7m thick. The attack damaged the roof, bringing down large sections of concrete inside the building, and it was not completed before ground troops overran the site. The building was used for post-war testing of the Grand Slam by 15 Squadron during the joint UK/USA Project Ruby; the Americans also tested their own Amazon and Samson penetration weapons on the building (all these drops used inert-filled bombs).

LEFT Aerial reconnaissance photo of the Valentin U-boat factory at Farge, which has been marked with the aiming point in the middle of the roof. *(Crown Copyright via The Science Museum)*

BELOW LEFT The Valentin bunker showing the massive construction; the roof beams were further covered in reinforced concrete to form a flat roof over 7m thick. *(The Science Museum)*

BELOW Inside the Valentin bunker showing the penetration of a Grand Slam. *(Crown Copyright)*

127
THE EARTHQUAKE BOMB RAIDS

TARGET PROFILE

Oil storage facility, Farge

Type: underground oil storage facility
Location: 53° 13' 13" N 8° 32' 18" E (NE of Farge, Germany)
Built: 1943–45
Attacked: 27 March 1945 (15 Tallboys), hit but results not recorded
Current status: site in use for oil storage

Just a few miles from the Valentin facility, the oil storage depot at Farge is a much more enigmatic target. Comprising a number of oil tanks buried beneath the ground, it was one of Germany's largest storage facilities, with access to loading piers on the Weser as well as railway connections. Underground oil tanks were one of the main targets which Wallis intended for Tallboy, but this was the only time such a target was attacked with the weapon, and it seems to have largely been missed by post-war bombing surveys, so the extent of the damage caused is not recorded in detail.

Grand Slams were dropped, six Tallboys hitting the roof and causing tons of debris to fall into the pens. One week later, after several aborted attempts to reach the Baltic port of Swinemünde, they bombed the cruisers *Prinz Eugen* and *Lützow* there with fourteen Tallboys, damaging the latter so badly that she settled onto the seabed.

Both squadrons came together again on the 19th for an attack on the island of Heligoland in the German Bight. Although there were U-boat pens on the island, these were not the target, which was the gun batteries on the cliffs situated around the north part of

BELOW Map of the Farge area, showing the oil storage facilities and rail links; the black rectangle is the Valentin bunker. *(USAF Museum)*

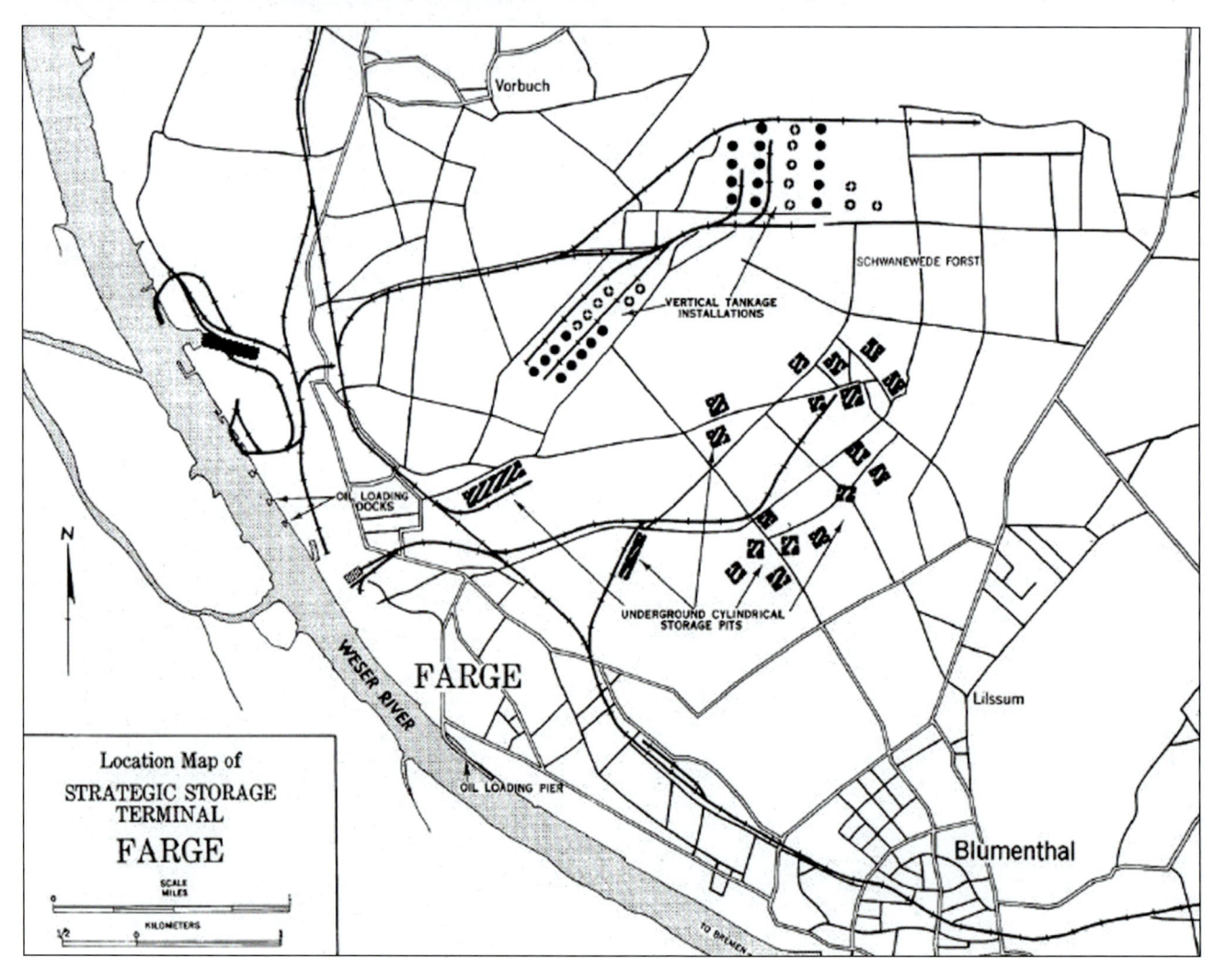

the island to defend the approaches to the German ports. Twenty-eight Tallboys and six Grand Slams fell on the island, but only two direct hits were scored and although other damage was caused, the raid was considered unsuccessful.

Finally, on 25 April, Tallboy had its last outing of the war when 9 and 617 formed part of a Main Force raid on Berchtesgaden, Hitler's Bavarian home. The two squadrons dropped thirteen Tallboys each, and the 'Eagle's Nest' was damaged, although Hitler himself was in Berlin.

Post-war developments

As the Allies liberated France and the Low Countries, and fought their way into Germany, various inspection parties were sent out to investigate the effects of the bombing war, including teams with particular interest in concrete structures and the V-weapon sites, and their reports describe the results of the earthquake bomb attacks, often with detail on a bomb-by-bomb basis.

There was interest in further testing their penetrating power against concrete targets, and the Valentin site at Farge was chosen for the joint US/UK Project Ruby, conducted in 1946–47 (the blockhouse at Éperlecques had also been considered, but was not used). This programme saw numerous penetration weapons dropped on the site: (inert) Grand Slams, Disney bombs (a 4,500lb UK-designed rocket-assisted penetration bomb which had been used operationally by the Americans without much success) and American-developed Amazon and Samson bombs.

Although some work was done in Britain on a Tallboy Mk.III, it was in the USA where the earthquake bomb idea was taken forward. B-29 Superfortresses could be modified to carry Tallboys and Grand Slams, either semi-recessed in the two-section bomb bay or on inner wing pylons, and the Northrop XB-35 flying wing was also designed to carry the bombs (although this aircraft did not go into service). The Americans also designed a remotely controlled version of Tallboy, called Tarzon, which could be steered as it fell, and this saw limited operational use in Korea. A 44,000lb penetration bomb was also developed, although not deployed operationally, nuclear weapons by then being the weapon of choice for substantial targets.

Review of the deep-penetration bombs

Although the Tallboy became available less than a year before the end of the war, and the Grand Slam only two months before, these weapons and the two squadrons that dropped them at last allowed the RAF to deliver what they always purported to be able to deliver – destruction of substantial pinpoint targets. More importantly, they were able to damage targets which other types of bombs had no chance of being able to damage, such as the reinforced concrete U-boat pens and V-weapon bunkers. The Wizernes V-2 rocket site and the Marquise–Mimoyecques V-3 gun site in particular had the potential to inflict massive damage on London, and were untouchable by conventional bombs. The destruction of the *Tirpitz* was another significant Tallboy victory. The 'earthquake bombs' have been described as the most effective of the air-dropped weapons of the war, short of the atom bombs.

Examples of most of the bombs described here can now be seen in museums – a list of these can be found in Appendix 4.

ABOVE Rare aerial reconnaissance photo of the bombing of the Farge oil storage facility. *(Crown Copyright via The Science Museum)*

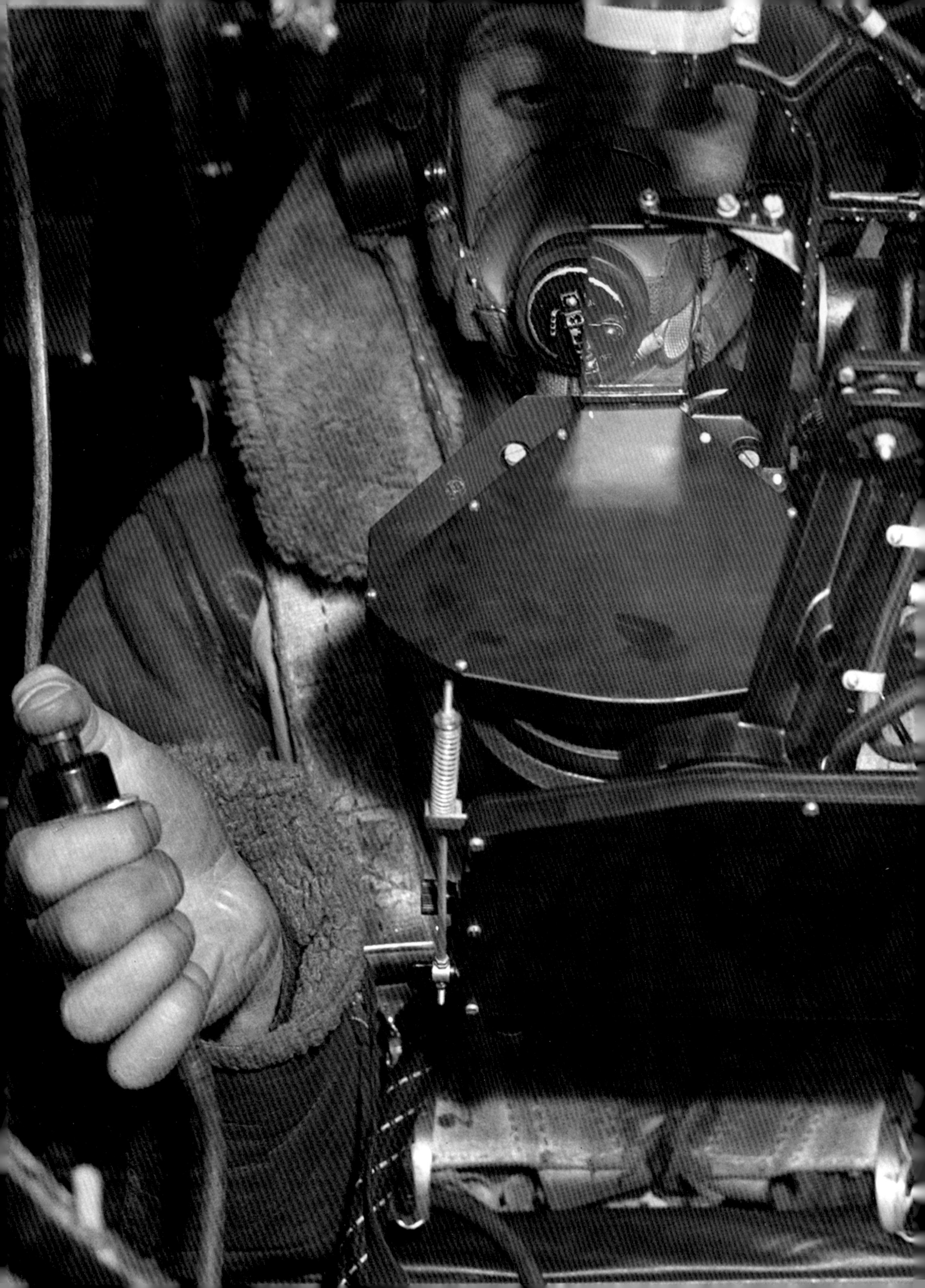

Chapter Seven

High-level Bomb Aiming

Over the course of the war, bomb aiming technology developed from simple sights relying on manual configuration to highly automated sights which could direct the pilot accurately towards the target.

OPPOSITE The bomb aimer in his natural environment, looking through the graticule glass of a Mk.XIV bomb sight, ready to press the 'tit' in his right hand and call 'bomb gone!' *(Imperial War Museum CH12283)*

Key principles – the bomb aiming problem

The 'ideal' bombing problem is illustrated in the diagram. If a bomber releases a bomb while flying straight and level with speed V at height H above the target 'T', the bomb will continue to move forward with horizontal speed V while accelerating downwards due to gravity, following a parabolic course to the target. At the moment of release, the bomb aimer's direct line of sight to the target is at a certain angle θ below the horizontal, this being known as the 'bombing angle' or 'sighting angle'. For a known V and H, θ can be pre-calculated and the resulting line-of-sight vector displayed via a simple bomb sight to the bomb aimer, who then simply needs to guide his pilot so that the vector passes through the target, at which point the bomb is released.

However, there are several factors which make the problem more complex in reality. Firstly, due to air resistance, the speed of a real bomb is retarded from the ideal path, and it will always experience a 'ground trail' causing it to fall some distance short of the target at L (the shortfall being dependent on properties of the bomb and the atmospheric conditions). If the bomb is light, it may reach its terminal velocity during its fall, after which its path will be a straight line, further complicating the calculation. To cope with this, the characteristics of the bomb must be included in the calculation performed to find the correct sighting angle.

Wind offers another complication, as the wind will move the bomb off target by a distance equal to the time of fall multiplied by the wind speed. This wind drift must also be allowed for in the calculation to maintain accuracy.

The final problem is that, as the bombing angle displayed is for straight-and-level flight, any deviation from this would cause the bomb to miss its target. As well as the possibility of the bomber climbing, diving or turning at the moment of release, there is also the fact that an attacking aircraft is likely to meet enemy resistance from aircraft or ground fire, resulting in some degree of rapid aircraft motion during the bombing run. A good bomb sight should be able to cope with this range of motions in order to prevent the run from having to be restarted.

LEFT The bombing problem: an aircraft flying at speed V and height H above the target will theoretically be in position to hit the target when the sighting angle is θ, but trail will cause the bomb to fall short at L; wind and other factors will further complicate the problem. *(Author)*

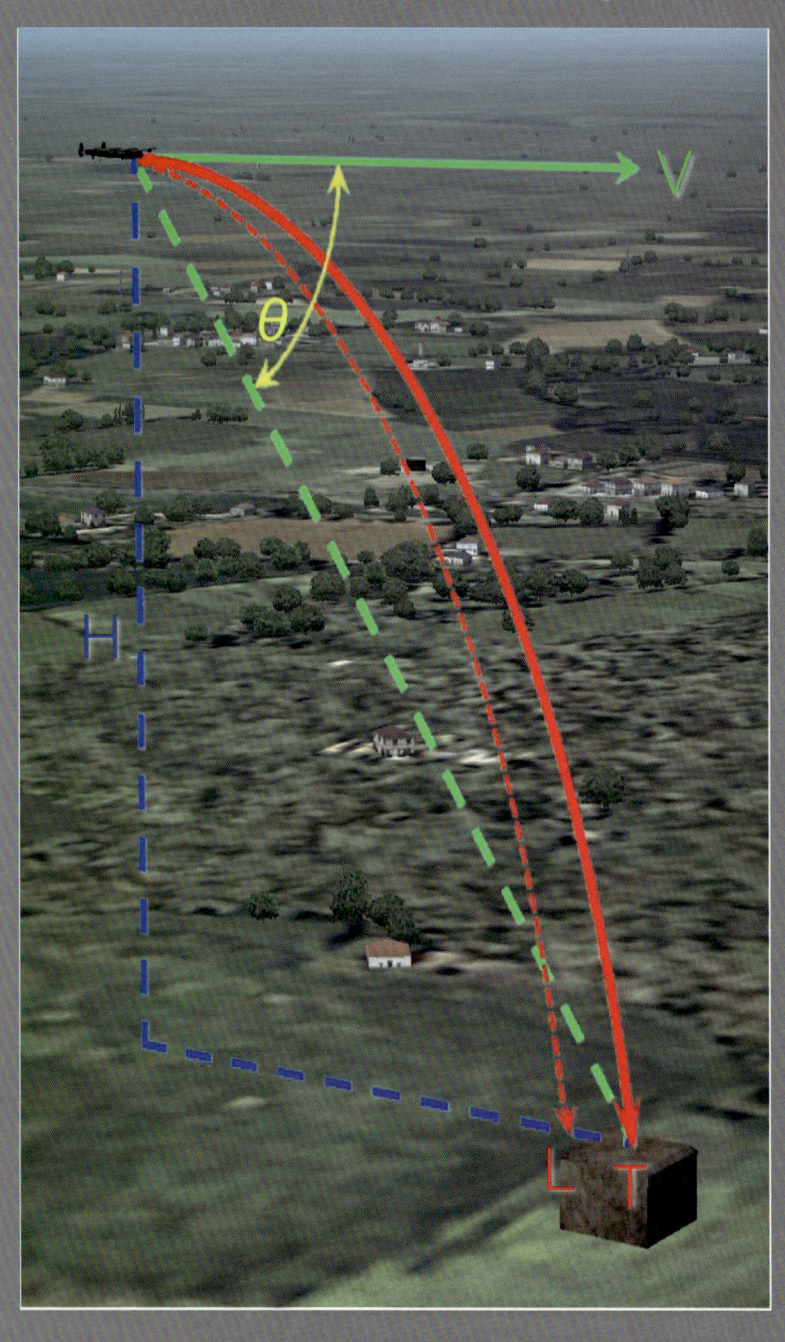

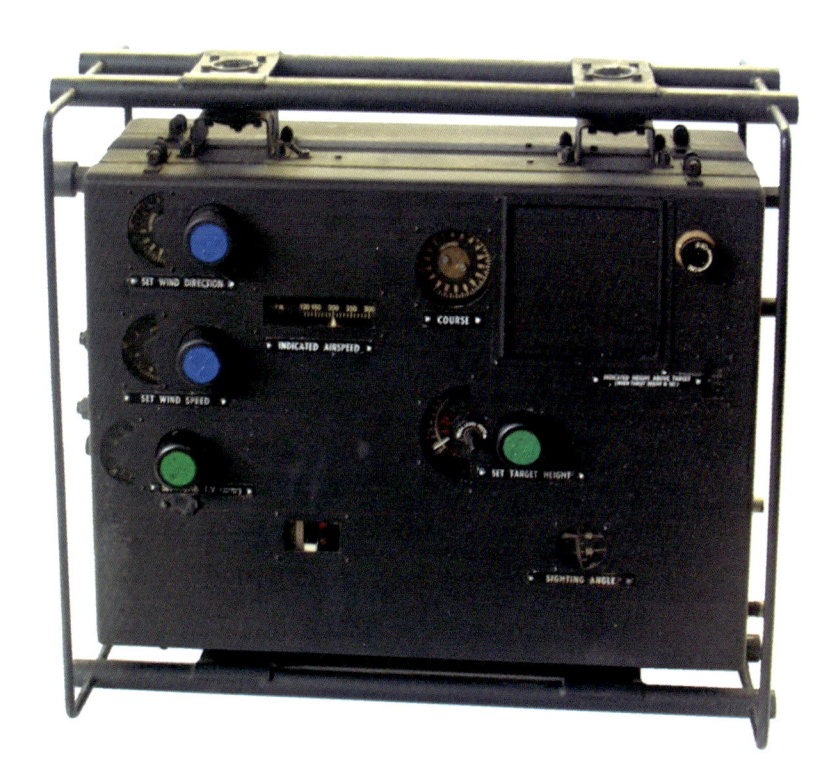

Bomb aiming

The problem of hitting a target with a bomb from a high-flying aircraft is not a trivial one. At the start of the war, the primary bomb sight in use by Bomber Command was the course setting bomb sight (CSBS), often known as the Wimperis sight after its developer. This was a manually operated vector sight (described in Patent GB415523 awarded in 1934, though its roots date back to the First World War), which allowed the bomb aimer to set up a number of bombing parameters on a series of scales which projected from the front of the sight to produce a line-of-sight vector. This had been developed to a Mk.VII by the early 1930s and the Mk.IX (which handled a wider range of aircraft speeds) was in common use by 1939 (and training on this sight continued throughout the war). With good training, the sight was reasonably accurate (and it could also cope with wind drift), but the line-of-sight vector was fixed (relative to the aircraft), so no allowance was made for the aircraft deviating from a pre-determined height or straight-and-level flight during the bombing run.

Operationally, as a straight-and-level run was the exception rather than the rule, some means of coping with unexpected aircraft motion was required; there was also a need to reduce the amount of computation to be performed by the bomb aimer. These demands were taken to the Committee for the Scientific Study of Air Defence at the end of 1939, and Prof. Patrick Blackett (Director of Naval Operational Research) undertook to design a suitable sight, which he did with a small team of engineers at RAE Farnborough (applying for Patent GB581970 at the end of 1941). The sight, known as the Mk.XIV, consisted of a mechanical analogue computer unit

ABOVE LEFT The Mk.XIV computer could continuously calculate the point of impact of a bomb, even when the aircraft was manoeuvring. *(Author)*

ABOVE The rear of the Mk.XIV computer. *(Author)*

LEFT The mounting bracket for the Mk.XIV sighting head was fixed on the left side of the bomb aimer's compartment. *(Author)*

133

HIGH-LEVEL BOMB AIMING

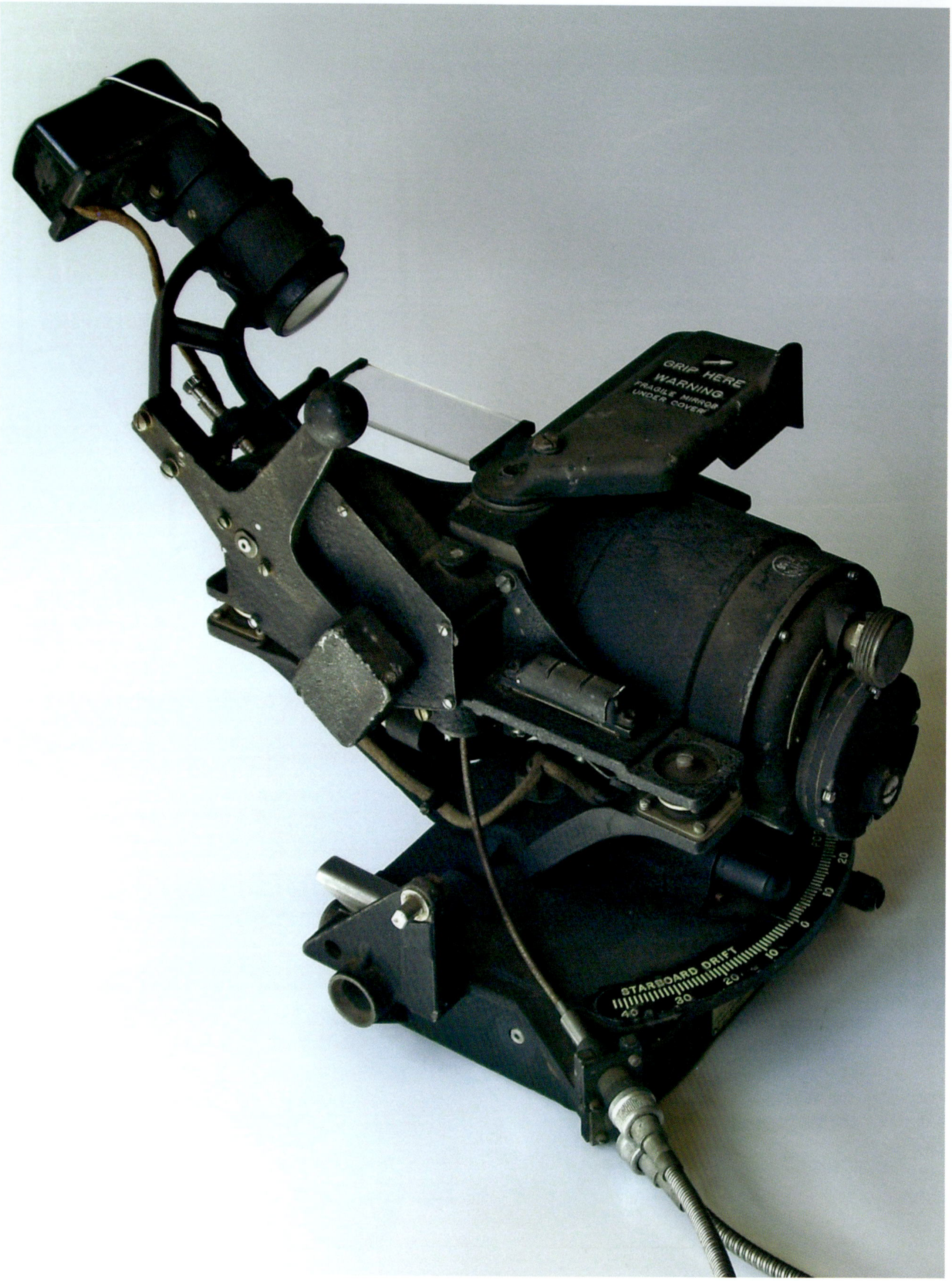
GRIP HERE
WARNING
FRAGILE MIRROR UNDER COVER
STARBOARD DRIFT

('computor' on the original) in the bomb aimer's compartment which performed the necessary calculations in real time and continuously modified the position of a graticule projected on the separate sighting head, mounted in the nose, which the bomb aimer viewed (thus although the computer performed most of the aiming calculations, this was still a vector sight). The graticule represented the position where a bomb released *at that instant* would land – the bomb aimer's task was thus to instruct the pilot to steer the aircraft so that the graticule would pass over the target, at which point he would release the bomb.

Five preset parameters, such as the bomb's terminal velocity and target height, were input on the computer's front panel before flight; height and airspeed were obtained from miniature bellows inside. Supplied with electrical power (for the motor), compressed air, suction (for the gyros), a continuous input of aircraft course and pitot pressure (for airspeed measurement), the computer was thus able to measure airspeed, height and pitch, and from these to calculate (entirely mechanically) the sighting angle (via a ground speed calculation) and drift angle. These angles were continuously output via the angular position of two flexible drive shafts; the drift angle shaft rotated the sighting head about a vertical axis, and the sighting angle shaft changed the elevation of the graticule projector, together thus controlling the line of sight seen by the bomb aimer. The graticule brightness, as well as scale illumination, could be altered using a separate control box mounted between the computer and the sighting head. The aircraft's course was fed into the computer from the aircraft's central Direct Reading (gyro) compass, the current course being displayed on the bomb aimer's course setting indicator; if a DR compass was not fitted, the course (as given by the navigator) was input manually via the handle on the indicator unit, which was connected to the computer via a flexible shaft.

The computer allowed for wind drift, if the wind speed and direction were preset. This required the use of 'wind finders' – lead aircraft in a formation would track a landmark, then fly a 'racetrack' circuit with two standard-rate turns and two straight legs. If flown accurately, when the aircraft completed the circuit, it would come back to the same position – if there was no wind. If there was wind, its effect would be to offset the apparent position of the landmark. By measuring the size and angle of the offset

OPPOSITE The T.1 sighting head was interchangeable with the Mk.XIV; the light (top) projected a graticule onto the glass slide, kept steady by the roll gyro (large drum). *(Author)*

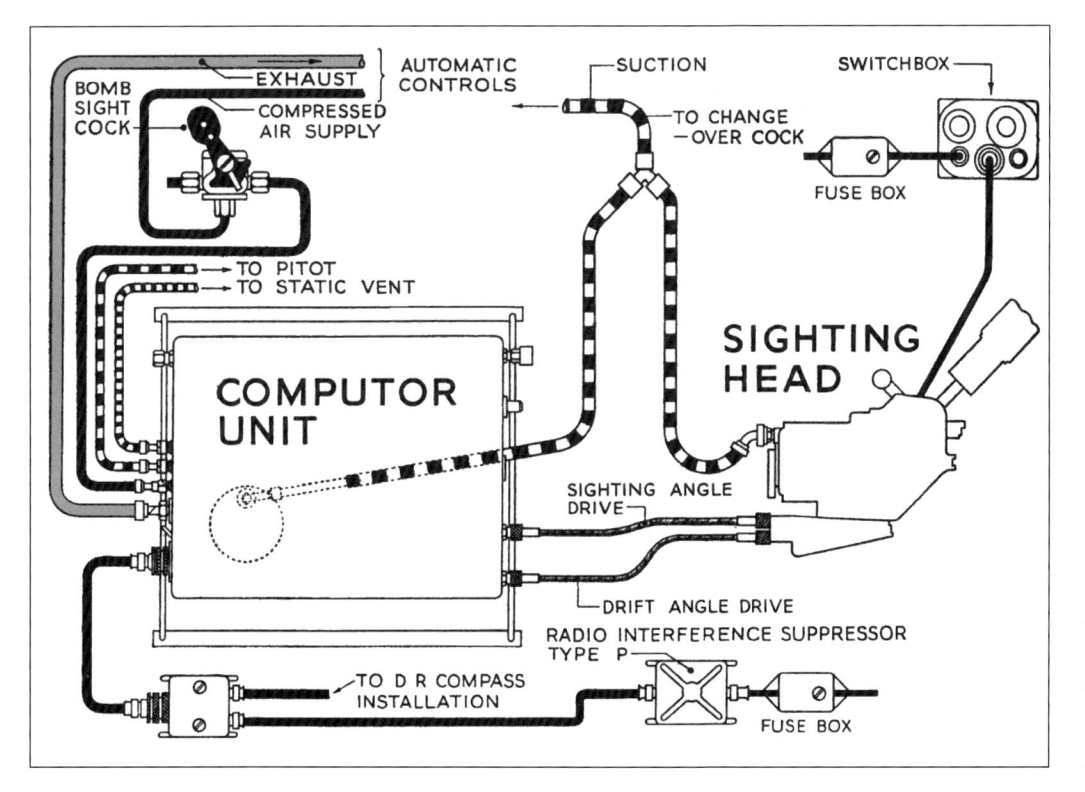

LEFT Schematic showing the connections between the Mk.XIV computer, sighting head and the aircraft. *(Crown Copyright via RAF Museum – AP 1730A)*

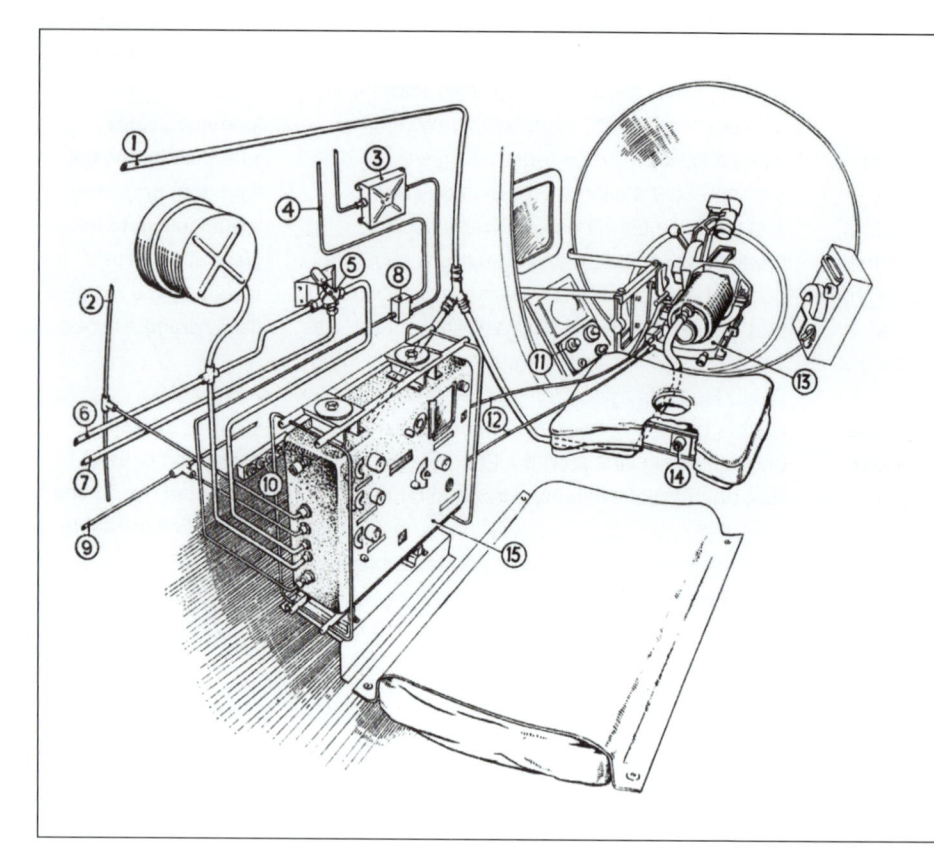

The bomb aimer's compartment with the Mk.XIV bomb sight and its connections. *(Crown Copyright via RAF Museum – AP 1730A)*

1 To suction
2 To static vent
3 Radio interference suppressor
4 To DR compass
5 Bomb sight on/off cock
6 Exhaust
7 Compressed air supply from air drier
8 Distribution box
9 To pitot head
10 Stowage for services
11 Switchbox (for illumination)
12 Flexible shafts between computer and sighting head
13 Sighting head
14 Stowage for sighting head suction pipe
15 Mk.XIV computer unit

The bomb aimer's compartment in BBMF Lancaster PA474. *(Author)*

1 Corner of Mk.XIV computer
2 T.1 switch/dimmer control box *
3 Mk.XIV switch/dimmer control box *
4 Sighting head mounting bracket
5 Collimator handle (to advance graticule)
6 Sighting head gyro
7 Cushion
8 Collimator to project graticule
9 Reflector glass
10 Reflector glass protective cover (open)
11 Clear view panel within nose blister
12 Bomb distributor
13 Bomb selection switches
14 Bomb pre-selector

* *normally only one of these would have been fitted*

Note: wiring harnesses and flexible shafts between computer and sighting head are not fitted

136
DAM BUSTERS MANUAL

(which could be done using the sighting head itself), the wind speed and direction could be calculated, and this value was radioed to other aircraft in the formation to input into their computers; often there were several wind finding aircraft, and average figures were used.

The key innovation of the Mk.XIV sight was that the sight was stabilised in pitch and roll. The computer unit was mounted on the left side of the bomb aimer's compartment, and a vacuum-driven gyroscope built into it kept the graticule stable in pitch. The sighting head contained a second gyroscope which stabilised the roll of the reflector glass onto which the graticule was projected. Thus stabilised, the sight required a run onto the target of only ten seconds and (in theory) could also cope with a range of aircraft pitch angles (up to 5° climb and 20° dive) although the wings had to be level ... in practice, however, a straight-and-level run of *at least* ten seconds was made whenever possible to maintain accuracy. The graticule was in the shape of a sword, with the blade foremost – the bomb aimer thus guided the pilot so that the target passed beneath the tip of the sword (by using the collimator handle, he could temporarily move the graticule forward over the ground in order to acquire the line to the target as early as possible), then down the blade (the 'drift line'). When it met the sword hilt (the 'release line'), he pressed the button to release the bomb.

The Mk.XIV was being trialled in spring 1942, and new production aircraft were being fitted

BELOW Internal schematic of the T.1 computer; the different calculation elements are colour coded. *(BAE SYSTEMS)*

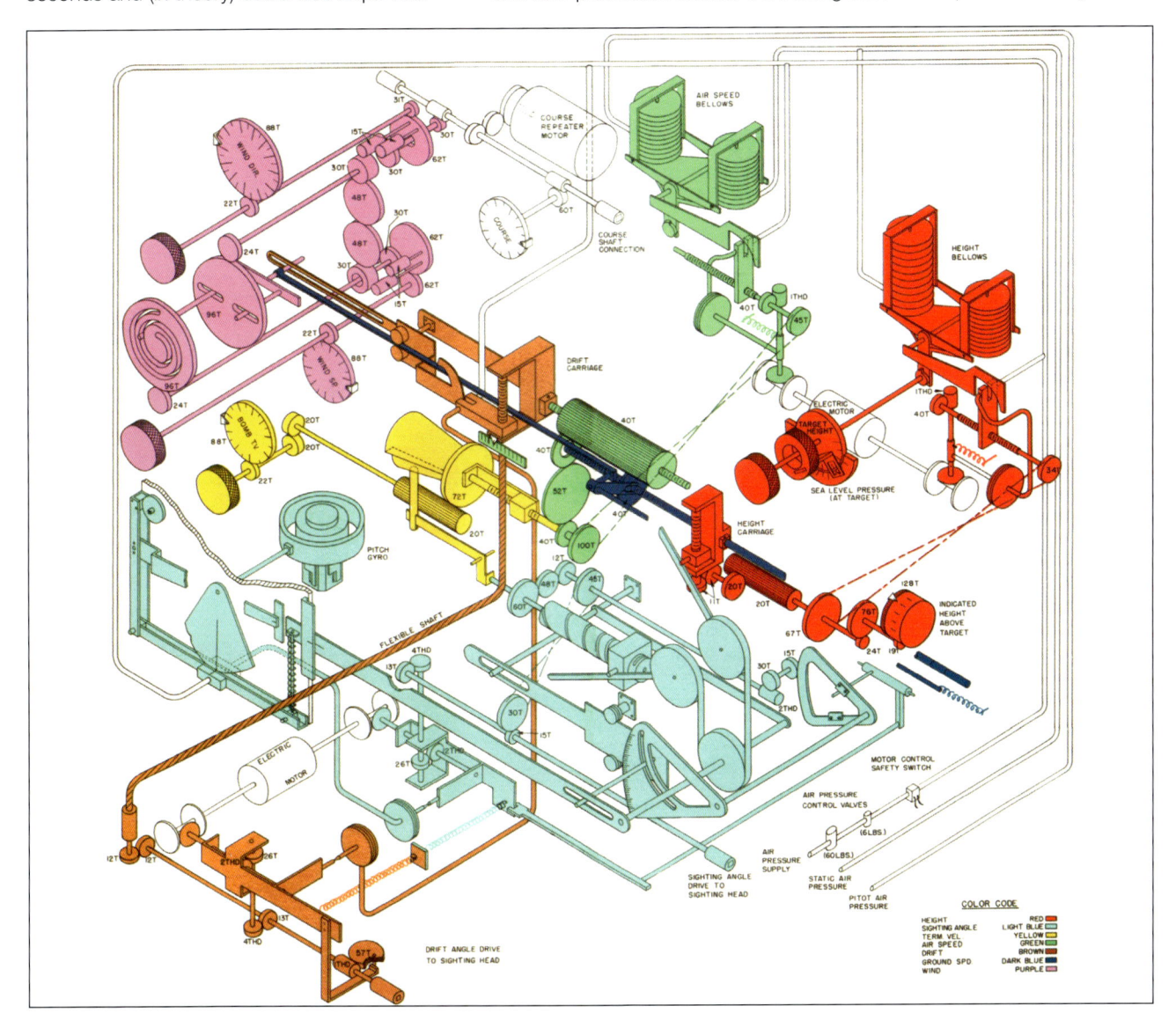

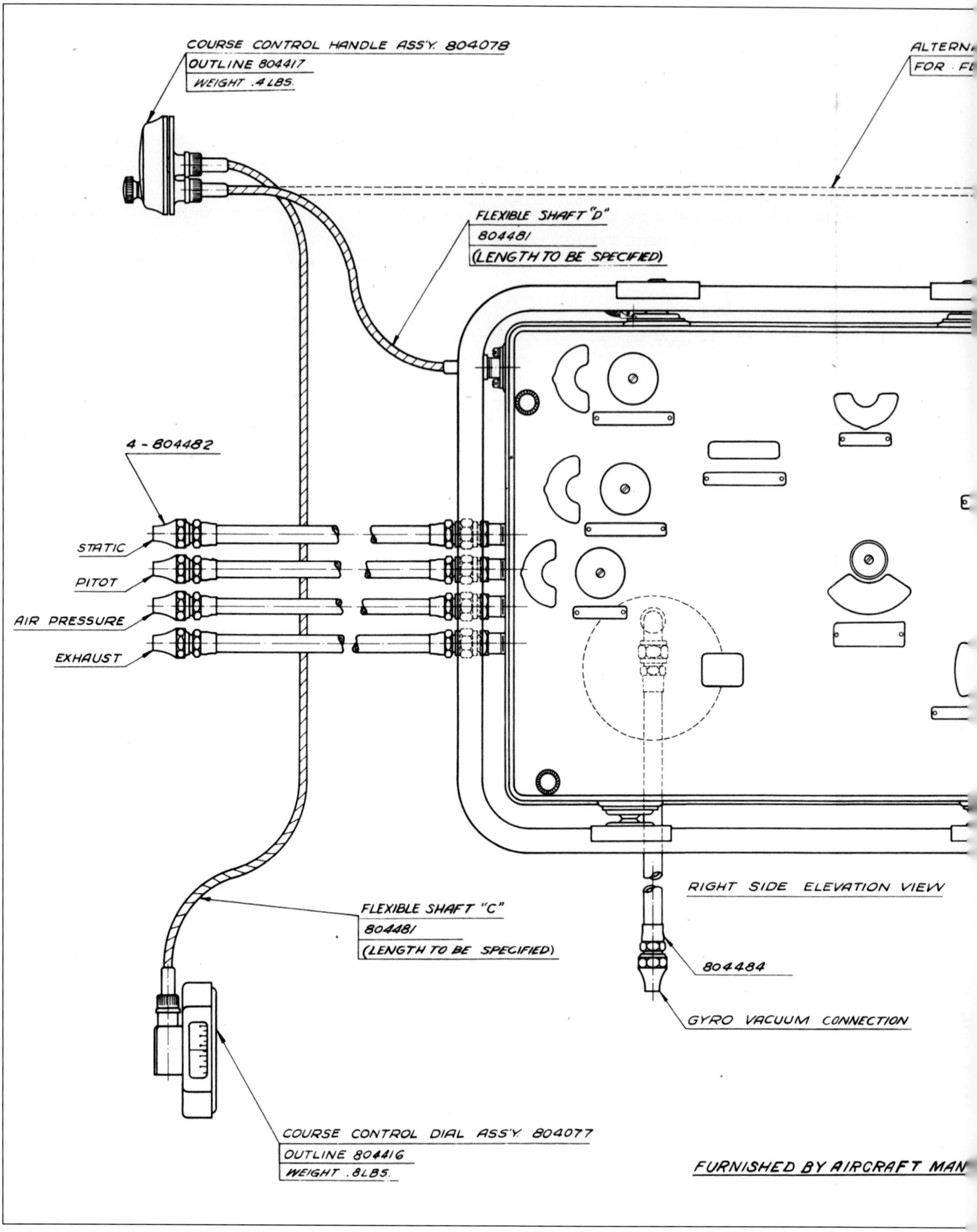
COURSE CONTROL HANDLE ASS'Y. 804078
OUTLINE 804417
WEIGHT .4 LBS.
ALTERN
FOR FL
FLEXIBLE SHAFT "D"
804481
(LENGTH TO BE SPECIFIED)
4 - 804482
STATIC
PITOT
AIR PRESSURE
EXHAUST
RIGHT SIDE ELEVATION VIEW
FLEXIBLE SHAFT "C"
804481
(LENGTH TO BE SPECIFIED)
804484
GYRO VACUUM CONNECTION
COURSE CONTROL DIAL ASS'Y. 804077
OUTLINE 804416
WEIGHT .8LBS.
FURNISHED BY AIRCRAFT MAN

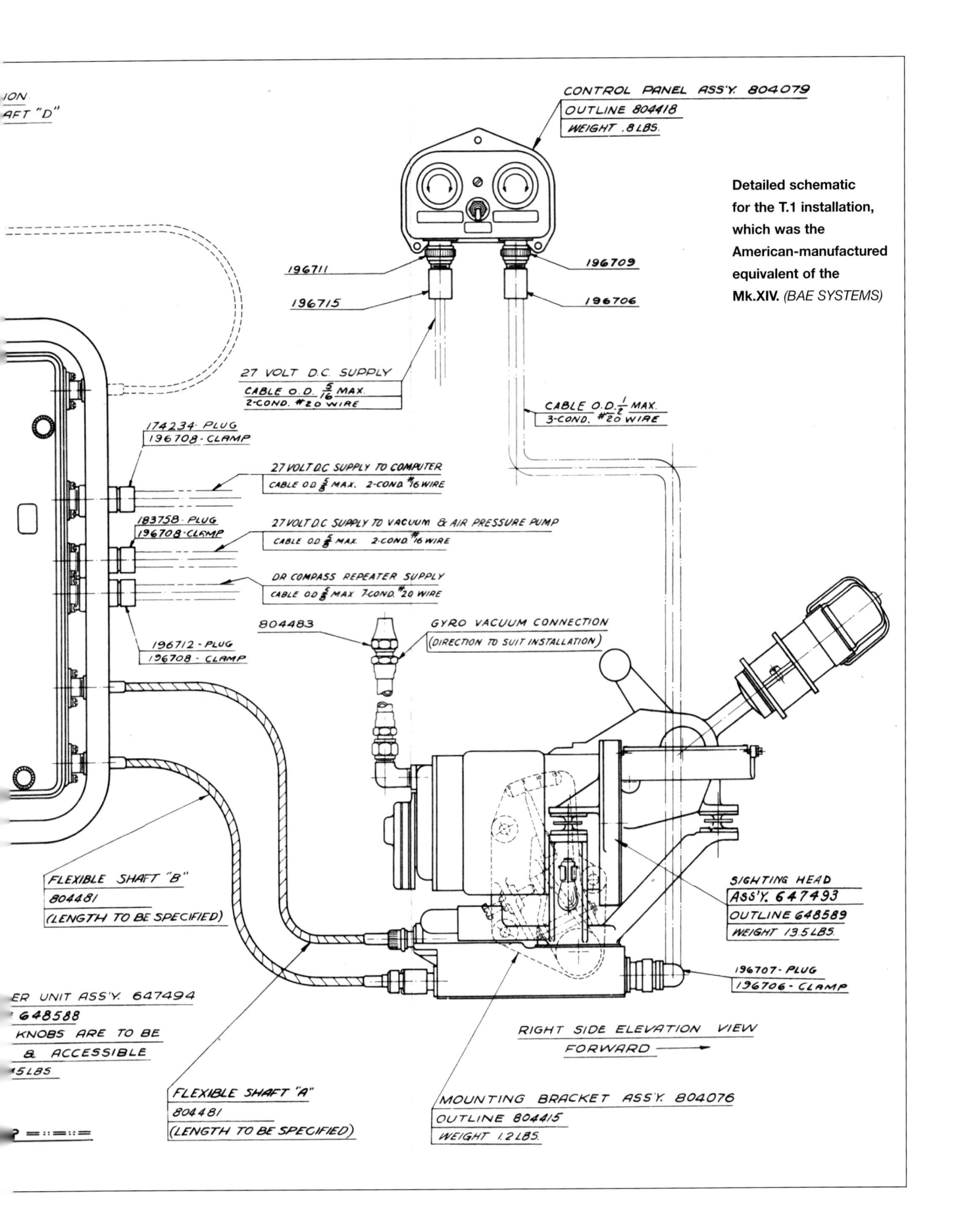

Detailed schematic for the T.1 installation, which was the American-manufactured equivalent of the Mk.XIV. *(BAE SYSTEMS)*

with it by the autumn, with priority being given to heavy bombers.

Performance was increased in the Mk.XIVA version, with the allowable climb angle increased to 11° at the expense of allowable dive angle being reduced slightly to 19°, and slightly faster turns could also be handled. Maximum bombing height was increased from 20,000 to 25,000ft. The original sight required a different computer for each aircraft type, but the Mk.XIVA had a standard computer, with an internal cam being changed to allow for the differences in airspeed calculation between aircraft types. The new sight became available towards the end of 1944.

In addition to UK production, the sight was also manufactured in the USA by Sperry Gyroscope (subcontracted to a division of General Motors), this version being known as the T.1 (and later T.1A). Despite some cosmetic differences, the two types of sight were completely compatible externally, with

ABOVE Front of the T.1 computer; the bomb aimer only needed to input five settings on the front panel, of which three could be set before take-off. *(Author)*

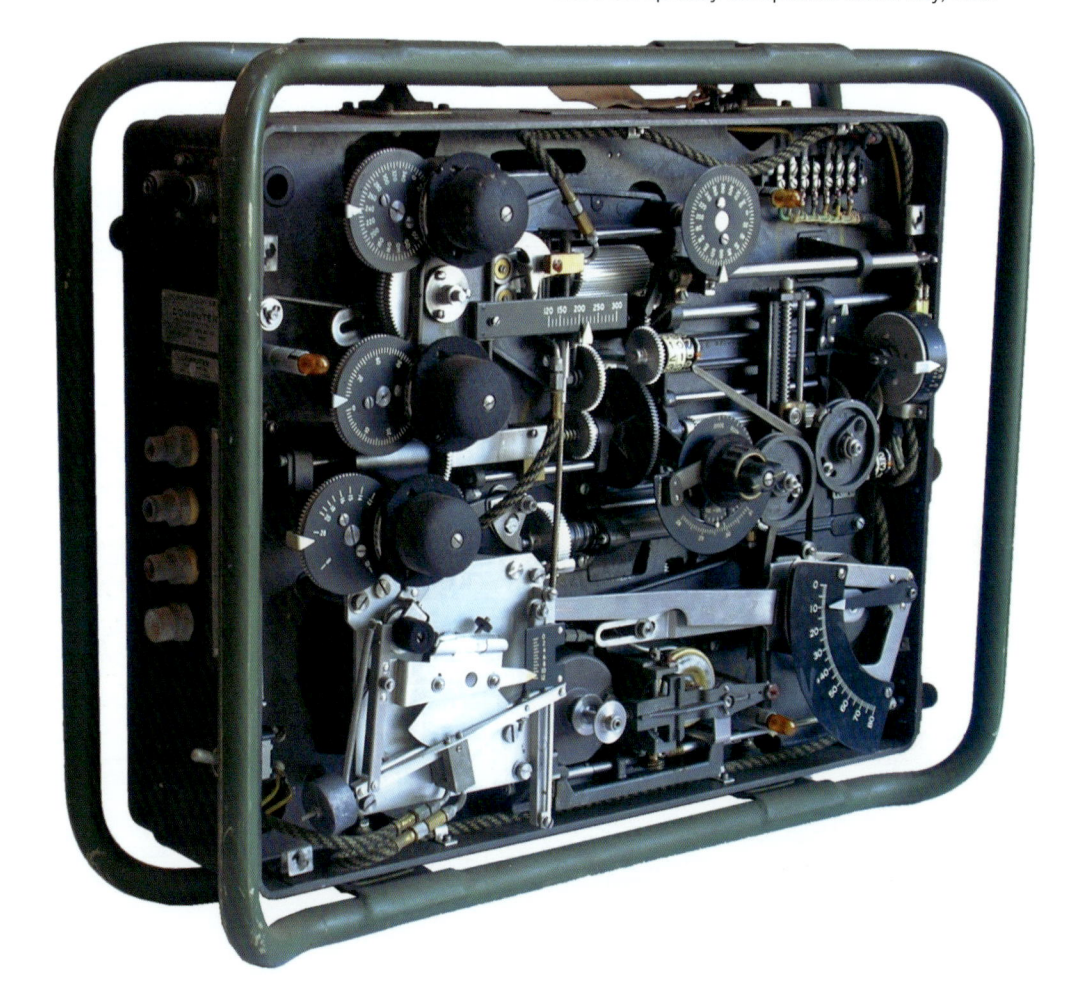

RIGHT T.1 computer with the front panel removed, showing the mechanism. *(Author)*

heads and computers interchangeable (internal parts, though functionally identical, were not interchangeable due to different manufacturing standards); the T.1 often had its own vacuum-pressure pump to provide suction for the gyros, rather than using the main aircraft supply.

In case the computer became unserviceable, the bomb aimer carried an 'emergency computor' – a simple rotating plastic disc on a base – which allowed the main calculations to be performed manually (if there was time) and the sighting head positioned accordingly; in practice, however, an earthquake bomb would often be brought back if there was a problem with the bomb sight.

The Mk.XIV/T.1 was the standard 'area sight' used by Bomber Command up to the end of the war, and in daylight Tallboy raids analysed in February and March 1945, it achieved an average radial error of 195yd from an average height of 13,000ft. More than 23,000 T.1s were made, so surviving examples are not

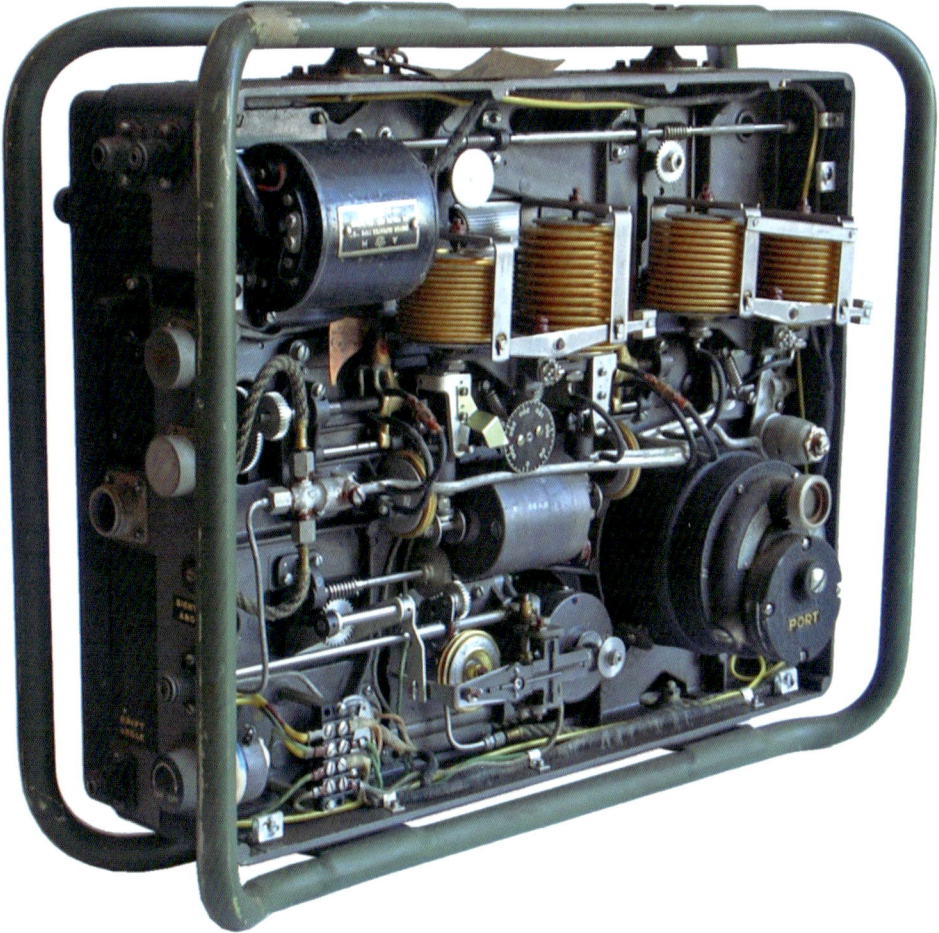

ABOVE The rear of the T.1 computer, showing the pitch gyro (right). *(Author)*

LEFT T.1 computer with the rear panel removed; the brass coils are the airspeed and height bellows. *(Author)*

ABOVE If the sight computer became unserviceable, the bomb aimer could perform the main sighting calculations using a simple emergency computer and enter the results directly into the sighting head. *(Author)*

ABOVE Poor performance on the bombing range could be used to trace common faults with the bomb sight. *(Author)*

Main particulars – Mk.XIV bomb sight

Type	vector sight (computer-assisted)
Length (computer)	21in
Height (computer)	20in
Width (computer)	11in
Length (sighting head)	17.5in (max)
Height (sighting head)	15.25in (max)
Width (sighting head+bracket)	11.25in
Weight	85lb (complete)
Speed range	120–300mph
Height range	1,000–20,000ft (Mk.XIV)/ 1,000–25,000ft (Mk.XIVA)
Pitch movement limit	–20° to +5° (Mk.XIV) / –19° to +11° (Mk.XIVA)
Azimuth movement limit	±40°
Roll movement limit	±60°
Electricity supply	12V or 24V DC
Compressed air supply	60lb/in^2
Gyro suction supply	4.5in of mercury

uncommon. British-manufactured developments of the T.1, the T.2, T.3 and T.4 continued in use with the RAF well after the war. In later examples, the vacuum gyros were replaced with electric gyros.

OUTLINE OPERATING PROCEDURE – Mk.XIV/T.1

Prior to air test
Check lamps and dimmers, clean reflector glass.

Air test flight
Check reflector becomes horizontal in straight flight; turn on compressed air cock and electric power switch; after zeroing target height, check that airspeed and height indicated on sight corresponds with values on pilot's instruments; check that spirit-level bubble on sighting head is central when flying straight and level; calculate sighting angle using manual computer, and check that this is within 2° of angle calculated by sight computer.

LEFT Simulated view through a T.1 sight approaching a target; the bomb aimer would direct the pilot so that the target moved down the long line of the graticule; when it reached the cross, he would release the bomb. *(Author)*

Prior to operational flight
Input forecast wind speed/direction, bomb terminal velocity (Tallboy's TV of 3,800fps was set one-third of the way between the scale marks at 2,800fps and infinity), target height above sea level and levelling scales (to allow for different aircraft attitudes in flight).

Approaching target
Turn on compressed air cock, electric power switch and graticule lamp, reset wind speed and direction from latest information (e.g. wind finders); pilot opens bomb doors (if fitted) and trims aircraft for level flight.

Bombing run
Push down collimator handle to extend graticule drift line ahead of aircraft, and direct pilot towards target (continually calling 'right', 'left left' or 'steady' as appropriate), release collimator handle, continue to direct pilot so that target follows drift line in graticule.

Drop position
When target reaches graticule release line, release bomb, call 'bomb gone'.

After bombing
Switch off computer and close compressed air cock (if done immediately, this preserves the sighting angle at release for future reference); the pilot would need to re-trim the aircraft at this point, as the release of a large bomb load would cause the aircraft to surge upwards by around 500ft.

Evasive action could be taken during the bomb run almost up to the release point, as long as the pitch and bank limits were not

BELOW The range unit of a SABS Mk.IIa sight. *(Author)*

exceeded – this caused the gyros to topple, and re-erection of the gyros took approximately fifteen minutes.

Automatic bomb sights

The largest factor contributing to the imprecision of vector sights was often the accuracy of the wind drift calculation, and the idea of allowing for wind automatically (without the need to calculate it explicitly) was central to the automatic bomb sight (ABS) developed by the RAE from the mid-thirties. Development, however, was slow, and in its original form, the sight would have required a very long run-up to the target. As with the vector sight, stabilisation was the key to this, and the stabilised version of the automatic bomb sight (SABS Mk.II) became available in early 1942, although it required considerable training to use and seems to have been reserved for attacks on moving targets, of which there were very few, with only one operational use of the sight recorded in the second half of the year.

SABS was a tachometric (rather than a vector) sight and (after pre-setting some bombing parameters on the sight) it was used in a slightly different way. As in the Mk.XIV, the bomb aimer viewed an aiming graticule projected onto a reflector glass, but with the SABS the target was bracketed by the graticule

LEFT The SABS controlled a Bombing Direction Indicator to show the pilot if a course correction was required. *(Crown Copyright via RAF Museum – AP 1730A)*

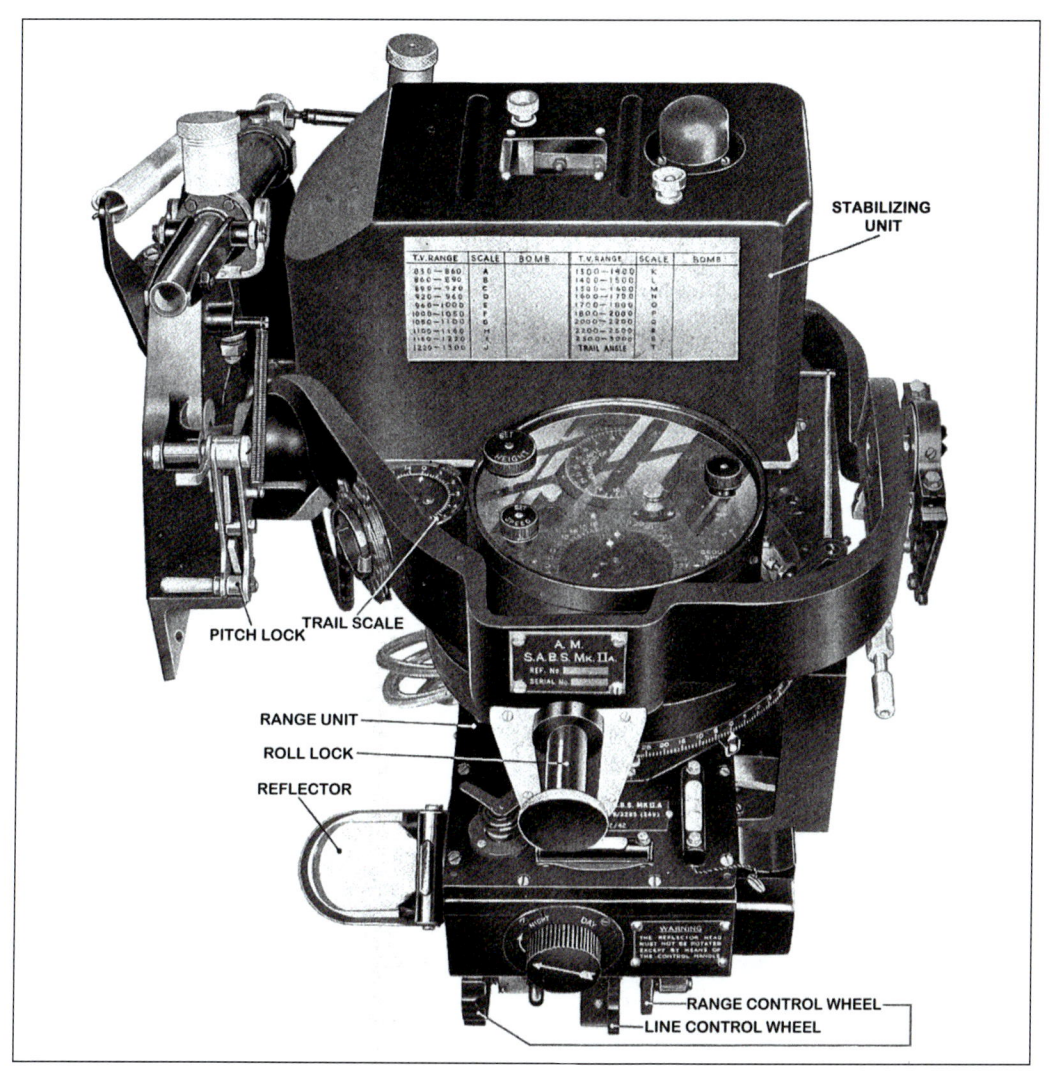

LEFT The complete SABS consisted of the range unit (bottom), stabilising unit (top) and the gimbal mounting frame. *(Crown Copyright via RAF Museum – AP 1730A)*

throughout the bombing run. If the target deviated from the graticule during the approach, the bomb aimer used the sight's controls to line it up again, and over time the sight could thus automatically accumulate the aircraft's ground speed and wind drift. The output from the sight was an indication of which direction the pilot should steer, this being relayed to him automatically by a bombing direction indicator (BDI) on his instrument panel. If both aircrew followed their instruments accurately, with the pilot making correctly banked turns with no sideslip, then the aircraft would track correctly towards the target. The moment of bomb release was calculated automatically by the sight, and it released the bomb itself when this point was reached. A few seconds before release, a red light on the sight (and a duplicate in the cockpit) came on, going out again at the moment of release; warning time was proportional to the square root of height and inversely proportional to ground speed, giving 10 seconds warning at 10,000ft/200mph and 15.75 seconds at 25,000ft.

The SABS was mounted in the nose of the aircraft and consisted of three main components: a range unit (incorporating a mechanical analogue computer to perform the sighting calculations) which was operated by the bomb aimer, a stabilisation unit attached to the range unit, and a gimbal frame which allowed the sight freedom of movement relative to the aircraft. The stabilisation unit contained two gyroscopes driven by compressed air, one keeping the unit steady in both pitch and roll within the frame, the other providing the azimuth corrections for the BDI. The range unit was smaller than the Mk.XIV computer, although more complex to manufacture and to maintain. Less than 1,000 SABSs were made, and although several range units can be found in museums, no complete SABS installations are known to have survived.

As wind was handled automatically, the sight was (in theory) more accurate than vector sights and also easier to use, although it was found operationally that considerable practice was required by the bomb aimers

BELOW Schematic showing the connections between the SABS and the aircraft. *(Crown Copyright via RAF Museum – AP 1730A)*

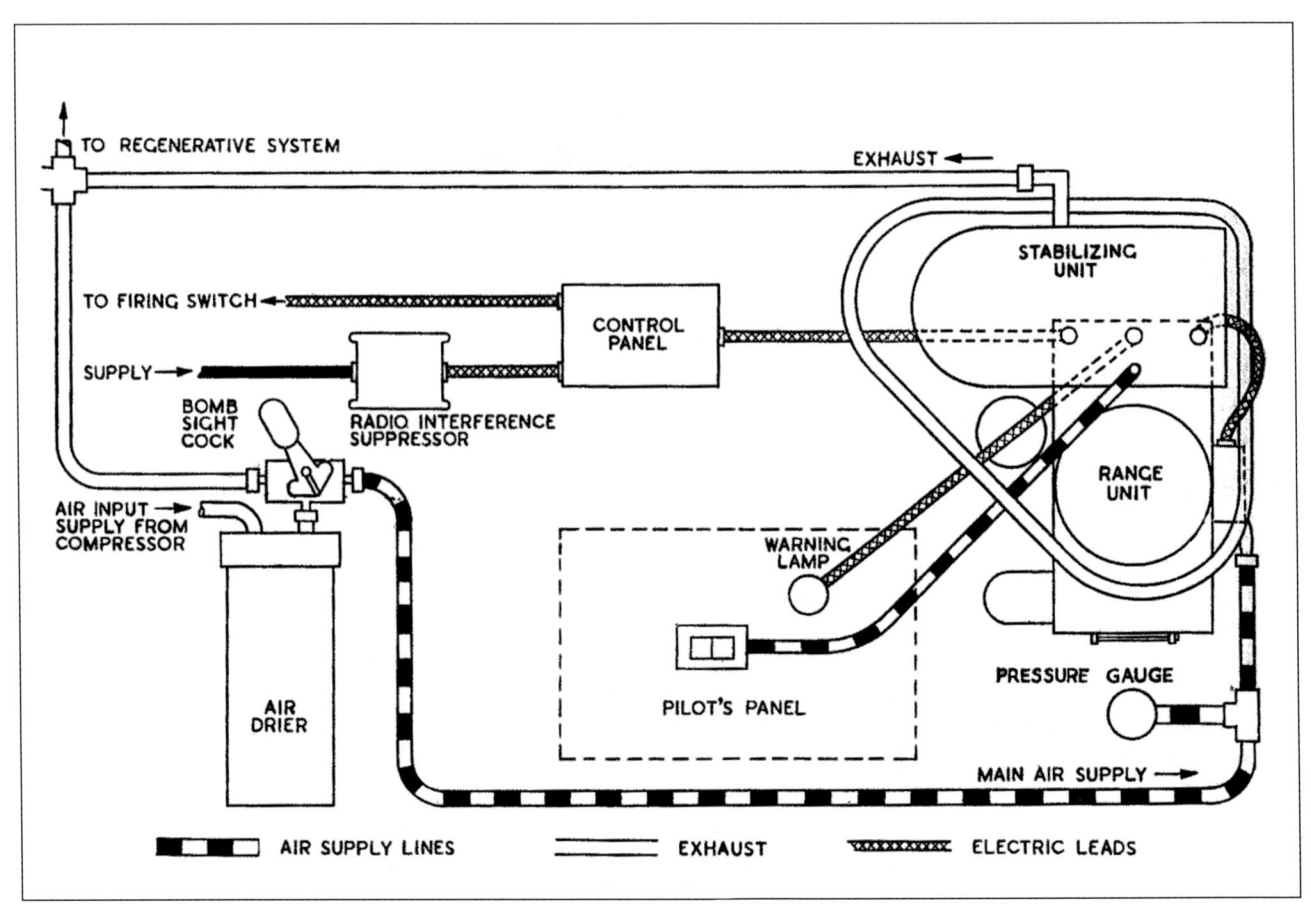

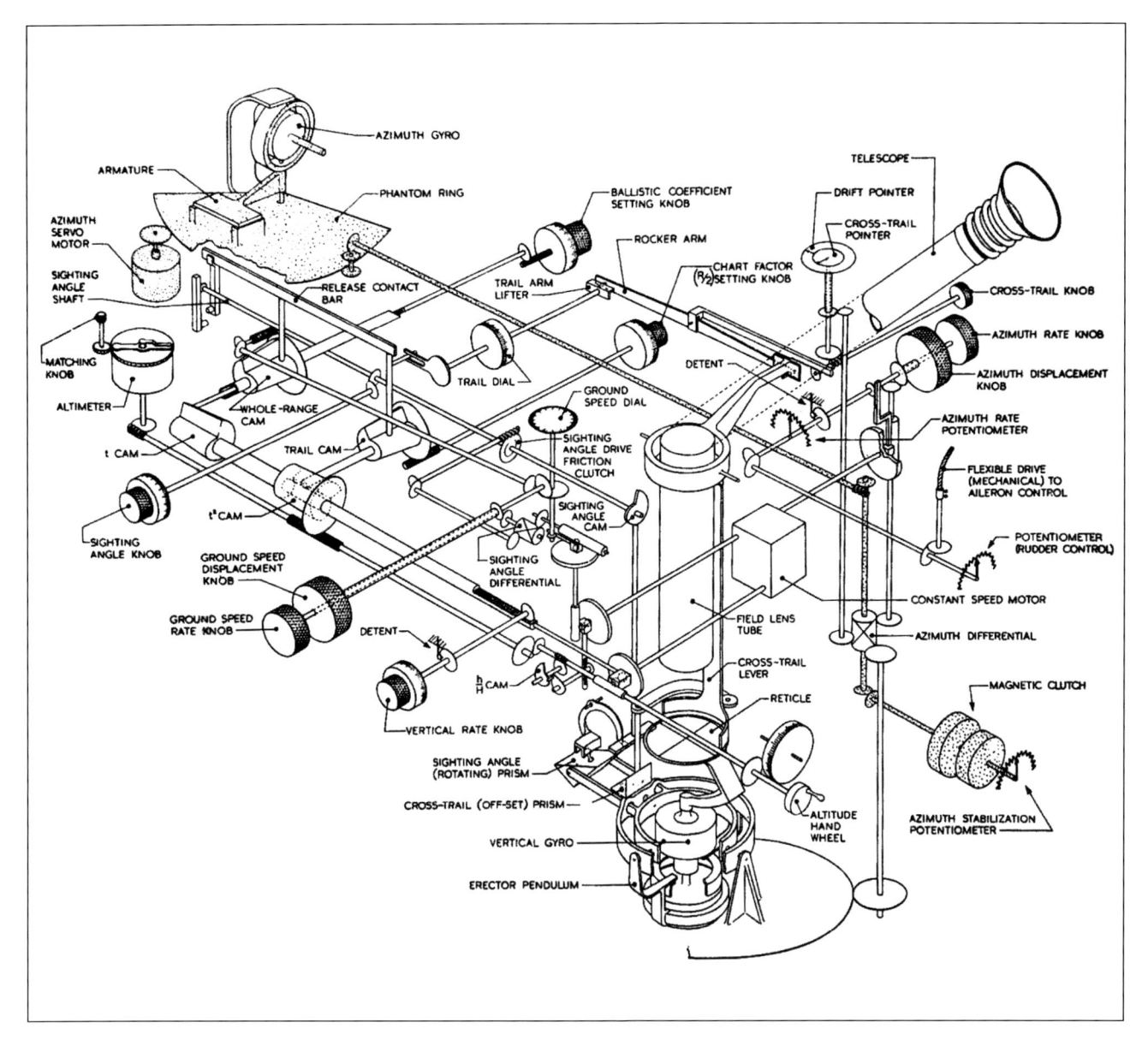

to maintain accuracy. By early 1943, two full squadrons (97 and 207 Squadrons) plus a few aircraft in three other squadrons had been equipped with SABS Mk.II, but it was decided to replace these with Mk.XIVs due to several factors: the training burden imposed by the SABS, problems with the compressor required to provide air pressure to the sight (which meant that performance deteriorated above 12,000ft), and concerns over the relatively long target run required for successful operational use. In August 1943, Harris decided that 617 Squadron would be used for special operations, and that they would be equipped with SABS Mk.IIA (a slightly improved version) and kept in training to use it effectively. Thus, although not the first squadron to use it, 617 became the primary user of the sight operationally; 9 Squadron began to receive the SABS in the last few months of the war.

The one shortcoming of the SABS which remained unresolved was the long run up to the target required by the sight in order to accumulate the wind drift. Fortunately, fighter attacks became increasingly rare towards the end of the war, but radar-predicted flak remained a problem. During the bombing run, the pilot also had to maintain a constant height (within 50ft) and a constant speed, and follow the BDI accurately with correctly banked turns with no sideslip. However, in

LEFT Internal schematic of the SABS. *(Crown Copyright via RAF Museum – AP 1730A)*

Main particulars – SABS Mk.IIA bomb sight

Type	tachometric ('automatic') sight
Length	19.5in
Width	16in
Depth	20in
Weight	65lb (complete)
Speed range	100–300mph
Height range	5,000–25,000ft
Pitch movement limit	±20°
Azimuth movement limit	±25°
Roll movement limit	±30°
Electricity supply	24V DC
Compressed air supply	60lb/in^2

skilled hands, the SABS 'precision sight' was able to achieve great accuracy – analysis of drops between June and August 1944 showed an average radial error of 170yd from an average height of 13,000ft, and a second survey between December 1944 and March 1945 showed that the error had reduced to only 125yd.

The American Norden tachometric sight was technically comparable to the SABS, although rarely achieving the same levels of accuracy in practice. The Norden had the further sophistication of actually flying the aircraft during the bomb run by controlling its automatic pilot.

OUTLINE OPERATING PROCEDURE – SABS MK.IIA

Prior to flight
Set switches appropriately, fit trail scale (corresponding to terminal velocity of bomb being carried), check that sight functional parts and windows are clean and dry, perform basic checks.

20 minutes prior to reaching target
Unlock sight, turn on compressed air to activate pitch and roll gyro, illuminate graticule, enter initial values for drift on sight, set range control well forward, check bomb is selected and fuzed, obtain values for drift, true airspeed and true height above target (from navigator) and enter these on sight, guide pilot verbally towards target; pilot opens bomb doors (if fitted) and trims aircraft for level flight.

Start of bombing run (approx. 40 seconds to target)
Target acquired in graticule, range motor activated, azimuth gyro activated, call 'run started'.

Bombing run
Graticule kept on target by adjusting range and line control wheels as required, pilot follows course corrections given by BDI; 10–25 seconds before drop position reached, red warning light is illuminated on sight and in cockpit, call 'warning light'.

Drop position
Bomb released automatically via electrical signal to bomb slip, red lights are extinguished, call 'bomb gone'.

After bombing
Switch off and lock sight; the aircraft would again need to be re-trimmed by the pilot due to the reduced loading.

Evasive action was now possible, although when feasible the straight run would be maintained for 30 seconds to allow an aiming point photograph to be taken, and the bomb aimer to visually track the bomb down to the ground.

OPPOSITE Simulated view through a SABS approaching a target; the bomb aimer would use the control wheels (bottom) to keep the graticule on the target; the sight released the bomb automatically.
(Author)

149
HIGH-LEVEL BOMB AIMING

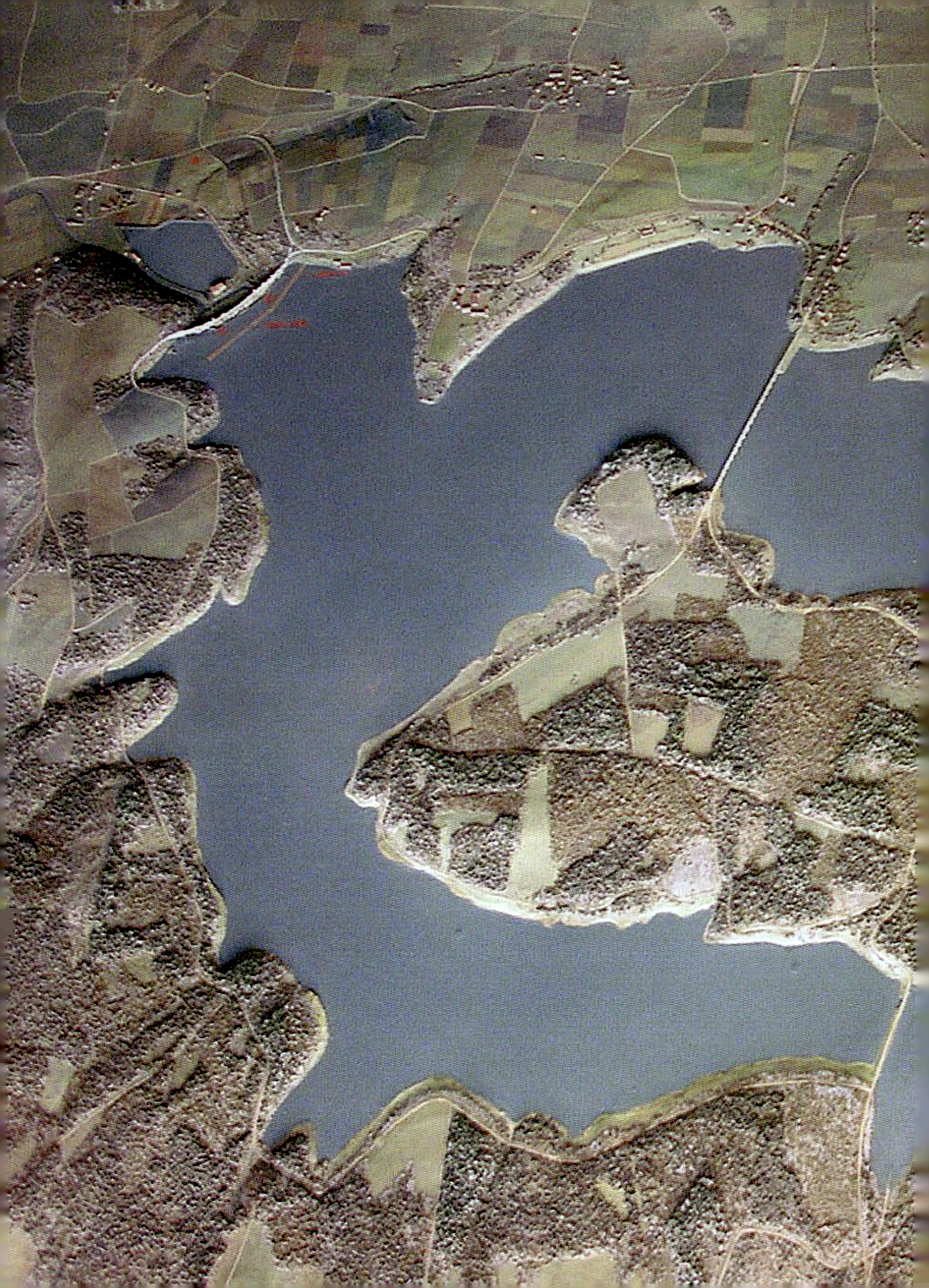

Appendices

Appendix 1
617 Squadron crews on Operation Chastise, 16–17 May 1943

Appendix 2
Type 464 Provisioning Lancasters

Appendix 3
Lancaster B.I Specials

Appendix 4
Bombs on display

Bibliography

OPPOSITE The briefing models for the dam raids are now held by the Imperial War Museum. This is the Möhne model, with the dam at the top left. *(Author)*

Appendix 1

617 Squadron crews on Operation Chastise, 16–17 May 1943

Pilot	Flight Engineer	Navigator	Wireless Operator	Bomb Aimer	Front Gunner	Rear Gunner	Aircraft	Wave
Gibson, G.P.	Pulford, J.	Taerum, H.T.	Hutchison, R.E.G.	Spafford, F.M.	Deering, G.A.	Trevor-Roper, R.D.	ED932 'G'	1, 1st flight
Hopgood, J.V.	Brennan, C.	Earnshaw, K.	Minchin, J.W.	Fraser, J.W.	Gregory, G.H.F.G.	Burcher, A.F.	ED925 'M'	1, 1st flight
Martin, H.B.M.	Whittaker, I.	Leggo, J.F.	Chambers, L.	Hay, R.C.	Foxlee, B.T.	Simpson, T.D.	ED909 'P'	1, 1st flight
Young, H.M.	Horsfall, D.T.	Roberts, C.W.	Nichols, L.W.	MacCausland, V.S.	Yeo, G.A.	Ibbotson, W.	ED877 'A'	1, 2nd flight
Maltby, D.J.H.	Hatton, W.	Nicholson, V.	Stone, A.J.B.	Fort, J.	Hill, V.	Simmonds, H.T.	ED906 'J'	1, 2nd flight
Shannon, D.J.	Henderson, R.J.	Walker, D.R.	Goodale, B.	Sumpter, L.J.	Jagger, B.	Buckley, J.	ED929 'L'	1, 2nd flight
Maudslay, H.E.	Marriott, J.	Urquhart, R.A.	Cottam, A.P.	Fuller, M.J.D.	Tytherleigh, W.J.	Burrows, N.R.	ED937 'Z'	1, 3rd flight
Astell, W.	Kinnear, J.	Wile, F.A.	Garshowitz, A.A.	Hopkinson, D.	Garbas, F.A.	Bolitho, R.	ED864 'B'	1, 3rd flight
Knight, L.G.	Grayston, R.E.	Hobday, H.S.	Kellow, R.G.T.	Johnson, E.C.	Sutherland, F.E.	O'Brien, H.E.	ED912 'N'	1, 3rd flight
Barlow, R.N.G.	Whillis, S.L.	Burgess, P.S.	Williams, C.R.	Gillespie, A.	Glinz, H.S.	Liddell, J.R.G.	ED927 'E'	2
Munro, J.L.	Appleby, F.E.	Rumbles, F.G.	Pigeon, P.E.	Clay, J.H.	Howarth, W.	Weeks, H.A.	ED921 'W'	2
Byers, V.W.	Taylor, A.J.	Warner, J.H.	Wilkinson, J.	Whittaker, A.N.	Jarvis, C. McA.	McDowell, J.	ED934 'K'	2
Rice, G.	Smith, E.C.	MacFarlane, R.	Gowrie, C.B.	Thrasher, J.W.	Maynard, T.W.	Burns, S.	ED936 'H'	2
McCarthy, J.C.	Radcliffe, W.G.	MacLean, D.A.	Eaton, L.	Johnson, G.L.	Batson, R.	Rodger, D.	ED825 'T'	2
Ottley, W.H.T.	Marsden, R.	Barrett, J.K.	Guterman, J.	Johnston, T.B.	Strange, H.J.	Tees, F.	ED910 'C'	3
Burpee, L.J.	Pegler, G.	Jaye, T.	Weller, L.G.	Arthur, J.L.	Long, W.C.A.	Brady, J.G.	ED865 'S'	3
Brown, K.W.	Feneron, H.B.	Heal, D.P.	Hewstone, H.J.	Oancia, S.	Allatson, D.	MacDonald, G.S.	ED918 'F'	3
Townsend, W.C.	Powell, D.J.D.	Howard, C.L.	Chalmers, G.A.	Franklin, C.E.	Webb, D.E.	Wilkinson, R.	ED886 'O'	3
Anderson, C.T.	Paterson, R.C.	Nugent, J.P.	Bickle, W.D.	Green, G.J.	Ewan, E.	Buck, A.W.	ED924 'Y'	3

133 men; dark shading indicates those killed on Operation Chastise (53); light shading indicates others killed before the end of the war (32)

RIGHT Two additional crews trained for Operation Chastise, but did not take part due to illness, those of Divall and Wilson. From left to right: Flt Sgt J.H. Payne (gunner), Plt Off T.W. Johnson (flight engineer), Sgt W.E. Hornby (gunner), Sgt L.G. Mieyette (wireless operator), Plt Off C.H. Coles (bomb aimer), Flg Off J.A. Rodger (navigator) and Flt Lt H.S. Wilson; both crews were carrying Blockbusters to the Dortmund–Ems Canal on the night of 15–16 September 1943, but both failed to return. *(Imperial War Museum TR1126)*

Appendix 2

Type 464 Provisioning Lancasters

Aircraft	Pilot on Operation Chastise	Aircraft History
ED765		1st prototype; to Farnborough 8/4/1943; to Manston 10/4/1943 including Upkeep spin trials 13/4/1943; crashed at Ashley Walk 5/8/1943 during overland Upkeep trials (Kellaway)
ED817 'C'		2nd prototype; to Farnborough 16/4/1943; to Manston 20/4/1943; to Scampton 30/4/1943; ORB lists 2 operations 22/4/1944 (Carey to Brunswick) and 24/4/1944 (Carey to Milan); SOC 23/9/1946
ED825 'T'	McCarthy	3rd prototype; to Farnborough 17/4/1943; to A&AEE Boscombe Down 22/4/1943; to Manston 24/4/1943; to A&AEE 27/4/1943; to Scampton 16/5/1943 as spare aircraft; flew on Operation Chastise due to ED915 being U/S; ORB lists 2 further operations – 11/11/1943 (O'Shaughnessy to Anthéor) and 10/12/1943 (Weeden FTR SOE arms drop, crashed at Doullens NE of Amiens)
ED864 'B'	Astell	Used for Manston trials; to Scampton 22/4/1943; lost on Operation Chastise (crashed near Marbeck)
ED865 'S'	Burpee	To Scampton 22/4/1943; lost on Operation Chastise (crashed near Gilze-Rijen)
ED877 'A'	Young	To Scampton 22/4/1943; lost on Operation Chastise (crashed into sea near IJmuiden)
ED886 'O'	Townsend	To Scampton 23/4/1943; ORB lists 2 further operations – 11/11/43 (Bull to Anthéor) and 10/12/43 (Bull FTR SOE arms drop, crashed at Terramesnil NE of Amiens)
ED906 'J'	Maltby	To Scampton 23/4/1943; ORB lists 5 further operations – 11/11/43 (Clayton to Anthéor), 10/12/1943 and 16/12/1943 (Clayton, abandoned SOE missions), 22/12/1943 (Clayton to Noball site) and 4/1/44 (Clayton to Noball site); to MU for storage 15/4/1944; used for Operation Guzzle (Upkeep disposal) in 1946; SOC 29/7/1947
ED909 'P'	Martin	To Scampton 23/4/1943; caught fire on non-operational flight 10/11/43 (Bull); ORB lists 1 further operation – 8/6/44 (Sanders to Saumur); used for Operation Guzzle (Upkeep disposal) in 1946; SOC 29/7/1947
ED910 'C'	Ottley	To Scampton 28/4/1943; lost on Operation Chastise (crashed near Hamm)
ED912 'N'	Knight	To Scampton 3/5/1943; ORB lists 4 further operations – 11/11/43 (Kearns to Anthéor), 16/12/1943 (Kearns to Noball site), 20/12/1943 (Kearns to Liege) and 22/12/1943 (Kearns to Noball site); to MU for storage 2/1946; SOC 26/9/1946
ED915 'Q'		To Scampton 3/5/1943; ORB shows no operations; SOC 8/10/1946
ED918 'F'	Brown	To Scampton 30/4/1943; ORB shows no more operations; training for a possible Italian dams raid 21/1/1944, aircraft crashed at Snettisham (O'Shaughnessy)
ED921 'W'	Munro	To Scampton 23/4/1943; ORB shows no more operations; SOC 26/5/1946
ED924 'Y'	Anderson	To Scampton 30/4/1943; ORB shows no more operations; SOC 23/9/1946
ED925 'M'	Hopgood	To Scampton 30/4/1943; lost on Operation Chastise (crashed near Ostönnen)
ED927 'E'	Barlow	To Scampton 3/5/1943; lost on Operation Chastise (crashed near Haldern)
ED929 'L'	Shannon	To Scampton 30/4/1943; ORB shows no more operations; SOC 7/10/1946
ED932 'G'	Gibson	To Scampton 30/4/1943; ORB lists 4 further operations – 11/11/1943 (Wilson to Anthéor), 16/12/1943 (Wilson to Noball site), 20/12/1943 (Wilson to Liege), 22/12/1943 (Wilson to Noball site) and 30/12/43 (Ross to Noball site); to MU for storage 7/2/1945; used for Operation Guzzle (Upkeep disposal) in 1946; SOC 29/7/1947
ED933 'X'		To Scampton 3/5/1943; splash damaged performing test drop at Manston 12 or 13/5/1943 (not repaired before Operation Chastise); ORB lists 1 further operation – 8/6/1944 (Watts to Saumur); used for disposal of two Upkeeps in spring 1945; SOC 7/10/1946
ED934 'K'	Byers	To Scampton 3/5/1943; lost on Operation Chastise (crashed into Waddenzee)
ED936 'H'	Rice	To Scampton 12/5/1943; damaged on Operation Chastise, returned from repair 17/7/1943; ORB shows no more operations; SOC 29/7/1946
ED937 'Z'	Maudslay	To Scampton 6/5/1943; lost on Operation Chastise (crashed near Netterden)

23 aircraft (19 flew on Operation Chastise); dark shading indicates those lost on Operation Chastise (8);
light shading indicates others lost before the end of the war (4)

Notes:
FTR – Failed To Return; MU – Maintenance Unit; ORB – Operational Record Book; SOC – Struck Off Charge (scrapped);
SOE – Special Operations Executive

Appendix 3

Lancaster B.I 'Specials'

	617 Squadron YZ code letter	15 Squadron LS code letter	13/3/1945 Bielefeld (aborted)	14/3/1945 Bielefeld Viaduct (rail)	15/3/45 Arnsberg Viaduct (rail) Ruhr	19/3/45 Arnsberg Viaduct (rail) Ruhr	21/3/1945 Arbergen Bridge (rail) at Dreys/Bremen	22/3/1945 Neinburg Bridge (rail) S of Bremen	23/3/1945 Bremen Bridge (rail)	27/3/1945 Farge U-boat construction site	6/4/1945 Sperrbrecher (ship) at IJmuiden (aborted)	7/4/1945 Sperrbrecher (ship) at IJmuiden	9/4/1945 Finkenwerder U-boat pens at Hamburg	13/4/1945 Shipping at Swinemunde (aborted)	15/4/1945 Shipping at Swinemunde (aborted)	16/4/1945 Shipping at Swinemunde	19/4/1945 Coastal guns at Heligoland	25/4/1945 Berchtesgaden	Notes/fate
PB592																			Dropped prototype Grand Slam 13/3/1945 – had mid-upper turret
PB995																			A&AEE prototype B.I Special – had mid-upper turret
PB996	C/K			g	G	G	G	Gj	G		T	T	t	t	T				
PB997	E			t	T	G	G		G	t	T	T	t	t	T		T		
PB998	N/D			T	T		T				T	T		t	T	T	T		
PD112	S/Z		g	G			g	G				G							Dropped first operational Grand Slam 14/3/1945
PD113	B/T				T		T	G	t		T		t	T					
PD114	B			G		T	G	G	G		T		t			T	G	T	
PD115	C/K				T	T			G		T	T	t	t	Tj	G			
PD116	W/A			T	T				G				t	t	Tj	T	t		
PD117	L				T														Shot down by flak 21/3/45, Gumbley and crew killed
PD118	B/M			T	T		T	G	t		T	T	t	T	G				
PD119	J (T?)	?	g		G	T*	G	G			G	t	t	T					To 15 Squadron then RAE Farnborough; SOC 20/9/1950
PD120																			Aircraft history unknown
PD121	S/Z	?		T		t	G				t	t			G		t		To 15 Squadron; SOC 19/5/1947
PD122		?																	To 15 Squadron; SOC 25/3/1948
PD123																			Aircraft history unknown
PD124																			Aircraft history unknown
PD125		?																	To 15 Squadron; SOC 25/3/1948
PD126	L	?			G														To 15 Squadron; SOC 25/3/1948
PD127	F	S																T	To 15 Squadron; sold for scrap 16/10/1947
PD128	N/D	R				T	T		G	t	T		t	t	T	T			To 15 Squadron; SOC 25/3/1948
PD129	O				G	T			G	t	T								
PD130	D/W/U				G	T		T	g**	t	T	T		t	T		T		
PD131	A/V	V			G		T	T	G	t	T	T					t		To 15 Squadron; SOC 19/5/1947
PD132	X				T		T	T	t		t	T		t		T	T	t	
PD133	P					T		T				T		t	T	T			
PD134	Y/U						G	G		t	T	T		t			G	T	
PD135	W/A					T			t	T	T	t				G	t		
PD136	N/D																		Aircraft history unknown
PD137																			To Bomb Ballistics Unit, Woodbridge then to RAE Farnborough
PD138																			Aircraft history unknown
PD139	W/L						G		G	t	T	t	t	T	T	T			Crash landed in Germany 16/5/1945, scrapped
Grand Slams			0	1	1	6	1	5	6	13	0	0	2	0	0	0	6	0	**41 in total**
Tallboys			0	0	0	5	13	5	6	0	0	12	12	0	0	14	6	7	**80 in total**

KEY

T – Tallboy dropped
G – Grand Slam dropped
j – jettisoned

t – Tallboy carried but brought back
g – Grand Slam carried but brought back
SOC – Struck off change (scrapped)

* may have been a Grand Slam
** may have been jettisoned

Appendix 4

Bombs on display

Examples of Upkeep can be seen at:
- Brooklands Museum, Weybridge, Surrey (complete, on loan from RAF Museum)
- Newark Air Museum, Notts (complete, on loan from Barnes Wallis Memorial Trust)
- IWM Duxford, Cambs (complete)
- Lincolnshire Aviation Heritage Centre, East Kirkby, Lincs (complete)
- Brenzett Aeronautical Museum, Kent (complete, with three hydrostatic pistols)
- Petwood Hotel, Woodhall Spa, Lincs (damaged)
- EOD TIC, Chattenden, Kent (concrete core only) [site not publicly accessible]
- Grantham Museum, Lincs (end fragment with exploder pockets)
- Ringwood Town & County Experience, Ringwood, Hants (reconstructed from original parts)
- 617 Squadron, RAF Lossiemouth, Moray (reconstructed from original parts) [site not publicly accessible]
- Dover Castle, Kent (blank end plate and up to 28in of cylinder)

Examples of other 'bouncing bombs' can be seen at:
- Spitfire and Hurricane Memorial Museum, Manston (Highball core cylinder)
- RAF Scampton Museum (Highball core cylinder)
- Herne Bay Museum (Highball core cylinder)
- Brooklands Museum (prototype, poor condition, on loan from Holland House Estates, Dorchester)
- Fleet Air Arm Museum, Yeovilton, Somerset (prototype, poor condition)
- Nothe Fort, Weymouth, Dorset (prototype, poor condition)
- The Swannery, Abbotsbury, Dorset (prototype, dimpled)

LEFT Wallis and his two sons investigate one of the prototype 'bouncing bombs' at Chesil Beach. *(Mary Stopes-Roe)*

RIGHT 617 Squadron have examples of Upkeep, Tallboy and Grand Slam at their base at RAF Lossiemouth. *(Author)*

- Haverfordwest (Withybush) Airport (Highball casing fragments)
- Several complete Highballs were located in Loch Striven by divers from Underwater Science Ltd in July 2010; work is ongoing to recover some of these for museum display

Replica Upkeeps can be seen at:
- RAF Museum, Hendon, London (full size, cutaway)
- Lincolnshire Aviation Heritage Centre, East Kirkby, Lincs (full size)
- Thameside Aviation Museum, East Tilbury, Essex (half scale)
- Eder Dam Museum, Germany (full size)

An example Blockbuster can be seen at:
- RAF Museum, Hendon, London (with Type E trolley)

Examples of the 'earthquake' bombs can be seen at:
- Brooklands Museum, Weybridge, Surrey (Tallboy and Grand Slam with Type E trolleys, and Tallboy (small))
- RAF Museum, Hendon, London (Grand Slam with Type H trolley)
- Yorkshire Air Museum, Elvington, Yorks (Tallboy and Grand Slam (casing only, no tail))
- 617 Squadron, RAF Lossiemouth (Tallboy and Grand Slam) [site not publicly accessible]
- BBMF, RAF Coningsby, Lincs (Tallboy and Grand Slam) [site not publicly accessible]
- Explosive Ordnance Disposal TIC, Chattenden, Kent (Tallboy and Grand Slam) [site not publicly accessible]
- Site of former Holton Le Clay railway station, Lincs (Tallboy with replica tail)
- Belgian Army base, Meerdaal (Tallboy with replica tail) [site not publicly accessible]
- Pakistan Air Force Museum, Karachi (Tallboy)

A replica 'earthquake' bomb can be seen at:
- Nanton Lancaster Society Air Museum, Canada (Tallboy full-size replica)

Bibliography

Brickhill, Paul, *The Dam Busters* (Evans Brothers, 1951)
Cooper, Alan, *The Men Who Breached the Dams* (William Kimber, 1982)
Cooper, Alan, *Beyond the Dams to the Tirpitz* (William Kimber, 1983)
Cotter, Jarrod and Blackah, Paul, *Avro Lancaster Owner's Workshop Manual* (Haynes, 2008)
Curtis, Des, *Most Secret Squadron: the Story of 618 Squadron* (Skitten Books, 1995/Grub Street, 2009)
Euler, Helmuth, *The Dams Raid: Through the Lens* (After the Battle, 2001)
Falconer, Jonathan, *The Dam Busters* (Sutton, 2003/Haynes 2010)
Flower, Stephen, *A Hell of a Bomb* (Tempus, 2001)
Gibson, Guy P., *Enemy Coast Ahead* (Michael Joseph, 1946)
Morpurgo, Jack E., *Barnes Wallis* (St Martin's, 1972/Penguin, 1973/Ian Allan, 1981)
Murray, Iain R., *Bouncing-Bomb Man: The Science of Sir Barnes Wallis* (Haynes, 2009)
Sweetman, John, *The Dambusters Raid* (Cassell Military Classics, 1999)
Sweetman, John, *Tirpitz: Hunting the Beast* (Sutton, 2000)
Ward, Chris, Lee, Andy and Wachtel, Andreas, *The Dambusters: the Definitive Story of 617 Squadron at War 1939–1945* (Red Kite, 2003)

Crown Copyright

Index

A&AEE Boscombe Down 35, 37, 41, 75, 100, 125
Aerial reconnaissance 42, 47, 50, 53, 65, 67, 90, 99-100, 103, 105, 117, 119, 121, 127, 129
Aero engines
    Packard Merlin 28 23
    Rolls-Royce Merlin 24 92, 117
Aircraft crashes and collisions 23, 44-45, 49, 55-56, 89, 92
Aircrew 41, 48, 152
    bomb aimer 4, 31, 33, 35-36, 40, 46, 48, 52, 66, 83, 90, 131-132, 135-136, 141-142, 148, 152
    flight engineer 35, 48, 152
    gunners 4, 46, 49, 92, 152
    navigator 4, 35, 40, 48, 152
    pilot 4, 35, 48, 152
    wireless operator 41, 48, 152
Air Ministry 70
Airship *R.100* 8
Air Staff 8
Anderson, C.T. 45, 52, 55
Anti-torpedo nets 9, 14
Astell, W. 45, 49
Avro Lancaster 13, 31, 33, 37, 40-42, 55, 60-61, 64, 67, 75-76, 114-115, 122, 125, 136
    modifications 25, 27, 31, 40, 43, 63, 81
    B.I Special 91-92, 124-125, 154
    B.III 23
    Type 464 Provisioning 23, 25, 27, 41, 56-57, 61, 92, 118, 153
Avro Lincoln 92

Barlow, R.N.G. 23, 44-45, 56
Battle of Britain Memorial Flight (BBMF) 136
Bazin, Wg Cdr J.M. 113
Bismarck battleship 14, 115
Blackett, Prof Patrick 133
Boeing B-29 Superfortress 129
Bomb aiming 8, 36, 131-149
    Aldis height lamps 13, 30, 34, 41, 46, 52
    bomb sights and computers 36, 41, 66, 89, 118, 131-148
    CSBS 133
    Dann sight 36
    Mk.III low-level 118
    Mk.XIV/T.1 133-144
    SABS 64, 145-148

Bomb carrying and release equipment 16, 27-30, 43, 57, 83, 89
    bomb bay and doors 27-31, 33, 60, 63, 81, 83, 92, 144
    calliper arms 13, 23, 27, 30, 32, 36, 43, 57
    hydraulic motor and belt 27-28
    slip and sling 29-30, 32, 82-84, 92
Bomb construction 16-21, 60-63, 70, 72-76, 91
    detonators and pistols 18-21, 37, 45, 60, 63-64, 74, 78-81, 88-89, 91
    fuzes 18, 20-23, 45-46, 60, 63, 74, 76, 78, 88-89, 91, 97
Bomb dropping 15, 144, 148
    drogue parachutes 60
    heights 10, 33-34, 37, 64, 66, 69, 76, 92, 97, 115, 132, 135
    release distance 35, 132, 135
    tests 14, 16, 32-33, 37, 41, 57, 70, 76, 126, 129
    spinning 14-15, 27-28, 36, 56, 64
Bomb ground handling 63-64
    transport frames 63
    trollies 31, 63-64, 84-85, 87-88
    winches 31, 85
Bomb loading 31-32, 41, 63, 75, 87-89, 91
Bomb plans and drawings 9, 17-18, 37, 63, 72-73, 77, 90-92, 114
Bombing tactics 89-90
Bomb tails 60, 75, 84-86, 91
Bombing targets 8, 10, 44, 54, 56-57, 64, 90, 96, 121
    aero engine factories 65-66
    barrages 118-119, 121
    Berchtesgaden 129
    canals 56-57, 64, 117-118, 125
    dams 8-11, 28, 39, 42, 44-46, 48-57, 64, 117-118, 120-121
    E-boat pens 98-100, 113, 121-122
    factories 66-67, 69, 121, 126-129
    Heligoland 128-129
    marshalling yards 64, 67
    military camps 96
    oil refineries 126, 128-129
    shipping 42, 57, 78, 121, 125-126, 128
    towns and cities 60, 67, 121, 125
    U-boat pens 69, 110-113, 122
    underground 96-98, 128
    viaducts and bridges 8, 44-45, 64-66, 97, 110, 122-126
    V-weapon sites 65, 100-110, 129

Bomb and mine types
    blast (High Capacity)
        2,000lb HC 59
        4,000lb HC Cookie 29, 59-60, 64
        8,000lb HC Super Cookie 59-60, 63, 67
        12,000lb HC Blockbuster 59-62, 65-67, 81, 97, 121, 125
    bouncing 10, 13-16, 46, 57, 155
        Baseball 57
        Highball 14, 28, 57, 115
        Kurt (German) 56
        Upkeep 14-23, 28-29, 31-32, 36-37, 40-41, 43-47, 56-57, 70, 120
    deep penetration/earthquake (Medium Capacity) 10, 21, 69-129
        Amazon (American) 126, 129
        Samson (American) 126, 129
        Tarzon (American) 129
        4,000lb MC (test specimen) 70-71
        12,000lb MC Tallboy 8, 53, 61, 65, 67, 70-88, 91-92, 96-103, 105-115, 117-118, 120-126, 128-129, 141, 144
        22,000lb (ten-ton prototype) 9-11, 70
        22,000lb MC Grand Slam 69-71, 77, 82, 84-85, 87, 90-95, 122-129
        44,000lb (American) 129
    General Purpose (GP) 8, 60, 101, 110
        40lb 95
        250lb 8
        500lb 59-60
        1,000lb 59-60, 64, 66-67, 97, 110
    incendiary 60, 66-67
    Johnny Walker (JW) mine 114
    4,500lb Disney rocket-assisted 101, 129
Brooklands 9, 71
Brown, K.W. 45, 52, 55
Building Research Station 11
Burhill Golf Club 8
Burpee, L.J. 45
Byers, V.W. 44

Chadwick, Roy 23, 27, 56
Cheshire, Sqn Ldr G.L. 61, 65-67, 97
Chesil Beach 15, 155
Churchill, Winston 37, 51
Cochrane, Sir Ralph 40, 42, 44, 76
Cockshott, Sqn Ldr J.V. 124
Coles, C.H. 152

Dann, Wg Cdr C.L. 35
Davis, LAC 95
D-Day 56
Deering, G.A. 4
de Havilland Mosquito 57, 60-61, 65, 67, 117, 121
Dewberry, LA 95
Divall, William 41, 152
Douglas A-26 Invader 57

English Steel Corporation 73
Fairey Swordfish 9
Fauquier, Gp Capt J. 121, 125
Fice, Ted 37
Fleet Air Arm 115
Fleet lagoon 15
Fritzlar airfield 56

Gaggle (flying formation) 89
Gibson, Wg Cdr Guy 4, 13, 39, 41-42, 45-46, 48-49, 55-56, 60

Handley Page Halifax 60
Harris, Sir Arthur 'Bomber' 16, 40, 44, 51, 147
Hitler, Adolf 129
Hopgood, J.V. 45-46
Hornby, W.E. 152
Hutchinson, R.E.G. 4

Jeffries, Cpl 95
Johnson, T.W. 152

King George VI 56
Knight, L.G. 45-46, 49, 55, 64
Korea 129

Lockspeiser, Sir Benjamin 33
Loch Striven 57, 156
Longbottom, Sqn Ldr M.V. 'Shorty' 37

Maltby, D.J.H. 36, 45-49, 55, 64
Martin, H.B.M. 45-46, 49, 55, 66
Maudslay, H.E. 41, 45-46, 49
McCarthy, J.C. 44-45, 51-52, 55
Michael Nairn & Co. Ltd 74
Mieyette, L.G. 152
Ministry of Aircraft Production 10, 15
Ministry of Supply 33
Model dams 11, 42, 120, 150
Munro, J.L. 44, 66

Nant-y-Gro Dam 11
National Physical Laboratory 15
Navigation 8
    Oboe 61, 65
Nigger (dog) 40-41, 48
North American P-51 Mustang 61
Northrop XB-35 129

Operation Catechism 115, 117
Operation Chastise 37, 39-57, 66, 118, 152

Operation Glimmer 96
Operation Guzzle 57
Operation Obviate 117
Operation Paravane 114-115
Operation Taxable 96-97
Ottley, W.H.T. 45
Oxley Engineering Co. 15

Payne, Flt Sgt J.H. 152
Portal, Lord Charles 51
Project Ruby 126, 129

RAE Farnborough 23, 133, 145
RAF (Royal Air Force) 17, 115
    Bomber Command 7-8, 114, 133, 141
    Coastal Command 33, 118
    5 Group 40, 44, 117
    8 (Pathfinder) Group 61, 67
    9 Squadron 53, 60-61, 67, 89, 113-114, 117, 121, 122, 125, 126, 147
    15 Squadron 92
    76 Squadron 60
    83 Squadron 97
    97 Squadron 147
    106 Squadron 60
    207 Squadron 147
    218 Squadron 96
    617 Squadron 37, 40, 56, 59-61, 64-65, 67, 89, 92, 96, 102, 110, 113, 117, 121-122, 125-126, 147, 152, 156
    618 Squadron 57
RAF bases and airfields
    Bardney 88, 113
    Carnaby 125
    Coningsby 61
    Ford 66
    Lossiemouth 117, 156
    Manston 23, 37
    Medmenham 42
    Scampton 23, 40-42, 44-45, 55-56
    Woodhall Spa 65
RAF Museum, Hendon 28, 32, 34, 64, 83-84
Reculver 13, 41, 57
Rice, G. 44
River Fulda 56
River Weser 56
Road Research Laboratory 11
Rodger, J.A. 152
ROF Chorley 17
ROF Risley 72
ROF Woolwich 17, 72
Royal Engineers 108
Royal Navy
    A-class submarines 28
    Department of Miscellaneous Weapons Development 57
    HMS *Alderney* 28
    S-class submarines 28
X-craft submarines 57, 114-115

Shannon, D.J. 45, 48, 55
Short Bros, Rochester 72
Signal code words 42, 46, 48
Silvermere Lake, Weybridge 14
Spafford, F.M. 4
Speer, Albert 52
Summers, Chief Test Pilot Joseph 'Mutt' 15
Surviving bombs 17-18, 71, 155-156

Taerum, H.T. 4
Tait, Wg Cdr J.B. 'Willie' 114
Target marking 61, 65
    low-level 65-67
    'Newhaven' 61
    'Paramatta' 61
    'Wanganui' 61
Target Profiles (see also Bombing targets) 46, 52, 54, 65, 97-98, 101, 106, 108-110, 115, 117-118, 120, 122-123
Tirpitz battleship 42, 57, 78, 114-118, 121, 129
Torpex explosive 16-17, 72, 76, 78
Townsend, W.C. 45, 52, 55
Training flights 41
    Ashley Walk range 56, 125
    Derwent Dam 40-41
    Eyebrook Reservoir 41
    Howden Dam 41
    low flying 40, 56
    night flying 40-41
    Wainfleet range 41

U-boats 33, 69, 110-113, 122, 126-127, 129
USAAF 65, 101-103, 125

VHF radios 31, 41, 44
Vickers-Armstrongs Ltd. 23, 98
    Barrow-in-Furness 17
    Elswick 7
    Walker 7, 28
    Weybridge 8-9, 28
Vickers
    Warwick 57
    Wellesley 8
    Wellington 7-8, 15, 117
Victoria Cross 56
V-weapons (Crossbow) 64-65, 100-110, 129
    V-1 ('Noball') 65, 100, 103, 106
    V-2 rockets 100-101, 103-104, 129
    V-3 101, 103, 108, 129

Wallis, Barnes 7-10, 13-16, 28, 32-33, 40-41, 44, 48, 52, 56-57, 69, 96-98, 128, 155
Wallis, Molly 28
Weaver, Ernest W. 69
Whitworth, Gp Capt J.N.H. 42
Wilson, H.S. 41, 152
Wilson, D.J.B. 66
'Window' strips 96

Young, H.M. 45-47, 49, 55

RIGHT 617 Squadron's 'finest hour' – the breached Möhne Dam on 17 May 1943. Even Barnes Wallis recognised that 'no such spectacular target remains to be brought down'. *(Author's collection)*